New Perspectives in History

Forces of Order and Movement in Europe Since 1815

Edited by

ROBERT J. SCALLY

New York University

Houghton Mifflin Company • **Boston**

New York • Atlanta • Geneva, Ill. • Dallas • Palo Alto

Printed in the U.S.A.

Library of Congress Catalog Card Number: 71-160412

ISBN: 0-395-12659-2

Contents

Introduction

The library of intellectual history contains some of the boldest and most imaginative creations of the historian's craft. But it is a house built with borrowed tools, of diverse materials, its shape and genus as mysterious to its creators as the proverbial elephant to the three blind men. Intellectual history has always been an eclectic, loosely defined study. A glance at the files of the *Journal of the History of Ideas*, the principal forum of discussion on the subject, is enough to see the broad demarcations, or their absence, which constrain the historian of ideas. One is apt to find thoughts on anything from modern chemical warfare to "Animate Motion in the Seventeenth Century" or "Poetic Inspiration in Greek Literature" under the same cover. This is as it should be; for history at its best has always added to the mind and world of dead men some revelation of the fancies and concerns of the living. It has been literature as well as science, expression as well as analysis, both whimsical and serious. How, then, do we prescribe limits? What is outside the province of intellectual history?

Western history and Western art share in the same distinct tradition. From the earliest times Europeans have demonstrated a strong inclination to maintain a rather unhappy tension between the spirit and body, form and matter, conscious and unconscious, myth and reality, ideal and praxis, thought and action—this tendency being the most distinctive unity in European culture. From Euripides to Sartre, from the Manichees to Christian Existentialists, in the literature, religion, and architecture of the Western tradition, the resolution of elemental conflicts has pleased the taste and spirit of Europeans. It is therefore not surprising to find the dualism in our philosophy of history. In virtually every discussion of the nature of intellectual history some "line" is described which separates "deeds" and "ideas," "passion" and "reason," "sentiment" and "science," or "propaganda" and "philosophy." When H. Stuart Hughes describes the history of social thought he distinguishes between "higher" and "lower" levels, the first being "intellectually clear and significant statements" and the latter "popular effusions in the nature of slogans."[1] In the classic *The Idea of History*, R. G. Collingwood speaks of the "inside" and "outside" of historical events: that "which can be described in terms of bodies and their movements . . . ," and that "which can only be described in terms of thought . . . ."[2] To be sure, absolute separations either of "higher" and "lower" or "inside" and "outside" are not commonly found in any kind of history whether in theory or practice. This is necessarily so because the study of history is the study of integral human behavior, of the acts of the whole man, performed with motivation or, as it is sometimes said, with reason:

> Man is regarded as the only subject of the historical process, because man is regarded as the only animal that thinks, or thinks enough, and clearly enough, to render his actions the expression of his thoughts.[3]

The dynamics of this expression in the human past is the subject matter of the science, the philosophy, and the art of history. And it is in this passage between thought and action that most of the battles of intellectual history are fought.

With the not always welcome aid of the new social sciences, historians over the past century have begun to examine the question of motivation, the catalyst of thought and action, far more explicitly and rigorously than ever before. Since the medieval chroniclers, the proper function of the historian has been not merely to record (that Caesar's blood was spilled on the floor of the senate house) but to interpret (what thought was in the minds of the "honourable men?"). It is the difference between what Collingwood called the "outside" and the "inside" of the event.[4] If the available data were sufficient to do so, the modern historian might be expected to examine, with tools borrowed from the psychologist, the emotional condition and clinical history of Brutus and the assassins; with the tools of the sociologist, the collective imperatives and loyalties of the Roman senatorial class; with the tools of the anthropologist, the force of the kingship taboo in Roman society; and so on in the attempt to understand the "whole act." Even if the new techniques serve only

---

[1] H. Stuart Hughes, *Consciousness and Society: The Reorientation of European Social Thought, 1890-1930* (New York, Vintage, 1958), p. 9.

[2] R. G. Collingwood, *The Idea of History* (Oxford, Clarendon Press, 1946), p. 213.

[3] *Ibid.*, p. 216.

[4] *Ibid.*, p. 213.

to raise more questions, he must at least be conscious that such questions exist.

Like the weapons of war, the existence of the tools of science has compelled their use. Whether as scientist, artist, antiquarian, or philosopher, the historian has always picked up what implements came to hand in the hope of exposing a discernible form in his material, of penetrating the "tale told by an idiot" to discover a rational process. At least some part of the agitated discussion which now enlivens the history of ideas seems to have come from the feeling that the new techniques tend to reduce rather than enlarge that rational element. Consequently, as Hughes quite bluntly concedes, historians have been somewhat squeamish in the presence of modern social science, which has stirred an old gnawing premonition that "the basic characteristic of human experience was the limited nature of its freedom."[5] Since the historian's traditional concern was what men had done, the apparent promise of the social sciences to expose human deeds as the mere product of "vast impersonal forces" and psychological programming threatened to rob him of his subject and its mysteries, to render his skills as obsolete as the alchemist's. Should science carry off the thought as well as the deed with such soulless scrutiny, little indeed would appear to remain for the historian as such save the quaint and nostalgic—and for the scholar of ideas, nothing at all.

Although the history of ideas has been an integral part of the craft since Herodotus, its status as a distinct discipline has passed through numerous phases. The notion that ideas have a motive force in determining events large or small is somewhere at the root of this kind of history, although the point is seldom pressed dogmatically. As a widely-shared consensus, that belief can certainly be traced back as far as the eighteenth century. And it has never been wholly extinguished, despite the shattering doubts and assaults of the past hundred years. It was initially in the defense of those sanctuaries of the Enlightenment—creative rationality, emancipation from nature, and cultural progress—that the history of ideas was reconstructed from the wreckage left by the Romantics, Positivists, and Irrationalists. In the context of the eighteenth century the momentous political and ideological force of the rationalist principle is highly visible, yet the implications of its contemporary revival are rather

---

[5] Hughes, *op. cit.*, p. 4.

obscure. But perhaps something of the significance of the movement is suggested by the fact that it received its major impetus in America where both the idea of Progress retained greatest vitality into the twentieth century and where the social sciences had proceeded furthest. American scholars had not been engulfed by massive social and political upheavals as had the Europeans; they were able to maintain, until recent years, the comforting illusion of the spectator, sympathetic, partisan, but at the same time detached. Not having been cowed, suborned, or coerced by enthroned ideologies, the American scholar has found it easier to commune serenely with the past, and to see in it the steady march of reason and potent ideas; in a sense, the eighteenth century lasted longer in America than anywhere else.

The late Arthur O. Lovejoy, one of the greatest American scholars of the Enlightenment and a prime mover of the revived history of ideas, devoted a celebrated book, *The Great Chain of Being* (1936), to the study of what he called a "unit-idea" underlying the thought of an entire cultural era. The working principle of the book itself was the notion that rational activity, conceived similarly to the "intellectually clear and significant statements" defined by Hughes, was not only the most dominant meaningful activity of man but the most worthy of note in reflecting on the past. A variety of views approximating this concept have come to be the prevailing orthodoxy in intellectual history since the 1920's, particularly in American scholarship, and it has altered only slowly with the revelations of the decades after 1936.[6] The bewildering experiences of these recent years appear to have offered scant reinforcement for the defense of the sanctuaries of reason. When ideas have been grotesqued and reason prostituted by men for their purposes, we have abstracted them to the academic groves, disembodied and untainted, and forgotten the men. Among the consequences, as one perceptive critic has put it, intellectual history becomes a history of ideas rather than a history of thinking:

> A rationalistic concept of mind commits us to a theory which conceives ideas as entities lodged in a mind, prefigures the history of ideas, and transforms it into a biography of mental development. . . . And the mind under this theory is the Greek mind, the mind which

grasps, the spectator of endless transmutation unconnected with events.[7]

The Humanities, the study of philosophy and literature in particular, have had great influence in the development of intellectual history, that influence tending generally toward the rationalistic and "intrinsic" approach: "the internal relationship between what some men write and say and what other men write and say," more or less independent of the social context—"the relation between what a few men write and say and what many men actually do."[8] Naturally, the main body of writing in intellectual history falls somewhere between the "intrinsic" and social methods, though the most formative and prominent works in the field have leaned decisively toward the former. Thus, the guiding principles in the study of ideas have departed only slightly from those laid down at the founding of the seminal History of Ideas Club at Johns Hopkins University in 1922:

. . . the historical study of the development and influence of general philosophical conceptions, ethical ideas, and aesthetic fashions, in occidental literature, and the relations of these to manifestations of the same ideas and tendencies in the history of philosophy, of science, and of political and social movements.[9]

Despite the commitment to relate the study of ideas to their manifestations in political and social movements, intellectual history has generally shunned the frontal encounter with this formidable historical puzzle. Furthermore, as the language of the Club's manifesto clearly suggests, a preferential hierarchy is established in which the sort of ideas malleable to subtle, systematic, or formal expression are accorded not only the superior elevation worthy of a humanist's attention but implicitly the generative role,[10] while "popular effusions"—ideology, political action, expressions of class

[7] *Ibid.*, p. 16.

[8] Crane Brinton, *Ideas and Men: The Study of Western Thought*, 2nd edition (Englewood Cliffs, N.J., Prentice-Hall, 1963), p. 4.

[9] Arthur O. Lovejoy, *Essays in the History of Ideas* (Baltimore, Johns Hopkins Press, 1948); in the "Foreward" by Don Cameron Allen, ix.

[10] John Higham, "Intellectual History and its Neighbors," *Ideas in Cultural Perspective*, Wiener and Noland, eds., (New Brunswick, Rutgers Univ. Press, 1962), p. 85; reprinted from *Journal of the History of Ideas*, vol. XV, No. 3, pp. 339-347.

consciousness and inchoate aspirations—are abandoned to the encroaching armies of social scientists.

The humanist cannot ignore the threat which he detects in the new sciences to his consoling concept of a "history of free men"—much of it a nurtured myth perhaps but one that has emancipated and sustained men since the Middle Ages. Yet the challenge is at times regarded less as an alternate and complementary search for the truth than as a heresy and therefore an ideological assault to be resisted in the name of free, disinterested, objective inquiry. The fluctuating line of defense drawn between the humanities and social sciences thus becomes not only one which separates divergent views about the way men act, a question that can be discussed dispassionately, but of how men should act, a tense conflict of moral philosophy and ideologies. In history, especially in intellectual history, it is neither possible nor desirable to detach method from subject entirely. The ideas of the past, as well as the acts of men in the past, are only discernable through the fickle selectivity of present bias and fashion—in Alfred North Whitehead's words: "our history of ideas is derived from our ideas of history."[11] This is to say no more than that the contemporary historian is himself an intellectual, part of a community, a member of a group, a class, a culture, a sharer in a world view, and therefore inseparable from the subject matter of intellectual history. Consequently, a critical examination of the "internal" genesis and ramifications of the "unit-ideas" in which our own intellectual era participates becomes necessary. If the history of intellectuals is germane to intellectual history, perhaps the richest area of study then becomes the behavior—both the thoughts and the acts—of the historian himself. How do the attitudes and methods of this generation of historian-intellectuals manifest the ideas, traditions, aesthetic fashions, myths, passions, and ideals of the past and of the contemporary mood? How does their intellectual behavior relate to the quantifiable social milieu "outside?"

Leonard Krieger's article in this collection, written in 1951, examines the background of the social and political orientation of the liberal European intellectual, a category broad enough to encompass most students of ideas, lay and professional. By "liberal" Krieger means to include " . . . not only representatives of the familiar secular political tradition nor only the intellectuals free of

---

[11] Alfred North Whitehead, *Adventures of Ideas* (New York, Macmillan, 1933), p. 8; cited in Loewenberg, *op. cit.*, p. 17.

all institutional attachment, but rather all those intellectuals who, whatever their mundane ties, are responsive to general currents which come from beyond those associations and create a tension in them."[12] In cameo, the history of the European intellectual community which Krieger describes reflects the general confrontation of reality and ideal, engagement and withdrawal persisting in the European world since the eighteenth century. The dilemma of the liberal intellectual since then has been to confront the social realities which have been increasingly impervious to his ideals while at the same time to resist a lofty isolation which might blind his only window into the real world and personal meaningfulness. As Krieger observes, and Hughes and Stern corroborate, in the generation preceding the First World War the intellectuals' response to the stifling certainties of Positivism took the form of an attempt "to impregnate a balky reality with value."[13] Whether its expression was neo-idealism or neo-Marxism, reaction or revolutionism, the compelling force of his plea to personalize reality, and thereby to humanize history, marked a rising discontent with the new industrial realities and an episode in the continuous struggle of the intellectual against alienation and forlornness. Unlike his counterpart of the eighteenth century, the modern intellectual found increasing difficulty in making "inner" and "external" reality consonant. He chose, or was forced to choose, either withdrawal, the rejection of an external reality subject to reason, or engagement through the existential act. Rather tragically, whichever path he selected required some abandonment of his sustaining creed—the reassuring faith which E. J. Hobsbawm discovers even in the illiterate Andalusian peasant—that knowledge of the truth is of itself enough to liberate. Sadly, as many of the intellectuals discussed in this collection felt, the truth had exiled them from the community of men or flung them willy-nilly into a choiceless, faceless, and philistine world.

In our own generation it is difficult to imagine that there ever was a time when ideals and reality, "inner" and "external" realities, were consonant; when the role of the intellectual could be anything other than a critical and discontented one. What function do ideas have but to change things, to increase our control over circumstances, to

---

[12] Leonard Krieger, "The Intellectuals and European Society," *Political Science Quarterly*, vol. LXVII, No. 2 (June, 1952), 227.

[13] *Ibid.*, p. 231.

rationalize a random reality, or at least, as Lenin saw it, to understand necessity. In this light, ideas become weapons in the struggle of men against circumstance as they were in the struggle against dumb nature and often are in the conflicts between men and men. All men have perforce been involved in this fate—Bodo the peasant and Sir Isaac Newton, bandits, philosophers, bricklayers, clowns, and Messiahs—and all have learned to use ideas in their different ways. The ideas encompassed by this broad interpretation need not, of course, be systematic, elevated, subtle, or even distinguishable from myth, but they may often share with philosophy the power to illuminate reality, to relieve confusion, or to justify action. And like philosophy, even in its most pristine form, they appear to be capable at times of giving direction to discontent.

The political consciousness which E. P. Thompson traces in the semi-literate English artisan, the anarchism of Hobsbawm's Spanish peasants, or the Volkish ideology of the German Youth Movement are examples of such ideas, crude, unsystematic, derivative, and clumsily articulated, yet containing the catalyst which renders the human condition meaningful and turns perplexity into passionate conviction for large masses of people. In the function they perform, as weapons or merely as instruments to blunt the pain of hopelessness, they do not differ from the complex profundities of Hegel, Nietzsche, or Croce. They are of the "lower" order of ideas which have most often been left to the social historian, the *idées-forces* which "united the imagination with the will, the anticipated vision of things with their execution."[14] If we are to exclude these from intellectual history by calling politically useful ideas "ideologies" we are hard put to find any "pure" thought, anywhere in man's intellectual history.

Needless to say, as our definition becomes more inclusive, selecting the significant material from the expanding historical record becomes more difficult. The readings in this collection were chosen to provide a few examples of how men singly, in groups, and in masses have adapted ideas to their understanding of political and social realities. Intellectuals of varying status make up a significant part of the subject matter of the following studies because, first, it is they who must spend their life's effort struggling with that adaptation. Second, as Leonard Krieger points out in his

[14] Alfred Fouilée, *Morale des Idées-Forces* (Paris, Alcan, 1908), p. 353; cited in Fritz Stern, *The Politics of Cultural Despair* (New York, Anchor, 1965), p. 4.

essay on "The Intellectuals and European Society," they have been forced in a specially intense way into the struggle between idea and social reality. Between the Andalusian farmer and the professional intellectual, the illiterate and the learned, the selections are designed to reflect the course of that struggle at graduated levels of intellectual complexity and to represent various approaches to the analysis, or self-analysis in the case of George Orwell, of the passage between a political thought and a political act. All of the men represented in the collection, both the subjects and the narrators, are involved in a personal rebuttal of Alexander Herzen's melancholy reading of history:

> History is all improvisation, all will, all extemporised. There are no frontiers, there are no time-tables, no itineraries. All that exists is specific conditions, and sacred discontent, the flow of life. . . .[15]

[15] Isaiah Berlin, "A Marvellous Decade, IV," *Encounter,* vol. VI, No. 5 (May, 1956), 25.

Dynamics

E. P. THOMPSON

Radical Culture

The following selection, from Edward Palmer Thompson's recent masterpiece, *The Making of the English Working Classes,* is an example of a revived British school of social history in the tradition of Booth, Mayhew, the Hammonds, and the Coles, using many of the contemporary techniques of the social sciences. The special concern of this chapter on the "Radical Culture" of the English working classes of the 1820's is one of the most persistent and knotty problems of intellectual history: the emergence of political consciousness among the working classes, forged from their own experience and the "filtering down" of ideas from the Radical tradition of the previous decades. Of particular interest is the manner in which the semi-literate and the autodidactic working man receives, internalizes, and transmits the values and concepts of the Radical culture and the process through which he makes it his own in the pubs, reading circles, chapels, and newsrooms attended by working men.

As in the second selection on the Andalusian peasants, the confines of intellectual history are broadened in Thompson's work to include mass culture and popular consciousness. Since in every age of history it is the anonymous mass of ordinary men who, in sheer quantity at least, perform most acts and think most thoughts, the history of Thompson's and Hobsbawm's variety seems to be widening the window on what was once the invisible mainland of the past.

WHEN CONTRASTED with the Radical years which preceded and the Chartist years which succeeded it, the decade of the 1820's seems strangely quiet—a mildly prosperous plateau of social peace. But many years later a London costermonger warned Mayhew:

> People fancy that when all's quiet that all's stagnating. Propagandism is going on for all that. It's when all's quiet that the seed's agrowing. Republicans and Socialists are pressing their doctrine.[1]

[1] H. Mayhew, *London Labour and the London Poor* (1884), I, p. 22.

These quiet years were the years of Richard Carlile's contest for the liberty of the press; of growing trade union strength and the repeal of the Combination Acts; of the growth of free thought, co-operative experiment, and Owenite theory. They are years in which individuals and groups sought to render into theory the twin experiences . . . of the Industrial Revolution, and the experience of popular Radicalism insurgent and in defeat. And at the end of the decade, when there came the climactic contest between Old Corruption and Reform, it is possible to speak in a new way of the working people's consciousness of their interests and of their predicament *as a class.*

There is a sense in which we may describe popular Radicalism in these years as an intellectual culture. The articulate consciousness of the self-taught was above all a *political* consciousness. For the first half of the 19th century, when the formal education of a great part of the people entailed little more than instruction in the Three R's, was by no means a period of intellectual atrophy. The towns, and even the villages, hummed with the energy of the autodidact. Given the elementary techniques of literacy, labourers, artisans, shopkeepers, clerks and schoolmasters, proceeded to instruct themselves, severally or in groups. And the books or instructors were very often those sanctioned by reforming opinion. A shoemaker, who had been taught his letters in the Old Testament, would labour through the *Age of Reason*; a schoolmaster, whose education had taken him little further than worthy religious homilies, would attempt Voltaire, Gibbon, Ricardo; here and there local Radical leaders, weavers, booksellers, tailors, would amass shelves of Radical periodicals and learn how to use parliamentary Blue Books; illiterate labourers would, nevertheless, go each week to a pub where Cobbett's editorial letter was read aloud and discussed.

Thus working men formed a picture of the organisation of society, out of their own experience and with the help of their hard-won and erratic education, which was above all a political picture. They learned to see their own lives as part of a general history of conflict between the loosely defined "industrious classes" on the one hand, and the unreformed House of Commons on the other. From 1830 onwards a more clearly-defined class consciousness, in the customary Marxist sense, was maturing, in which working people were aware of continuing both old and new battles on their own.

It is difficult to generalise as to the diffusion of literacy in the early years of the century. The "industrious classes" touched, at one pole, the million or more who were illiterate, or whose literacy amounted to little more than the ability to spell out a few words or write their names. At the other pole there were men of considerable intellectual attainment. Illiteracy (we should remember) by no means excluded men from political discourse. In Mayhew's England the ballad-singers and "patterers" still had a thriving occupation, with their pavement farces and street-corner parodies, following the popular mood and giving a Radical or anti-Papal twist to their satirical monologues or Chaunts, according to the state of the market.[2] The illiterate worker might tramp miles to hear a Radical orator, just as the same man (or another) might tramp to taste a sermon. In times of political ferment the illiterate would get their workmates to read aloud from the periodicals; while at Houses of Call the news was read, and at political meetings a prodigious time was spent in reading addresses and passing long strings of resolutions. The earnest Radical might even attach a talismanic virtue to the possession of favoured works which he was unable, by his own efforts, to read. A Cheltenham shoemaker who called punctually each Sunday on W. E. Adams to have "Feargus's letter" read to him, nevertheless was the proud owner of several of Cobbett's books, carefully preserved in wash leather cases.[3]

Recent studies have thrown much light on the predicament of the working-class reader in these years.[4] To simplify a difficult discussion, we may say that something like two out of every three working men were able to read after some fashion in the early part of the century, although rather fewer could write. As the effect of the Sunday schools and day schools increasingly became felt, as well as the drive for self-improvement among working people themselves, so the number of the illiterate fell, although in the worst child labour areas the fall was delayed. But the ability to read was only the elementary technique. The ability to handle abstract and consecutive argument was by no means inborn; it had to be discovered against almost overwhelming difficulties—the lack of leisure, the cost of candles (or of spectacles), as well as educational deprivation.

[2] See esp. Mayhew, *op. cit.*, I, p. 252 ff.
[3] W. E. Adams, *Memoirs of a Social Atom* (1903), I, p. 164.
[4] See especially R. K. Webb, *The British Working Class Reader, 1790-1848* (1955), the same author's article, "Working-Class Readers in Early Victorian England," *English Hist. Rev.*, LXV (1950); R.D. Altick, *The English Common Reader* (Chicago, 1957), esp. Chs. IV, VII, XI; and J. F. C. Harrison, *Learning and Living* (1961), Part One.

Ideas and terms were sometimes employed in the early Radical movement which, it is evident, had for some ardent followers a fetishistic rather than rational value. Some of the Pentridge rebels thought that a "Provisional Government" would ensure a more plentiful supply of "provisions"; while, in one account of the pitmen of the north-east in 1819, "Universal Suffrage is understood by many of them to mean universal suffering . . . 'if one member suffers, all must suffer.'"[5]

Such evidence as survives as to the literary accomplishment of working men in the first two decades of the century serves only to illustrate the folly of generalisation. In the Luddite times (when few but working men would have supported their actions) anonymous messages vary from self-conscious apostrophes to "Liberty with his Smiling Attributes" to scarcely decipherable chalking on walls. We may take examples of both kinds. In 1812 the Salford Coroner, who had returned a verdict of "Justifiable Homicide" upon the body of a man shot while attacking Burton's mill was warned:

> . . . know thou cursed insinuater, if Burton's infamous action was "justifiable", the Laws of Tyrants are Reasons Dictates.—Beware, Beware! A months' bathing in the Stygian Lake would not wash this sanguinary deed from our minds, it but augments the heritable cause, that stirs us up in indignation.[6]

The letter concludes, "Ludd finis est"—a reminder that Manchester boasted a grammar school (which Bamford himself for a short time attended) as well as private schools where the sons of artisans might obtain Latin enough for this. The other paper was found in Chesterfield Market. It is much to the same purpose but (despite the educational disadvantages of the writer) it somehow carries a greater conviction:

> I Ham going to inform you that there is Six Thousand men coming to you in Apral and then We Will go and Blow Parlement house up and Blow up all afour hus/labring Peple Cant Stand it No longer/dam all Such Roges as England governes but Never mind Ned lud when general nody and is harmey Comes We Will soon bring about the greate Revelution then all these greate mens heads gose of.

⁵ *Political Observer,* 19 December 1819.
⁶ Another letter ("Eliza Ludd" to Rev. W. R. Hay, 1 May 1812) commences: "Sir, Doubtless you are well acquainted with the Political History of America;" both in *Home Office Papers,* 40. 1.

Others of the promised benefits of "general nody" were: "We will Nock doon the Prisions and the Judge we Will murde whan he is aslepe."[7]

The difference (the critics will tell us) is not only a matter of style: it is also one of sensibility. The first we might suppose to be written by a bespectacled, greying, artisan—a cobbler (or hatter or instrument-maker) with Voltaire, Volney and Paine on his shelf, and a taste for the great tragedians. Among the State prisoners of 1817 there were other men of this order from Lancashire: the seventy-year-old William Ogden, a letter-press printer, who wrote to his wife from prison: "though I am in Irons, I will face my enemies like the Great Caractacus when in the same situation"; Joseph Mitchell, another printing worker, whose daughters were called Mirtilla, Carolina and Cordelia, and who—when another daughter was born while he was in prison—wrote in haste to his wife proposing that the baby be called Portia: or Samuel Bamford himself, whose instructions to his wife were more specific: "a Reformers Wife ought to be an heroine".[8] The second letter (we can be almost sure) is the work of a collier or a village stockinger. It is of much the same order as the more playful letter left by a pitman in the north-east coalfield in the house of a colliery viewer in 1831, into which he and some mates had broken during a strike riot:

I was at yor hoose last neet, and meyd mysel very comfortable. Ye hey nee family, and yor just won man on the colliery, I see ye hev a greet lot of rooms, and big cellars, and plenty wine and beer in them, which I got ma share on. Noo I naw some at wor colliery that has three or fower lads and lasses, and they live in won room not half as gude as yor cellar. I don't pretend to naw very much, but I naw there shudn't be that much difference. The only place we can gan to o the week ends is the yel hoose and hev a pint. I dinna pretend to be a profit, but I naw this, and lots o ma marrows na's te, that wer not tret as we owt to be, and a great filosopher says, to get noledge is to naw wer ignerent. But weve just begun to find that oot, and ye maisters and owners may luk oot, for yor not gan to get se much o yor own way, wer gan to hev some o wors now. . . .[9]

[7] *H.O.* 42.121.
[8] *H.O.* 42.163; *Blanketteer,* 20 November 1819.
[9] R. Fynes, *The Miners of Northumberland and Durham* (1923 edn.), p. 21.

"If the Bible Societies, and the Sunday School societies have been attended by no other good," Sherwin noted, "they have at least produced one beneficial effect;—they have been the means of teaching many thousands of children to read."[10] The letters of Brandreth and his wife, of Cato Street conspirators, and of other State prisoners, give us some insight into that great area between the attainments of the skilled artisan and those of the barely literate. Somewhere in the middle we may place Mrs. Johnston, addressing her husband ("My Dear Johnston"), who was a journeyman tailor, in prison:

> . . . believe me my Dear if thare is not a day nor a hour in the day but what my mind is less or more engage about you. I can appeal to the almighty that it is true and when I retire to rest I pray God to forgive all my enimies and change thare heart. . . .

Beside this we may set the letter of the Sheffield joiner, Wolstenholme, to his wife:

> Our Minaster hath lent me four vollams of the Missionary Register witch give me grat satisfaction to se ou the Lord is carin on is work of grais in distant contres.

The writing of this letter was attended with difficulties, since "Have broke my spettacles".[11] Such letters were written in unaccustomed leisure. We can almost see Wolstenholme laboriously spelling out his words, and stopping to consult a more "well-lettered" prisoner when he came to the hurdle of "satisfaction". Mrs. Johnston may have consulted (but probably did not) one of the "professional" letter-writers to be found in most towns and villages, who wrote the appropriate form of letter at ld. a time. For, even among the literate, letter-writing was an unusual pursuit. The cost of postage alone prohibited it except at infrequent intervals. For a letter to pass between the north and London might cost ls. 10d., and we know that both Mrs. Johnston and Mrs. Wolstenholme were suffering privations in the absence of their husbands—Mrs. Johnston's shoes were full of water and she had been able to buy no more since her husband was taken up.

---

[10] Sherwin's *Political Register*, 17 May 1817.

[11] *H.O.* 42.172. These correspondents, who were impatiently awaiting release from detention, knew that their mail was read by the prison governor, and were therefore especially prone to insert references to forgiveness, grace, and improving reading.

All the Cato Street prisoners, it seems, could write after some fashion. Brunt, the shoemaker, salted some sardonic verses with French, while James Wilson wrote:

> the Cause wich nerved a Brutus arm
> to strike a Tirant with alarm
> the cause for wich brave Hamden died
> for wich the Galant Tell defied
> a Tirants insolence and pride.

Richard Tidd, another shoemaker, on the other hand, could only muster: "Sir I Ham a very Bad Hand at Righting".[12] We cannot, of course, take such men as a "sample", since their involvement in political activity indicates that they belonged to the more conscious minority who followed the Radical press. But they may serve to warn us against *under*-stating the diffusion of effective literacy.[13] The artisans are a special case—the intellectual *elite* of the class. But there were, scattered throughout all parts of England, an abundance of educational institutions for working people, even if "institution" is too formal a word for the dame school, the penny-a-week evening school run by a factory cripple or injured pitman, or the Sunday school itself. In the Pennine valleys, where the weavers' children were too poor to pay for slates or paper, they were taught their letters by drawing them with their fingers in a sandtable. If thousands lost these elementary attainments when they reached adult life, on the other hand the work of the Nonconformist Churches, of friendly societies and trade unions, and the needs of industry itself, all demanded that such learning be consolidated and advanced. . . . In most artisan trades the journeymen and petty masters found some reading and work with figures an occupational necessity.

Not only the ballad-singer but also the "number man" or "calendar man" went round the working-class districts, hawking chapbooks,[14] almanacs, dying speeches and (between 1816 and 1820,

---

[12] See J. Stanhope, *The Cato Street Conspiracy*, pp. 161-7.

[13] Some of the earliest trade union correspondence which survives—that of the framework-knitters in the Nottingham City Archives—shows a widespread diffusion of literary attainment.

[14] Catnach's, "Trial of Thurtell", 500,000 (1823): "Confession and Execution of Corder", 1,166,000 (1828).

and at intervals thereafter) Radical periodicals. . . . One of the most impressive features of post-war Radicalism was its sustained effort to extend these attainments and to raise the level of political awareness. At Barnsley as early as January 1816 a penny-a-month club of weavers was formed, for the purpose of buying Radical newspapers and periodicals. The Hampden Clubs and Political Unions took great pains to build up "Reading Societies" and in the larger centres they opened permanent newsrooms or reading-rooms, such as that at Hanley in the Potteries. This room was open from 8 a.m. till 10 p.m. There were penalties for swearing, for the use of indecent language and for drunkenness. Each evening the London papers were to be "publicly read". At the rooms of the Stockport Union in 1818, according to Joseph Mitchell, there was a meeting of class leaders on Monday nights; on Tuesdays, "moral and political readings"; on Wednesdays, "a conversation or debate"; on Thursdays, "Grammar, Arithmetic, &c" was taught; Saturday was a social evening; while Sunday was school day for adults and children alike. In Blackburn the members of the Female Reform Society pledged themselves "to use our utmost endeavour to instil into the minds of our children a deep and rooted hatred of our corrupt and tyrannical rulers." One means was the use of "The Bad Alphabet for the use of the Children of Female Reformers": B was for Bible, Bishop, and Bigotry; K for King, King's evil, Knave and Kidnapper; W for Whig, Weakness, Wavering, and Wicked.

Despite the repression after 1819, the tradition of providing such newsrooms (sometimes attached to the shop of a Radical bookseller) continued through the 1820's. In London after the war there was a boom in coffee-houses, many of which served this double function. By 1833, at John Doherty's famous "Coffee and Newsroom" attached to his Manchester bookshop, no fewer than ninety-six newspapers were taken every week, including the illegal "unstamped." In the smaller towns and villages the reading-groups were less formal but no less important. Sometimes they met at inns, "hush-shops", or private houses; sometimes the periodical was read and discussed in the workshop. The high cost of periodicals during the time of the heaviest "taxes on knowledge" led to thousands of *ad hoc* arrangements by which small groups clubbed together to buy their chosen paper. During the Reform Bill agitation Thomas Dunning, a Nantwich shoemaker, joined with his shopmates and "our Unitarian minister . . . in subscribing to the Weekly Dispatch, price 8¹/₂d., the stamp duty being 4d. It was too expensive for *one* ill-paid crispin. . . ."[15]

The circulation of the Radical press fluctuated violently. Cobbett's 2d. *Register* at its meridian, between October 1816 and February 1817, was running at something between 40,000 and 60,000 each week, a figure many times in excess of any competitor of any sort.[16] The *Black Dwarf* ran at about 12,000 in 1819, although this figure was probably exceeded after Peterloo. Thereafter the stamp tax (and the recession of the movement) severely curtailed circulation, although Carlile's periodicals ran in the thousands through much of the Twenties. With the Reform Bill agitation, the Radical press broke through to a mass circulation once more: Doherty's *Voice of the People*, 30,000, Carlile's *Gauntlet*, 20,000, Hetherington's *Poor Man's Guardian*, 16,000, while a dozen small periodicals, like O'Brien's *Destructive*, ran to some thousands. The slump in the sale of costly weekly periodicals (at anything from 7d. to 1s.) during the stamp tax decade was to great degree made up by the growth in the sales of cheap books and individual pamphlets, ranging from *The Political House that Jack Built* (100,000) to Cobbett's *Cottage Economy* (50,000, 1822-8), *History of the Protestant Reformation*, and *Sermons* (211,000, 1821-8). In the same period, in most of the great centres there were one or more (and in London a dozen) dailies or weeklies which, while not being avowedly "Radical", nevertheless catered for this large Radical public. And the growth in this very large *petit-bourgeois* and working-class reading public was recognised by those influential agencies—notably the Society for the Promotion of Christian Knowledge and the Society for the Diffusion of Useful Knowledge—which made prodigious and lavishly subsidised efforts to divert the readers to more wholesome and improving matter.[17]

[15] For Radical reading-rooms, see A. Aspinall, *Politics and the Press* (1949), pp. 25-8, 395-6; Wearmouth, *op. cit.*, pp. 24-5, 88-9, 97-8, 111-12. For Dunning, "Reminiscences" (ed. W. H. Chaloner), *Trans. Lancs. & Cheshire Antiq. Soc.*, LIX, 1947, p. 97. For Stockport, see *Blanketteer*, 27 November 1819, and D. Read, *Peterloo* (Manchester, 1957), p. 48 f. For Blackburn, W. W. Kinsey, "Some Aspects of Lancashire Radicalism," (M. A. Thesis, Manchester 1927), pp. 66-7.

[16] In 1822 the circulation of the leading daily, *The Times*, was 5,730; the *Observer* (weekly), 6,860.

[17] I have accepted the figured given by R. D. Altick, *op. cit.*, pp. 381-93, although I doubt the claims for the *Voice of the People* and *Gauntlet*. For comparative figures of

This was the culture—with its eager disputations around the bookseller's stalls, in the taverns, workshops, and coffee-houses— which Shelley saluted in his "Song to the Men of England" and within which the genius of Dickens matured. But it is a mistake to see it as a single, undifferentiated "reading public". We may say that there were several different "publics" impinging on and overlapping each other, but nevertheless organised according to different principles. Among the more important were the commercial public, pure and simple, which might be exploited at times of Radical excitement (the trials of Brandreth or of Thistlewood were as marketable as other "dying confessions"), but which was followed according to the simple criteria of profitability; the various more-or-less organised publics, around the Churches or the Mechanic's Institutes; the passive public which the improving societies sought to get at and redeem; and the active, Radical public, which organised itself in the face of the Six Acts and the taxes on knowledge.

The struggle to build and hold this last public has been admirably told in W. D. Wickwar's *The Struggle for the Freedom of the Press*.[18] There is perhaps no country in the world in which the contest for the rights of the press was so sharp, so emphatically victorious, and so peculiarly identified with the cause of the artisans and labourers. If Peterloo established (by a paradox of feeling) the right of public demonstration, the rights of a "free press" were won in a campaign extending over fifteen or more years which has no comparison for its pig-headed, bloody-minded, and indomitable audacity. Carlile (a tinsmith who had nevertheless received a year or two of grammar school education at Ashburton in Devon) rightly saw that the repression of 1819 made the rights of the press the fulcrum of the Radical movement. But, unlike Cobbett and Wooler, who modified their tone to meet the Six Acts in the hope of living to fight another day (and who lost circulation accordingly), Carlile hoisted the black

---

the orthodox press, see Raymond Williams, *The Long Revolution* (1961), pp. 184-92. For the attempts to replace the radical press with safe and improving matter, see R. K. Webb, *op. cit.,* Chs. II, III, IV and J. F. C. Harrison, *op. cit.,* Chs. I and II.

[18] His account, covering the period 1817-1832 is mainly concerned with the first phase of the battle—the right of publication—particularly associated with Richard Carlile. The second phase, the struggle of the "Great Unstamped" (1830-5), associated particularly with the names of Carpenter, Hetherington, Watson, Cleave and Hobson, has not yet found its historian, although see C. D. Collett, *History of the Taxes on Knowledge* (1933 edn.), Ch. II, and A. G. Barker, *Henry Hetherington* (n.d.).

ensign of unqualified defiance and, like a pirate cock-boat, sailed straight into the middle of the combined fleets of the State and Church. As, in the aftermath of Peterloo, he came up for trial (for publishing the Works of Paine), the entire Radical press saluted his courage, but gave him up for lost. When he finally emerged, after years of imprisonment, the combined fleets were scattered beyond the horizon in disarray. He had exhausted the ammunition of the Government, and turned its *ex officio* informations and special juries into laughing-stocks. He had plainly sunk the private prosecuting societies, the Constitutional Association (or "Bridge-Street Gang") and the Vice Society, which were supported by the patronage and the subscriptions of the nobility, bishops and Wilberforce.

Carlile did not, of course, achieve this triumph on his own. The first round of the battle was fought in 1817, when there were twenty-six prosecutions for seditious and blasphemous libel and sixteen *ex officio* informations filed by the law officers of the Crown.[19] . . . Imprisonment as a Radical publisher brought, not odium, but honour. Once the publishers had decided that they were ready to go to prison, they outdid each other with new expedients to exhibit their opponents in the most ludicrous light. Radical England was delighted (and no one more than Hazlitt) at the resurrection by Sherwin of *Wat Tyler*—the republican indiscretion of Southey's youth. Southey, now Poet Laureate, was foremost in the clamour to curb the seditious licence of the press, and sought an injunction against Sherwin for infringement of copyright. Lord Eldon refused the injunction: the Court could not take notice of property in the "unhallowed profits of libellous publications". "Is it not a little strange," Hazlitt enquired, "that while this gentleman is getting an injunction against himself as the author of *Wat Tyler*, he is recommending gagging bills against us, and thus making up by force for his deficiency in argument?"[20] On the other hand, Carlile (who had taken over Sherwin's business) was more than pleased that the injunction was refused—for the sales of the poem were a staple source of profit in his difficult period at the start of the business. "Glory be to thee, O Southey!", he wrote six years later: "*Wat Tyler*

---

[19] Wickwar, *The Struggle for the Freedom of the Press* (1928), p. 315. See also *ibid.*, pp. 38-9 for the peculiarly unfair form of persecution, the *ex officio* information, which virtually permitted imprisonment without trial.

[20] Hazlitt, *Works*, VII, pp. 176ff. "Instead of applying for an injunction against *Wat Tyler*," Hazlitt opined, "Mr. Southey would do well to apply for an injunction against Mr. Coleridge, who has undertaken his defence in *The Courier*.

continued to be a source of profit when every other political publication failed. The world does not know what it may yet owe to Southey."[21]

The incidents of the pirating of *Queen Mab* and the *Vision of Judgement* were part of the same ebullient strategy. No British monarch has ever been portrayed in more ridiculous postures nor in more odious terms than George IV during the Queen Caroline agitation, and notably in Hone and Cruikshank's *Right Divine of Kings to Govern Wrong, The Queen's Matrimonial Ladder, Non Mi Ricordo,* and *The Man in the Moon.* The same author's *Slap at Slop and the Bridge-Street Gang* (1822), appeared in the format of the Government-subsidised *New Times,* complete with a mock newspaper-stamp with the design of a cat's paw and the motto: "On Every Thing He Claps His Claw", and with mock advertisements and mock lists of births and deaths:

MARRIAGE

His Imperial Majesty Prince Despotism, in a consumption, to Her Supreme Antiquity, The *ignorance* of Eighteen Centuries, in a decline. The bridal dresses were most superb.

While Carlile fought on from prison, the satirists raked his prosecutors with fire.

The second point is the real toughness of the libertarian and constitutional tradition, notwithstanding the Government's assault. It is not only a question of support in unexpected places—Hone's subscription list was headed by donations from a Whig duke, a marquis, and two earls—which indicates an uneasiness in the ruling class itself. What is apparent from the reports of the law officers of the Crown, in all political trials, is the caution with which they proceeded. In particular they were aware of the unreliability (for their purposes) of the jury system. By Fox's Libel Act of 1792 the jury were judges of the libel as well as of the fact of publishing; and however judges might seek to set this aside, this meant in effect that twelve Englishmen had to decide whether they thought the "libel" dangerous enough to merit imprisonment or not. One State prosecution which failed was a blow at the morale of authority which could only be repaired by three which succeeded. Even in 1819-21 when the Government and the prosecuting societies carried almost every

---

[21] Sherwin's *Republican*, 29 March 1817; Carlile's *Republican*, 30 May 1823.

case[22] (in part as a result of their better deployment of legal resources and their influence upon juries, in part because Carlile was at his most provocative and had shifted the battlefield from sedition to blasphemy), it still is not possible to speak of "totalitarian" or "Asiatic" despotism. Reports of the trials were widely circulated, containing the very passages—sometimes, indeed, whole books read by the defendants in court—for which the accused were sentenced. Carlile continued imperturbably to edit the *Republican* from gaol; some of his shopmen, indeed, undertook in prison the editing of another journal, as a means of self-improvement. If Wooler's *Black Dwarf* failed in 1824, Cobbett remained in the field. He did not like Carlile's Republicanism and Deism, nor their hold on the artisans of the great centres; and he turned increasingly back to the countryside and distanced himself from the working-class movement. (In 1821 he undertook the first of his *Rural Rides*, in which his genius seems at last to have found its inevitable form and matter.) But, even at this distance, the *Political Register* was always there, with its columns—like those of the Republican—open to expose any case of persecution, from Bodmin to Berwick.

The honours of this contest did not belong to a single class. John Hunt and Thelwall (now firmly among the middle-class moderates) were among those pestered by the "Bridge-Street Gang"; Sir Charles Wolseley, Burdett, the Reverend Joseph Harrison, were among those imprisoned for sedition. But Carlile and his shopmen were those who pressed defiance to its furthest point. The main battle was over by 1823, although there were renewed prosecutions in the late Twenties and early Thirties, and blasphemy cases trickled on into Victorian times. Carlile's greatest offence was to proceed with the unabashed publication of the *Political Works*, and then the *Theological Works*, of Tom Paine—works which, while circulating surreptitiously in the enclaves of "old Jacks" in the cities, had been banned ever since Paine's trial *in absentia* in 1792, and Daniel Isaac Eaton's successive trials during the Wars. To this he added many further offences as the struggle wore on, and as he himself moved from Deism to Atheism, and as he threw in provocations—such as the advocacy of assassination—which in any view of the case were incitements to prosecution. He was an indomitable man, but he was scarcely loveable, and his years of imprisonment did not improve him. His strength lay in two things. First, he would not even admit of

---

[22] In these three years there were 115 prosecutions and 45 *ex officio* informations.

the possibility of defeat. And second, he had at his back the culture of the artisans.

The first point is not as evident as it appears. Determined men have often (as in the 1790's) been silenced or defeated. It is true that Carlile's brand of determination ("THE SHOP IN FLEET STREET WILL NOT BE CLOSED AS A MATTER OF COURSE") was peculiarly difficult for the authorities to meet. No matter how much law they had on their side, they must always incur odium by prosecutions. But they had provided themselves, under the Six Acts, with the power to *banish* the authors of sedition for offences far less than those which Carlile both committed and proudly admitted. It is testimony to the delicate equilibrium of the time, and to the limits imposed upon power by the consensus of constitutionalist opinion, that even in 1820 this provision of the Act was not employed. Banishment apart, Carlile could not be silenced, unless he were to be beheaded, or, more possibly, placed in solitary confinement. But there are two reasons why the Government did not proceed to extreme measures: first, already by 1821 it seemed to them less *necessary*, for the increased stamp duties were taking effect. Second, it was apparent after the first encounters that if Carlile were to be silenced, half a dozen new Carliles would step into his place. The first two who did so *were*, in fact, Carliles: his wife and his sister. Thereafter the "shopmen" came forward. By one count, before the battle had ended Carlile had received the help of 150 volunteers, who—shopmen, printers, newsvendors—had between them served 200 years of imprisonment. The volunteers were advertised for in the *Republican*—men "who were free, able, and willing" to serve in General Carlile's Corps:

> It is most distinctly to be understood that a love of propagating the principles, and a sacrifice of liberty to that end . . . AND NOT GAIN, must be the motive to call forth such volunteers; for—though R. Carlile pledges himself to . . . give such men the best support in his power—should any great number be imprisoned, he is not so situated as to property or prospects as to be able to promise any particular sum weekly. . . .[23]

From that time forward the "Temple of Reason" off Fleet Street was scarcely left untenanted for more than a day. The men and women who came forward were, in nearly every case, entirely unknown to Carlile. They simply came out of London; or arrived on the coach from Lincolnshire, Dorset, Liverpool and Leeds. They came out of a culture.

It was not the "working-class" culture of the weavers or Tyneside pitmen. The people most prominent in the fight included clerks, shop assistants, a farmer's son; Benbow, the shoemaker turned bookseller; James Watson, the Leeds warehouseman who "had the charge of a saddlehorse" at a drysalter's; James Mann, the cropper turned bookseller (also of Leeds). The intellectual tradition was in part derived from the Jacobin years, the circle which had once moved around Godwin and Mary Wollstonecraft, or the members of the L.C.S. [London Corresponding Society, ed.], the last authentic spokesman of which—John Gale Jones—was one of Carlile's most constant supporters. In part it was a new tradition, owing something to Bentham's growing influence and something to the "free-thinking Christians" and Unitarians, such as Benjamin Flower and W. J. Fox. It touched that vigorous sub-culture of the "editors of Sunday newspapers and lecturers at the Surrey Institute" which *Blackwood's* and the literary Establishment so scorned—schoolmasters, poor medical students, or civil servants who read Byron and Shelley and the *Examiner*, and among whom, not Whig or Tory, but "right and wrong considered by each man abstractedly, is the fashion."[24]

It is scarcely helpful to label this culture *bourgeois* or *petit-bourgeois*, although Carlile had more than his share of the individualism which (it is generally supposed) characterises the latter. It would seem to be closer to the truth that the impulse of rational enlightenment which (in the years of the wars had been largely confined to the Radical intelligentsia) was now seized upon by the artisans and some of the skilled workers (such as many cotton-spinners) with an evangelistic zeal to carry it to "numbers unlimited"—a propagandist zeal scarcely to be found in Bentham, James Mill or Keats. The subscription lists for Carlile's campaign drew heavily upon London; and, next, upon Manchester and Leeds. The artisan culture was, above all, that of the self-taught. "During this

---

23 Wickwar, *op. cit.*, p. 231.

24 Keats to his brother George, 17 September 1819, *Works*, (1901), V, p. 108. The letter continues: "This makes the business of Carlile the bookseller of great moment in my mind. He has been selling deistical pamphlets, republished Tom Paine, and many other works held in superstitious horror . . . . After all, they are afraid to prosecute. They are afraid of his defence; it would be published in all the papers all over the empire. They shudder at this. The trials would light a flame they could not extinguish. Do you not think this of great import?"

twelve-month," Watson recalled of his imprisonment, "I read with deep interest and much profit Gibbon's *Decline and Fall of the Roman Empire*, Hume's *History of England*, and . . . Mosheim's *Ecclesiastical History*."[25] The artisans, who formed the nuclei of Carlile's supporting "Zetetic Societies" (as well as of the later Rotunda) were profoundly suspicious of an established culture which had excluded them from power and knowledge and which had answered their protests with homilies and tracts. The works of the Enlightenment came to them with the force of revelation.

In this way a reading public which was increasingly working class in character was forced to *organise itself*. The war and immediate post-war years had seen a "kept" press, on the one hand, and a Radical press on the other. In the Twenties much of the middle-class press freed itself from direct Government influence, and made some use of the advantages which Cobbett and Carlile had gained. *The Times* and Lord Brougham, who disliked the "pauper press" perhaps as much as Lord Eldon (although for different reasons), gave to the term "Radicalism" a quite different meaning—free trade, cheap government, and utilitarian reform. To some degree (although by no means entirely) they carried the Radical middle-class with them—the schoolmasters, surgeons, and shopkeepers, some of whom had once supported Cobbett and Wooler—so that by 1832 there were *two* Radical publics: the middle-class, which looked forward to the Anti-Corn Law League, and the working-class, whose journalists (Hetherington, Watson, Cleave, Lovett, Benbow, O'Brien) were already maturing the Chartist movement. Throughout the Twenties the working-class press struggled under the crushing weight of the stamp duties,[26] while Cobbett remained loosely and temperamentally affiliated to the plebeian rather than to the middle-class movement. The dividing-line came to be, increasingly, not alternative "reform" strategies (for middle-class reformers could on occasion be as revolutionary in their tone as their working-class counterparts) but alternative notions of political economy. The touchstone can be seen during the field labourer's "revolt" in 1830, when *The Times* (Cobbett's "BLOODY OLD TIMES") led the demand for salutary examples to be made of the rioters, while both Cobbett and

---

[25] W. J. Linton, *James Watson*, (Manchester, 1880), p. 19.

[26] In 1830 these taxes amounted to a 4d. stamp on each newspaper or weekly periodical, a duty of 3s.6d. on each advertisement, a small paper duty, and a large surety against action for libel.

Carlile were prosecuted once again on charges of inflammatory writing.

In 1830 and 1831 the black ensign of defiance was hoisted once again. Cobbett found a loophole in the law, and recommenced his *Twopenny Trash.* But this time it was Hetherington, a printing worker, who led the frontal attack. His *Poor Man's Guardian* carried the emblem of a hand-press, the motto "Knowledge is Power", and the heading: "Published contrary to 'Law' to try the power of 'Might' against 'Right'." His opening address, quoted clause by clause the laws he intended to defy:

> . . . the *Poor Man's Guardian* . . . will contain "*news, intelligence and occurrences,*" and "*remarks and observations thereon,*" and "*upon matters of Church and State tending,*" decidedly, "*to excite hatred and contempt of the Government and Constitution of* . . . *this country, as BY LAW established,*" and also, "*to vilify the ABUSES of Religion*". . . .

It would also defy every clause of the stamp tax legislation,

> or any other acts whatsoever and despite the "laws or the will and pleasure of *any tyrant* or *body of tyrants* whatsoever, any thing hereinbefore, or any-where-else . . . to the contrary notwithstanding.

His fourth number carried the advertisement, "WANTED": "Some hundreds of POOR MEN out of employ who have NOTHING TO RISK . . . to sell to the poor and ignorant" this paper. Not only were the volunteers found, but a score of other unstamped papers sprang up, notably Carlile's *Gauntlet,* and Joshua Hobson's *Voice of the West Riding.* By 1836 the struggle was substantially over, and the way had been opened for the Chartist press.

But the "great unstamped" was emphatically a working-class press. The *Poor Man's Guardian* and the *Working Man's Friend* were, in effect, organs of the National Union of the Working Classes; Doherty's *Poor Man's Advocate* was an organ of the Factory Movement; Joshua Hobson was a former hand-loom weaver, who had built a wooden hand-press by his own labour; Bronterre O'Brien's *Destructive* consciously sought to develop working-class Radical theory. These small, closely-printed, penny weeklies carried news of the great struggle for General Unionism in these years, the lock-outs of 1834 and the protests at the Tolpuddle case, or searching debate and exposition of Socialist and trade union theory. An examination of this period would take us beyond the limits of this study, to a time when the working-class was no longer in the making but (in its Chartist form) already made. The point we must note is the degree to which the fight for press liberties was a central formative influence upon the shaping movement. Perhaps 500 people were prosecuted for the production and sale of the "unstamped."[27] From 1816 (indeed, from 1792) until 1836 the contest involved, not only the editors, booksellers, and printers but also many hundreds of newsvendors, hawkers, and voluntary agents.[28]

Year after year the annals of persecution continue. In 1817 two men selling Cobbett's pamphlets in Shropshire, whom a clerical magistrate "caused . . . to be apprehended under the Vagrant Act . . . and had *well flogged at the whipping-post*"; in the same year hawkers in Plymouth, Exeter, the Black Country, Oxford, the north; in 1819 even a peep-show huckster, who showed a print of Peterloo in a Devon village. The imprisonments were rarely for more than a year (often newsvendors were committed to prison for a few weeks and then released without trial) but they could be more serious in their effects upon the victims than the more widely-publicised imprisonments of editors. Men were thrown into verminous "Houses of Correction"; often chained and fettered; often without knowledge of the law or means of defence. Unless their cases were noted by Cobbett, Carlile or some section of the Radicals, their families were left without any income and might be forced into the workhouse.[29] It was, indeed, in the smaller centres that the contest for freedom was most hard-fought. Manchester or Nottingham or Leeds had Radical enclaves and meetingplaces, and were ready to support the victimised. In the market town or industrial village, the cobbler or teacher who took in Cobbett or Carlile in the Twenties might expect to be watched and to suffer persecution in indirect forms. (Often Cobbett's parcels of *Registers* to country subscribers

[27] Abel Haywood, the Manchester bookseller, claimed the figure to be 750.

[28] Societies for the Diffusion of "Really Useful Knowledge" were formed to assist the "unstamped". See *Working Man's Friend*, 18 May 1833.

[29] See Wickwar, *op. cit.*, pp. 40, 103-14; *Second Trial of William Hone* (1818), p. 19; for the case of Robert Swindells, confined in Chester castle, while his wife and baby died from neglect, and his remaining child was placed in the poorhouse; Sherwin's *Political Register*, 14 March 1818, for the cases of Mellor and Pilling of Warrington, held for nineteen weeks chained to felons in Preston Gaol, sent for trial at the Court of King's Bench in London—the 200 miles to which they had to walk—the trial removed to Lancaster (200 miles back)—and then discharged.

simply failed to arrive—they were "lost" in the mail.) A whole pattern of distribution, with its own folklore, grew up around the militant press. Hawkers (Mayhew was told), in order to avoid "selling" the *Republican*, sold straws instead, and then *gave* the paper to their customers. In the Spen Valley, in the days of the "unstamped," a penny was dropped through a grating and the paper would "appear." In other parts, men would slip down alleys or across fields at night to the known rendezvous. More than once the "unstamped" were transported under the noses of the authorities in a coffin and with a godly cortege of free-thinkers.

We may take two examples of the shopmen and vendors. The first, a shop-*woman*, serves to remind us that, in these rationalist and Owenite circles, the claim for women's rights (almost silent since the 1790's) was once again being made, and was slowly extending from the intelligentsia to the artisans. Carlile's womenfolk, who underwent trial and imprisonment, did so more out of loyalty than out of conviction. Very different was Mrs. Wright, a Nottingham lace-mender, who was prosecuted for selling one of his *Addresses* containing opinions in his characteristic manner:

> A Representative System of Government would soon see the proprie-ty of turning our Churches and Chapels into Temples of Science and . . . cherishing the Philosopher instead of the Priest. Kingcraft and Priestcraft I hold to be the bane of Society . . . . Those two evils operate jointly against the welfare both of the body [and] of [the] mind, and to palliate our miseries in this life, the latter endeavour to bamboozle us with a hope of eternal happiness.

She conducted her long defence herself[30] and was rarely inter-rupted. Towards the end of her defence,

> Mrs. Wright requested permission to retire and suckle her infant child that was crying. This was granted, and she was absent from the Court twenty minutes. In passing to and fro, to the Castle Coffee House, she was applauded and loudly cheered by assembled thousands, all encouraging her to be of good cheer and to persevere.

Some time later she was thrown into Newgate, on a November night, with her six-months' baby and nothing to lie on but a mat. Such women as Mrs. Wright (and Mrs. Mann of Leeds) had to meet

---

[30] Most of Carlile's shopmen were provided with long written defences by Carlile, and this was probably so in her case.

not only the customary prosecutions, but also the abuse and insinuations of an outraged loyalist press. "This wretched and shameless woman," wrote the *New Times*, was attended by "*several females*. Are not these circumstances enough to shock every reflecting mind?" She was an "abandoned creature" (the conventional epithet for prostitutes) "who has cast off all the distinctive shame and fear and decency of her sex." By her "horrid example" she had depraved the minds of other mothers: "these monsters in female form stand forward, with hardened visages, in the face of day, to give their public countenance and support—*for the first time in the history of the Christian world*—to gross, vulgar, horrid blasphemy." She was a woman, wrote Carlile, "of very delicate health, and truly all spirit and no matter."[31] . . .

In the 20th-century rhetoric of democracy most of these men and women have been forgotten, because they were impudent, vulgar, over-earnest, or "fanatical." In their wake the subsidised vehicles of "improvement," the *Penny Magazine* and the *Saturday Magazine* (whose vendors no one persecuted) moved in: and afterwards the commercial press, with its much larger resources, although it did not really begin to capture the Radical reading public until the Forties and the Fifties. (Even then the popular press—the publications of Cleave, Howitt, Chambers, Reynolds, and Lloyd—came from this Radical background.) Two consequences of the contest may be particularly noticed. The first (and most obvious) is that the working-class ideology which matured in the Thirties (and which has endured, through various translations, ever since) put an exceptionally high value upon the rights of the press, of speech, of meeting and of personal liberty. The tradition of the "free-born Englishman" is of course far older. But the notion to be found in some late "Marxist" interpretations, by which these claims appear as a heritage of "bourgeois individualism" will scarcely do. In the contest between 1792 and 1836 the artisans and workers made this tradition peculiarly their own, adding to the claim for free speech and thought their own claim for the untrammelled propagation, in the cheapest possible form, of the products of this thought.

In this, it is true, they shared a characteristic illusion of the epoch, applying it with force to the context of working-class struggle. All the enlighteners and improvers of the time thought that the only

---

[31] See Wickwar, *op. cit.*, pp. 222-3; *Trial of Mrs. Susannah Wright* (1822), pp. 8, 44, 56; *New Times*, 16 November 1822.

limit imposed to the diffusion of reason and knowledge was that imposed by the inadequacy of the means. The analogies which were drawn were frequently mechanical. The educational method of Lancaster and Bell, with its attempt at the cheap multiplication of learning by child monitors, was called (by Bell) the "STEAM ENGINE of the MORAL WORLD." Peacock aimed with deadly accuracy when he called Brougham's Society for the Diffusion of Useful Knowledge the "Steam Intellect Society." Carlile was supremely confident that "pamphlet-reading is destined to work the great necessary moral and political changes among mankind":

> The Printing-press may be strictly denominated a Multiplication Table as applicable to the mind of man. The art of Printing is a multiplication of mind. . . . Pamphlet-vendors are the most important springs in the machinery of Reform.[32]

Owen contemplated the institution, by means of propaganda, of the NEW MORAL WORLD with messianic, but mechanical, optimism.

But if this was, in part, the rationalist illusion, we must remember the second—and more immediate—consequence: between 1816 and 1836 this "multiplication" seemed to *work*. For the Radical and unstamped journalists were seizing the multiplying-machine on behalf of the working class; and in every part of the country the experiences of the previous quarter-century had prepared men's minds for what they now could read. The importance of the propaganda can be seen in the steady extension of Radical organization from the great towns and manufacturing areas into the small boroughs and market towns. One of the Six Acts of 1819 (that authorising the search for weapons) was specifically confined only to designated "disturbed districts" of the Midlands and the North.[33] By 1832—and on into Chartist times—there is a Radical nucleus to be found in every county, in the smallest market towns and even in the larger rural villages, and in nearly every case it is based on the local artisans. In such centres as Croydon, Colchester and Ipswich, Tiverton and Taunton, Nantwich or Cheltenham, there were hardy and militant Radical or Chartist bodies. In Ipswich we find weavers, saddlers, harness-makers, tailors, shoemakers; in Cheltenham shoe-

---

[32] See Wickwar, *op. cit.*, p. 214.
[33] The counties of Lancaster, Chester, the West Riding, Warwick, Stafford, Derby, Leicester, Nottingham, Cumberland, Westmorland, Northumberland, Durham, the city of Coventry, and the county boroughs of Newcastle-upon-Tyne and Nottingham.

makers, tailors, stonemasons, cabinet-makers, garderners, a plasterer and a blacksmith—"earnest and reputable people—much above the average in intelligence."[34] These are the people whom Cobbett, Carlile, Hetherington and their newsvendors had "multiplied."

"Earnest and reputable people . . ."—this autodidact culture has never been adequately analysed.[35] The majority of these people had received some elementary education, although its inadequacy is testified from many sources:

> I well remember the first half-time school in Bingley. It was a cottage at the entrance to the mill-yard. The teacher, a poor old man who had done odd jobs of a simple kind for about 12s. a week, was set to teach the half-timers. Lest, however, he should teach too much or the process be too costly, he had to stamp washers out of cloth with a heavy wooden mallet on a large block of wood during school hours.[36]

This is, perhaps, the "schooling" of the early 1830's at its worst. Better village schools, or cheap fee-paying schools patronised by artisans, could be found in the Twenties. By this time, also, the Sunday schools were liberating themselves (although slowly) from the taboo upon the teaching of writing, while the first British and National schools (for all their inadequacies) were beginning to have some effect. But, for any secondary education, the artisans, weavers, or spinners had to teach themselves. The extent to which they were doing this is attested by the sales of Cobbett's educational writings, and notably of his *Grammar of the English Language,* published in 1818, selling 13,000 within six months, and a further 100,000 in the next fifteen years.[37] And we must remember that in translating sales (or the circulation of periodicals) into estimates of readership, the same book or paper was loaned, read aloud, and passed through many hands.

[34] W. E. Adams, *op. cit.*, p. 169. I am indebted to Mr. A. J. Brown for information about Ipswich. See also *Chartist Studies*, ed. A. Briggs, for Chartism in Somerset and East Anglia.

[35] J. F. C. Harrison's admirable account in *Learning and Living* tends to underestimate the vigour of redical culture before 1832. The best first-hand accounts are in William Lovett's autobiography and (for Chartist times) Thomas Frost, *Forty Years Recollections* (1880).

[36] Thomas Wood, *Autobiography* (1822-80) (Leeds, 1956). See also An Old Potter, *When I was a Child* (1903), Ch.I.

[37] M. L. Pearl, *William Cobbett* (1953), pp. 105-7. There were also many pirated editions.

But the "secondary education" of the workers took many forms, of which private study in solitude was only one. The artisans, in particular, were not as rooted in benighted communities as it is easy to assume. They tramped freely about the country in search of work; apart from the enforced travels of the Wars, many mechanics travelled abroad, and the relative facility with which thousands upon thousands emigrated to America and the colonies (driven not only by poverty but also by the desire for opportunity or political freedom) suggests a general fluency of social life. In the cities a vigorous and bawdy plebeian culture co-existed with more polite traditions among the artisans. Many collections of early 19th-century ballads testify to the fervour with which the battle between Loyalists and Radicals was carried into song. Perhaps it was the melodramatic popular theatre which accorded best with the gusto of the Jacobins and of the "old Radicals" of 1816-20. From the early 1790's the theatre, especially in provincial centres, was a forum in which the opposed factions confronted each other, and provoked each other by "calling the tunes" in the intervals. . . .

The vitality of the plebeian theatre was not matched by its artistic merit. The most positive influence upon the sensibility of the Radicals came less from the little theatres than from the Shakespearian revival—not only Hazlitt, but also Wooler, Bamford, Cooper, and a score of self-taught Radical and Chartist journalists were wont to cap their arguments with Shakespearian quotations. Wooler's apprenticeship had been in dramatic criticism; while the strictly trades unionist *Trades Newspaper* commenced, in 1825, with a theatre critic as well as a sporting column (covering prize-fighting and the contest between "the Lion Nero and Six Dogs").[38] But there was one popular art which, in the years between 1780 and 1830, attained to a peak of complexity and excellence—the political print.

This was the age, first, of Gillray and of Rowlandson, and then of George Cruikshank, as well as of scores of other caricaturists, some competent, some atrociously crude. Theirs was, above all, a metropolitan art. The models for the cartoonists drove in their coaches past the print-shops where their political (or personal) sins were mercilessly lampooned. No holds whatsoever were barred, on either

---

[38] *Trades Newspaper*, 31 July, 21 August 1825 et seq. The Editor felt called upon to apologise for carrying news of prize-fighting and animal-baiting; but the paper was governed by a committee of London trades unions, and the members' wishes had to be met.

side. Thelwall or Burdett or Hunt would be portrayed by the loyalists as savage incendiaries, a flaming torch in one hand, a pistol in the other, and with belts crammed with butchers' knives; while Cruikshank portrayed the King (in 1820) lolling blind drunk in his throne, surrounded by broken bottles and in front of a screen decorated with satyrs and large-breasted trollops. (The Bishops fared no better.) The popular print was by no means an art for the illiterate, as the balloons full of minute print, issuing from the mouths of the figures, testify. But the illiterate also could participate in this culture, standing by the hour in front of the print-shop window and deciphering the intricate visual minutiae in the latest Gillray or Cruikshank: at Knight's in Sweeting's Alley, Fairburn's off Ludgate Hill, or Hone's in Fleet Street (Thackeray recalled), "there used to be a crowd . . . of grinning, good-natured mechanics, who spelt the songs, and spoke them out for the benefit of the company, and who received the points of humour with a general sympathising roar." On occasions, the impact was sensational; Fleet Street would be blocked by the crowds; Cruikshank believed that his "Bank Restriction Note" (1818) resulted in the abolition of the death-penalty for passing forged money. In the 1790's the Government actually suborned Gillray into anti-Jacobin service. During the Wars the mainstream of prints was patriotic and anti-Gallican (John Bull took on his classic shape in these years), but on domestic issues the prints were savagely polemical and frequently Burdettite in sympathy. After the Wars a flood of Radical prints was unloosed, which remained immune from prosecution, even during the Queen Caroline agitation, because prosecution would have incurred greater ridicule. Through all its transformations (and despite the crudities of many practitioners) it remained a highly sophisticated city art: it could be acutely witty, or cruelly blunt and obscene, but in either case it depended upon a frame of reference of shared gossip and of intimate knowledge of the manners and foibles of even minor participants in public affairs—a patina of intricate allusiveness.[39]

The culture of the theatre and the print-shop was popular in a wider sense than the literary culture of the Radical artisans. For the keynote of the autodidact culture of the Twenties and early Thirties was moral sobriety. It is customary to attribute this to the influence

[39] Some motion of the complexity of this output can be gained from Dr. Dorothy George's very learned *Catalogues of Political and Personal Satire in the British Museum*, volumes VII, VIII, and IX and X. See also Blanchard Jerrold, *George Cruikshank* (1894), Ch. IV.

of Methodism, and undoubtedly, both directly and indirectly, this influence can be felt. The Puritan character-structure underlies the moral earnestness and self-discipline which enabled men to work on by candle-light after a day of labour. But we have to make two important reservations. The first is that Methodism was a strongly *anti-intellectual* influence, from which British popular culture has never wholly recovered. The circle to which Wesley would have confined the reading of Methodists (Southey noted) "was narrow enough; his own works, and his own series of abridgements, would have constituted the main part of a Methodist's library."[40] In the early 19th century local preachers and class leaders were encouraged to read more: reprints of Baxter, the hagiography of the movement, or "vollams of the Missionary Register." But poetry was suspect, and philosophy, biblical criticism, or political theory taboo. The whole weight of Methodist teaching fell upon the blessedness of the "pure in heart," no matter what their rank or accomplishments. This gave to the Church its egalitarian spiritual appeal. But it also fed (sometimes to gargantuan proportions) the philistine defences of the scarcely-literate. "It is *carte blanche* for ignorance and folly," Hazlitt exploded:

> Those . . . who are either unable or unwilling to think connectedly or rationally on any subject, are at once released from every obligation of the kind, by being told that faith and reason are opposed to one another.[41]

From the successive shocks of Paine, Cobbett, Carlile, the Methodist ministers defended their flocks: the evidence was abundant that unmonitored literacy was the "snare of the devil."

Some of the off-shoots from the main Methodist stem—the Methodist Unitarians (an odd conjunction) and notably the New Connexion—were more intellectual in inclination, and their congregations resemble the older Dissenting Churches. But the main Methodist tradition responded to the thirst for enlightenment in a different way. . . . Strange as it may seem, when we think of Bentham and his hatred of "juggical" superstition, the spirit of the times was working for a conjunction of the two traditions. If intellectual *enquiry* was discouraged by the Methodists, the acquisition of *useful* knowledge could be seen as godly and full of merit.

---

[40] Southey, *Life of Wesley*, p. 558.
[41] *Works*, IV, pp. 57ff., from *The Round Table* (1817).

The emphasis, of course, was upon the *use*. Work discipline alone was not enough, it was necessary for the labour force to advance towards more sophisticated levels of attainment. The old opportunist Baconian argument—that there could be no evil in the study of nature, which is the visible evidence of God's laws—had now been assimilated within Christian apologetics. Hence arose that peculiar phenomenon of early Victorian culture, the Nonconformist parson with his hand on the Old Testament and his eye on a microscope.

The effects of this conjunction can already be felt within the working-class culture of the Twenties. Science—botany, biology, geology, chemistry, mathematics, and, in particular, the applied sciences—the Methodists looked upon with favour, provided that these pursuits were not intermixed with politics or speculative philosophy. The solid, statistical, intellectual world which the Utilitarians were building was congenial also to the Methodist Conference. They also compiled their statistical tables of Sunday school attendances, and Bunting (one feels) would have been happy if he could have calculated degrees of spiritual grace with the accuracy that Chadwick calculated the minimum diet that might keep a pauper in strength to work. Hence came that alliance between Nonconformists and Utilitarians in educational endeavour, and in the dissemination of "improving" knowledge alongside godly exhortation. Already in the Twenties this kind of literature is well established, in which moral admonishments (and accounts of the drunken orgies of Tom Paine on his unvisited deathbed) appear side by side with little notes on the flora of Venezuela, statistics of the death-roll in the Lisbon earthquake, recipes for boiled vegetables, and notes on hydraulics. . . . And already in the Twenties, Political Economy can be seen as a third partner alongside Morality and Useful Knowledge, in the shape of homilies upon the God-given and immutable laws of supply and demand. Capital, even nicer in its taste than the hog, would select only the industrious and obedient worker and reject all others.

Thus Methodism and Evangelicism contributed few active intellectual ingredients to the articulate culture of the working people, although they can be said to have added an earnestness to the pursuit of *information*. (Arnold was later to see the Nonconformist tradition as deeply philistine, and indifferent to "sweetness and light.") And there is a second reservation to be made, when the sobriety of the artisan's world is attributed to this source. Moral sobriety was in fact demonstrably a product of the Radical and rationalist agitation itself; and owed much to the old Dissenting and Jacobin traditions. This is not to say that there were no drunken Radicals nor disorderly demonstrations. Wooler was only one of the Radical leaders who, it was said, was too fond of the bottle; while we have seen that the London taverns and Lancashire hush-shops were important meeting-places. But the Radicals sought to rescue the people from the imputation of being a "mob;" and their leaders sought continually to present an image of sobriety.

Moreover, there were other motives for this emphasis. One of the Rules of the Bath Union Society for Parliamentary Reform (established in January 1817) is characteristic:

> It is earnestly recommended to every Member not to spend his Money at public houses, because half of the said Money goes in Taxes, to feed the Maggots of Corruption.[42]

In the post-war years Hunt and Cobbett made much of the call for abstinence from all taxed articles, and in particular of the virtues of water over spirits or beer. The sobriety of the Methodists was the one (and only) attribute of their "sect" which Cobbett found it possible to praise: "I look upon drunkenness as the root of much more than half the mischief, misery and crimes with which society is afflicted."[43] This was not always Cobbett's tone; on other occasions he could lament the price, for the labourer, of beer. But a general moral primness is to be found in most quarters. It was, particularly, the ideology of the artisan or of the skilled worker who had held his position in the face of the boisterous unskilled tide. It is to be found in Carlile's account of his early manhood:

> I was a regular, active, and industrious man, working early and late . . . and when out of the workshop never so happy anywhere as at home with my wife and two children. The alehouse I always detested . . . I had a notion that a man . . . was a fool not to make a right application of every shilling.[44]

Many a day he had missed out a meal, and "carried home some

---

[42] *H.O.* 40.4.

[43] *Political Register*, 13 January 1821. The Temperance Movement can be traced to this post-war campaign of abstinence.

[44] See Wickwar, *op.cit.*, p. 68.

sixpenny publication to read at night." It is to be found, in its most admirable and moving form, in William Lovett's *Life and Struggles . . . in Pursuit of Bread, Knowledge and Freedom,* a title which, in itself, condenses all that we are seeking to describe.

It was a disposition strengthened, among the republicans and free-thinkers, by the character of the attacks upon them. Denounced in loyalist lampoons and from Church pulpits as disreputable exemplars of every vice, they sought to exhibit themselves as bearing, alongside their unorthodox opinions, an irreproachable character. They struggled against the loyalist legends of revolutionary France, which was presented as a sanguinary thieves' kitchen, whose Temples of Reason were brothels. They were particularly sensitive to any accusation of sexual impropriety, of financial misconduct, or of lack of attachment to the familial virtues.[45] Carlile published in 1830 a little book of homilies, *The Moralist,* while Cobbett's *Advice to Young Men* was only a more hearty and readable essay upon the same themes of industry, perseverance, independence. The rationalists, of course, were especially anxious to counter the accusation that the rejection of the Christian faith must inevitably entail the dissolution of all moral restraints. Alongside Volney's influential *Ruins of Empire* there was translated, and circulated as a tract, his *Law of Nature,* which served to argue—in the form of a dialogue—that the respectable virtues must all be adhered to according to the laws of social utility:

Q. Why do you say that conjugal love is a virtue?
A. Because the concord and union which are the consequence of the affection subsisting between married persons, establish in the bosom of their family a multitude of habits which contribute to its prosperity and conservation . . . .

So on for the greater part of a page. And so, through chapters on Knowledge, Continence, Temperance, Cleanliness, the Domestic Virtues, which read like a prospectus for the Victorian age. Where heterodoxy appeared on matters of sexual relations, as it did among the Owenite communitarians, it generally did so with a zeal charac-

---

[45]Cf. T. Frost, *Forty Years' Recollections,* p. 20. (of the anti-Owenite propaganda of the Thirties): "It was a very common device for complainants and witnesses to say of a person charged with larceny, wife desertion, or almost any other offence, 'He is a Socialist'; and reports of all such cases had the side-head, 'Effect of Owenism' . . .".

teristic of the Puritan temperament.[46] The very small group of neo-Malthusians who with considerable courage propagated among the working people, in the early Twenties, knowledge of the means of contraception did so out of the conviction that the only way in which the "industrious classes" could raise their physical and cultural standards was by limiting their own numbers. Place and his companions would have been utterly shocked if it had been suggested that these means contributed to sexual or personal freedom.[47]

Levity or hedonism was as alien to the Radical or rationalist disposition as it was to the Methodist, and we are reminded of how much the Jacobins and Deists owed to the traditions of old Dissent. But it is possible to judge too much from the written record, and the public image of the orator. In the actual movement, cheerfulness keeps breaking in, not only with Hone, but, increasingly, with Hetherington, Lovett and their circle, who were softer, more humorous, more responsive to the people, less didactic, but not less determined, than their master Carlile. It is tempting to offer the paradox that the rationalist artisans on Carlile's or Volney's model exhibited the same behaviour-patterns as their Methodist analogues; whereas in one case sobriety and cleanliness were recommended in obedience to God and to Authority, in the other case they were requisite virtues in those who made up the army which would overthrow Priestcraft and Kingcraft. To an observer who did not know the language the moral attributes of both might have appeared indistinguishable. But this is only partly so. For Volney's chapter-headings continue, "Of the Social Virtues, and of Justice." There was a profound difference between disciplines recommended for the salvation of one's own soul, and the same disciplines as means to the salvation of a class. The Radical and free-thinking artisan was at his most earnest in his belief in the *active* duties of citizenship.

[46] See, for example, William Hodson in the *Social Pioneer*, 20 April 1839 (*et passim*): "Allow me, Sir, to state . . . my views upon the /Marriage/Questio, . . . neither *man nor woman* can be happy, until they have *equal rights*; to marry each other for a home, as is often the case now, is the buying of human flesh; it is slave dealing of the worst description. . . . I contend that all unions ought to be solely from affection—to continue the unions when that affection ceases to exist is perfect . . . *prostitution.*"

[47] See Wallas, *Life of Francis Place* (1898), pp. 166-72; N. Himes, "J. S. Mill's Attitude toward Neo-Malthusianism," *Econ. Journal* (Supplement), 1926-9, I, pp. 459-62; M. Stopes, *Contraception* (1923); N. Himes, "The Birth Control Handbills of 1823," *The Lancet*, 6 August 1927; M. St. J. Packe, *Life of John Stuart Mill* (1954), pp. 56-9. See also below, p. 777.

Moreover, together with this sobriety, the artisan culture nurtured the values of intellectual enquiry and of mutuality. We have seen much of the first quality, displayed in the fight for press freedom. The autodidact had often an uneven, laboured, understanding, but it was *his own.* Since he had been forced to find his intellectual way, he took little on trust: his mind did not move within the established ruts of a formal education. Many of his ideas challenged authority, and authority had tried to suppress them. He was willing, therefore, to give a hearing to any new anti-authoritarian ideas. This was one cause for the instability of the working-class movement, especially in the years between 1825 and 1835; it also helps us to understand the rapidity with which Owenism spread, and the readiness of men to swing from one to another of the utopian and communitarian schemes which were put forward. (This artisan culture can be seen, also, as a leaven still at work in Victorian times, as the self-made men or the children of artisans of the Twenties contributed to the vigour and diversity of its intellectual life.) By mutuality we mean the tradition of mutual study, disputation, and improvement. We have seen something of this in the days of the LCS (London Corresponding Society). The custom of reading aloud the Radical periodicals, for the benefit of the illiterate, also entailed—as a necessary consequence—that each reading devolved into an *ad hoc* group discussion: Cobbett had set out his arguments, as plainly as he could, and now the weavers, stockingers, or shoemakers, debated them. . . .

We have spoken of the *artisan* culture of the Twenties. It is the most accurate term to hand, and yet it is not more than approximate. We have seen that *"petit-bourgeois"* (with its usual pejorative associations) will not do; while to speak of a "working-class" culture would be premature. But by artisan we should understand a milieu which touched the London shipwrights and Manchester factory operatives at one side, and the degraded artisans, the outworkers, at the other. To Cobbett these comprised the "journey-men and labourers," or, more briefly, "the people." "I am of opinion," he wrote to the Bishop of Llandaff in 1820, "that your Lordship is very much deceived in supposing the People, or the vulgar, as you were pleased to call them, to be *incapable of comprehending argument.*"

The people do not, I assure your Lordship, at all relish little simple tales. Neither do they delight in declamatory language, or in loose assertion, their minds have, within the last ten years, undergone a very great revolution. . . .

Give me leave . . . to say that . . . these classes are, to my certain knowledge, at this time, more enlightened than the other classes of the community. . . . They see further into the future than the Parliament and the Ministers.—There is this advantage attending their pursuit of knowledge.—They have no particular interest to answer; and, therefore, their judgement is unclouded by prejudice and selfishness. Besides which, their communication with each other is perfectly free. The thoughts of one man produce other thoughts in another man. Notions are convassed without the restraint imposed upon suspicion, by false pride, or false delicacy. And hence the truth is speedily arrived at.[48]

Which argument, which truths?

E. J. HOBSBAWM
The Andalusian Anarchists

Like E. P. Thompson, Hobsbawm is concerned with the emergence of "consciousness" in a class composed for the most part of illiterate or semi-literate men; in the world of people, as the author says, "who neither write nor read many books." In this case, however, it is the rural class of Andalusian peasants as opposed to the primarily urban working classes in England. Despite the differences of nationality, religion and the lower articulation of peasant radicalism, a number of resemblances are noticeable: the fervent, simplistic trust in "Science" and education, the home-spun methods of communicating "the Truth" through reading circles, travelling teachers and revolutionary pamphlets, and the grafting of indigenous meaning onto ideas and doctrines from outside the class culture. Though the contrast is not sharp, it will be noted that Hobsbawm places greater emphasis on "conditions"—e.g., the intrusion of capitalist relationships into the countryside—to account for the fluctuating receptivity of the *pueblos* to radical

[48] See J. F. C. Harrison, *op.cit.*, pp. 43 et seq.

From *Primitive Rebels: Studies in Archaic Forms of Social Movements in the 19th and 20th Centuries* (Manchester University Press, Manchester, 1963), pp. 74-92.

ideas and gives rather less weight to the role of intellectuals in molding consciousness than does Thompson. The difference between the Andalusian peasant and the English working man, as Hobsbawm puts it, is that the former was entering the world of capitalism as a first-generation immigrant. The following chapter describes one manner in which he tried to adapt to that world.

ANDALUSIA, it has been observed, is the "Sicily of Spain,"[1] and a great deal of the observations about that island apply equally to it. It consists, roughly, of the plain of the Guadalquivir and the mountains which enclose it like a shell. Taking it all in all, it is overwhelmingly a country of concentrated settlements (pueblos), an empty countryside into which the peasants went for long periods to live in shelters or barracks, leaving their wives in the town, of vast absentee-owned and inefficient estates, and a population of almost servile landless *braceros* or day-labourers. It is classical latifundist country, though this does not mean that all of it in the 19th century was directly cultivated in vast estates and ranches; part was let out in small farms on short leases. Only a very little—politically conservative islands in a revolutionary sea—was smallish or long-leased property. . . . It need hardly be said that the large estates normally occupied the best land. The general picture may be concisely summarized in the observation that in the provinces of Huelva, Seville, Cadiz, Cordoba and Jaen, 6,000 large landowners owned at least 56 per cent of the taxable income, 285,000 smaller owners shared the rest, and something like 80 per cent of the rural population owned no land at all.[2] It may be observed in passing that Andalusia, like Southern Italy, was undergoing a process of deindustrialization in the 19th century—if not from the time of the Moors—being incapable of holding off its northern and foreign competitors. An exporter of farm-produce and of unskilled labourers, who began to migrate to the industrialized north, its countrymen depended almost exclusively on a particularly miserable and chancy agriculture.

[1] Angel Marvaud, *La Question Sociale en Espagne*, Paris 1910, 42.
[2] Gerald Brenan, *The Spanish Labyrinth* (Cambridge, 1943), 114ff.; see also the maps, pp. 332-5; *La Reforma Agraria en Espana* (Valencia, 1937); "Spain: The distribution of property and land settlement," in *International Review of Agricultural Economics*, 1916, no. 5., which gives the percentage of landlords per hundred of rural inhabitants doing agricultural work as under 17 in Western and under 20 in Eastern Andalusia, as compared with almost 60 in Old Castile (pp. 95ff.).

A large literature unanimously paints their social and economic conditions in the most appalling colours. As in Sicily, the *braceros* worked when there was work for them and starved when there was none, as indeed they still do to some extent. An estimate of their food per month in the early 1900's makes them live virtually entirely on bad bread—2¹/₂ to 3 lb. per day—a little oil, vinegar, dry vegetables and a flavour of salt and garlic. The death-rate in the pueblos of the Cordovese hills at the end of the 19th century ranged from 30 to 38 per thousand. In Baena, 20 per cent of all deaths in the quinquennium 1896-1900 were from lung diseases, almost 10 per cent from deficiency diseases. Male illiteracy in the early 1900's ranged from 65 to 50 per cent in the various Andalusian provinces; hardly any peasant women could read. It is hardly necessary to continue this miserable catalogue beyond observing that parts of this unhappy region continue to be more poverty-stricken than any other part of Western Europe.[3]

It is not surprising that the area became solidly revolutionary as soon as political consciousness arose in Andalusia. Broadly speaking, the Guadalquivir basin and the mountain areas to the south-east of it were anarchist, that is, mainly the provinces of Seville, Cadiz, Cordoba and Malaga. The mining areas on the West and North (Rio Tinto, Pozoblanco, Almaden, etc.), working-class and socialist, sealed the anarchist zone off on one side; the province of Jaen, politically less developed and under the influence of both Castilian socialism and Andalusian anarchism, formed a frontier on another, Granada, in which conservatism was stronger—or at least the peasants more cowed—on the third. However, since Spanish election statistics give no reliable picture of the political complexion of this area, partly because the anarchists abstained from elections until 1936, and some may have abstained even then, partly because the influence of landlords and authorities vitiated them, the picture is bound to be impressionist rather than photographic.[4] Rural anarchism was by no means confined to the landless labourers.

[3] Marvaud, *op. cit.*, 137, 456-7; F. Valverde y Perales, *Historia de la Villa de Baena* (Toledo, 1903), 282 ff.

[4] Thus in the 1936 elections in Cadiz province there were Popular Front majorities everywhere except along part of the west coast and in the mountainous corner by Ronda, which, as it happened, contained some traditional and legendary strongholds of Anarchism, where the policy of abstention presumably operated. I have taken the figures of results published by the *Diario de Cadiz*, 17 Feb., 1936.

Indeed, it has been forcibly argued by Diaz del Moral and Brenan*
that smallholders as well as artisans played at least as important, and
some would say a more tenacious, part in it, since they were
economically less vulnerable and socially not so cowed. Anyone
who has seen a pueblo of *braceros*, in which, apart from the gentry,
the ranch foremen and others "born to rule," only the craftsmen and
the smugglers walk with the indefinable mark of self-respect, will
grasp the point.

Social revolution in Andalusia begins shortly after 1850. Earlier
examples have been quoted—the famous village of Fuenteovejuna
is Andalusian—but there is little evidence of specifically agrarian
revolutionary movements before the second half of the 19th century. The affair of Fuenteovejuna (1476) was, after all, a special revolt
against abnormal oppression by an individual lord, and, moreover,
concerted with the townsmen of Cordoba, though the legend and
drama do not stress this point. The hunger riots of the 17th century,
with their overtones of Andalusian separatism, appear also to have
been urban rather than rural, and reflect the disintegration of the
Spanish Empire at the time and the stronger contemporary revolts
of Portugal and Catalonia rather than agrarian unrest as such. In any
case there are few signs of any such movements specifically
envisioning a peasant millenium, though no doubt research would
reveal some. Andalusian peasants suffered and starved, as did
peasants in all pre-industrial periods, and what revolutionism was in
them found its outlet in an exceptionally passionate cult of social
banditry and smuggling; of

> Diego Corrientes, the brigand of Andalusia
> Who robbed the rich and succoured the poor.[5]

Perhaps also in a ferocious attachment to the Catholic Church
Militant, whose Holy Inquisition smote the heretic, however rich
and highly placed, whose (Spanish) theologians, like the Jesuit
Marians, defended the rising of Fuenteovejuna and attacked wealth
and proposed radical social remedies, and whose monasticism
sometimes embodied their primitive communist ideal. I have myself

*Gerald Brenan, *The Spanish Labyrinth.*

[5] Pitt-Rivers, *People of the Sierras* (1954), cap. xii, on the place of the bandit in the
scheme of things of a modern Andalusian pueblo. But this discussion does not show a
particularly good understanding of the phenomenon.

heard an old Aragonese peasant talk thus with approval of his son's order: "They have communism there, you know. They put it all together and everyone draws out enough to live by." While the Spanish Church retained that exceptional "populism" which made its parish priests fight as guerilla leaders at the head of their flocks in the French wars, it certainly functioned as a very effective outlet for sentiments which might otherwise have become revolutionary in a more secular manner.

In the late 1850's there is news of roaming peasant bands, and even of villages "taking power."[6] The first indigenous revolutionary movement which attracted specific attention was the revolt in Loja and Iznajar in 1861, several years before the irruption of the Bakuninist apostles. (However, I understand there is some question of left-wing "Carbonarist" Masonic influence in the Loja rising.[7]) The period of the International and the republican agitations of 1868-73 saw further movements: "cantonalism," that is, the demand for village independence, a characteristic of all Spanish peasant movements, in Iznajar and Fuenteovejuna, the demand for a division of lands in Pozoblanco and Benamejí, "this sadly famous pueblo, whose citizens in great number used formerly to practice contraband," where the bandits had often virtually besieged the rich and no crime was punished by the State, because nobody would inform.[8] As the "sons of Benamejí" (they still play their legendary role as individualist "men who make themselves respected" in Garcia Lorca's Gipsy Romances) added social revolution to individualist revolt, a new age in Spanish politics began. Anarchism appeared on the scene, propagated by the emissaries of the Bakuninist wing of the International. As elsewhere in Europe, the early 1870's saw a rapid expansion of mass political movements. The main strength of the new revolutionism lay in the classical latifundist provinces, notably in Cadiz and southern Seville. The strongholds of Andalusian anarchism begin to appear: Medina Sidonia, Villamartin, Arcos de la Frontera, El Arahal, Bornos, Osuna, El Bosque, Grazalema, Benaocaz.

[6] "The agrarian problem in Andalusia," in *Int. Rev. of Agric. Econ.* XI, 1920, 279.

[7] My friend Victor Kiernan, on whose profound knowledge of mid-19th-century Spanish affairs I have drawn, tells me that this is suggested—perhaps baselessly—in N. Diaz y Perez, *La Francmasoneria Espanola*.

[8] Julian de Zugasti, *El Bandolerismo*, Introduction, vol.I, 239-40. Iznajar, another of the pioneer centres of social revolution, also had an abnormally strong code of *omertà*, according to the same source.

The movement collapsed in the later 1870's—not so badly in Cadiz province as elsewhere—revived again in the early 1880's, to collapse again. The earliest of the peasant general strikes occurred at this time in the Jerez area—then as later a fortress of extreme physical force anarchism. In 1892 there was another outburst, which culminated in the easily repressed march of several thousands of peasants on Jerez. In the early 1900's another revival occurred, this time under the banner of the General Strike, a tactic which had not hitherto been systematically seen as a means of achieving social revolutions. General peasant strikes took place in at least sixteen pueblos, mainly in Cadiz province, in the years 1901-3.[9] These strikes show marked millenarian characteristics. After another period of quiescence the greatest of the hitherto recorded mass movements was set off, it is said, by news of the Russian Revolution, which penetrated into this remote region. In this "Bolshevik" period Cadiz for the first time lost its primacy among anarchist provinces to Cordoba. The Republic (1931-6) saw the last of the great revivals, and in 1936 itself the seizure of power in many anarchist pueblos. However, with the exception of Malaga and the Cordobese fringe, the anarchist zone fell under Franco's domination almost from the first days of the revolt, and even the Republican parts were soon conquered. 1936-7 therefore marks the end of at least this period of Andalusian anarchist history.

It is evident that, over the large area of Andalusia, peasant revolutionism was endemic from the late 1860's and epidemic at intervals of roughly ten years. It is equally clear that no movements of anything like comparable force and character existed in the first half of the 19th century. The reasons for this are not easy to discover. The rise of revolutionism was not simply a reflex of bad conditions, for conditions may have improved, though only to the point of eliminating the actual catastrophic famines, such as had occurred in 1812, 1817, 1834-5, 1863, 1868, and 1882. The last genuine famine (if we except some episodes since the Civil War) was that of 1905. Anyway, famine normally had its usual result of inhibiting rather than stimulating social movements when it came, though its approach sharpened unrest. When people are really hungry they are too busy seeking food to do much else; or else they

---

[9] In *Cadiz*: Arcos, Alcala del Valle, Cadiz, Jerez, La Linea, Medina Sidonia, San Fernando, Villamartin. *Seville*: Carmona, Moron. *Cordoba*: Bujalance, Castro del Rio, Cordoba, Fernan-Nunaz. *Malaga*: Antequera. *Jaen*: Linares.

die. Economic conditions naturally determined the timing and periodicity of the revolutionary outbreaks—for instance, social movements tended to reach peak intensity during the worst months of the year—January to March, when farm labourers have least work (the march on Jerez in 1892 and the rising of Casas Viejas in 1933 both occurred early in January), March-July, when the preceding harvest has been exhausted and times are leanest. But the rise of anarchism was not simply an index of growing economic distress. Again, it reflected outside political movements only indirectly. The relations between peasants and politics (which are a townsman's business) are peculiar in any case, and all we can say is that the vague news that some political cataclysm like a revolution or a "new law," or some event in the international labour movement which seemed to herald the new world—the International, the discovery of the General Strike as a revolutionary weapon—struck a chord among the peasants, if the time was ripe.

The best explanation is, that the rise of social revolutionism was the consequence of the introduction of capitalist legal and social relationships into the Southern countryside in the first half on the 19th century. Feudal rights on land were abolished in 1813, and between then and the revolution of 1854 the battle for the introduction of free contract in agrarian matters continued. By 1855 it was won: the general liberation of civil and ecclesiastical property (state, church and waste lands, etc.) was reaffirmed, and directions for their sale on the open market given. Thereafter the sales continued without interruption. It is hardly necessary to analyse the inevitably cataclysmic consequences of so unprecedented an economic revolution on the peasantry. The rise of social revolutionism followed naturally. What is peculiar about Andalusia is the remarkably clear and early transformation of social disturbance and revolutionary unrest into a specific and politically conscious movement of agrarian social revolution under anarchist leaders. For, as Brenan points out,[10] Andalusia in 1860 had the makings of much the same primitive and undifferentiated ferment as Southern Italy. It might have produced the Italian combination of social and Bourbon-revolutionary brigandage and occasional jacqueries, or the Sicilian combination of both with *Mafia*, itself a complex amalgam of social banditry, "landlords' banditry," and general self-defence against the outsiders. Clearly the preaching of the anarchist apostles, who

[10] Brenan, p. 156.

welded the separate rebellions of Iznajar and Benamejí, of Arcos dela Frontera and Osuna, together into a single movement, is partly responsible for this clarity of political outlines. On the other hand, anarchist apostles had also gone to Southern Italy, but without meeting anything like the same response.

It may be suggested that certain characteristics both of Church and State in Spain helped equally to produce the peculiar Andalusian pattern. The State was not a "foreigners" State as in Sicily (the Bourbon's or Savoyard's) or in Southern Italy (the Savoyards'); it was Spanish. To revolt against a legitimate ruler always requires considerably greater political consciousness than to reject a foreigner. Moreover, the Spanish State possessed a direct agency in every pueblo, omnipresent, efficient and the peasant's enemy: The *Guardia Civil*, formed in 1844 chiefly to suppress banditry, who watched over the villages from their fortified barracks, went about the countryside armed and in pairs, and were never "sons of the pueblo." As Brenan rightly observes, "every Civil Guard became a recruiting officer for anarchism, and, as the anarchists increased their membership, the Civil Guard also grew."[11] While the State forced the peasants to define their rebellions in terms of hostility to it, the Church also abandoned them. This is not the place to analyse the evolution of Spanish catholicism from the later 18th century.[12] We may merely note that, in the course of its losing struggle against the forces of economic and political liberalism, the Church became not simply a conservative-revolutionary force, as among the small proprietors of Navarre and Aragon (the backbone of the Carlist movement), but a conservative force *tout court*, in that it joined hands with the wealthy classes. To be the Church of the *status quo*, of the King and the past, does not disqualify an institution from also being the Church of the peasants. To be regarded as the Church of the rich does. As the social bandits became *bandoleros* protected by local rich *caciques* and the Church became the Church of the rich, the peasants' dream of a just and a free world had to find a new expression. This is what the anarchist apostles gave it.

The ideology of the new peasant movement was anarchist; or, to give it its more precise name, libertarian communist. Its economic

---

[11] An illustration: before the rising at Casas Viejas (1933) there were four Civil Guards stationed in the village; today (1956) there are supposed to be twelve or sixteen.

[12] Brenan's account is, as usual, both concise, lucid and perceptive.

programme aimed in theory at common ownership, in practice, in the early stages almost exclusively, at the *reparto*, the division of the land. Its political programme was republican and anti-authoritarian; that is, it envisaged a world in which the self-governing pueblo was the sovereign unit, and from which outside forces such as kings and aristocracies, policemen, tax-collectors and other agents of the supra-local State, being essentially agents of the exploitation of man by man, were eliminated. Under Andalusian conditions such a programme was less utopian than it seems. Villages had run themselves, both economically and politically, in their primitive way with a minimum of actual organization for administration, government and coercion, and it seemed reasonable to assume that authority and the State were unnecessary intrusions. Why indeed should the disappearance of a Civil Guard post or of a nominated mayor and a flow of official forms produce chaos rather than justice in the pueblo? However, it is misleading to express the anarchists' aspirations in terms of a precise set of economic and political demands. They were for a new moral world.

This world was to come about by the light of science, progress and education, in which the anarchist peasants believed with passionate fervour, rejecting religion and the Church, as they rejected everything else about the evil world of oppression. It would not necessarily be a world of wealth and comfort, for if the Andalusian peasants could conceive of comfort at all, it was of hardly more than that all should have enough to eat always. The pre-industrial poor always conceive of the good society as a just sharing of austerity rather than a dream of riches for all. But it would be free and just. The ideal is not specifically anarchist. Indeed, if the programme which haunted the minds of the Sicilian peasants or any other peasant revolutionaries were to have been carried out, the result would no doubt have resembled Castro del Rio in Cordoba province between the taking of power and its conquest by Franco's soldiers: the expropriation of land, the abolition of money, men and women working without property and without pay, drawing what they needed from the village store ("They put it all together and everyone draws out what he needs") and a great and terrible moral exaltation. The village bars were closed. Soon there would be no more coffee in the village store and the militants looked forward to the disappearance of yet another drug. The village was alone, and perhaps poorer than before: but it was pure and free and those who were unfit for freedom were killed.[13] If this programme bore the Bakuninist label, it was because no political movement has reflected the spontaneous aspirations of backward peasants more sensitively and accurately in modern times than Bakuninism, which deliberately subordinated itself to them. Moreover, Spanish anarchism, more than any other political movement of our period, was almost exclusively elaborated and spread by peasants and small craftsmen. As Diaz del Moral points out, unlike Marxism it attracted practically no intellectuals, and produced no theorist of interest. Its adepts were hedge-preachers and village prophets; its literature, journals and pamphlets which at best popularized the theories elaborated by foreign thinkers: Bakunin, Reclus, Malatesta. With one possible exception—and he a Galician—no important Iberian theorist of anarchism exists. It was overwhelmingly a poor men's movement and it is thus not surprising that it reflected the interests and aspirations of the Andalusian *pueblo* with uncanny closeness.

Perhaps it was closest of all to their simple revolutionism in its total and absolute rejection of this evil world of oppression, which found expression in the characteristic anarchist passion for burning churches, which has few parallels, and probably reflects the bitterness of the peasants' disappointment with the "betrayal" of the cause of the poor by the Church. "Malaga," says the 1935 Guide Bleu to Spain with a poker face, "is a city of advanced ideas. On the days of May 12th and 13th, 1931 forty-three churches and convents were burned there." And an old anarchist, looking down on the same burning city some five years later, had the following conversation with Brenan:

"What do you think of that?" he asked.
I said: "They are burning down Malaga."
"Yes," he said. "They are burning it down. And I tell you—not one stone will be left on another stone—no, not a plant nor even a cabbage will grow there, so that there may be no more wickedness in the world."[14]

And the conscientious anarchist did not merely wish to destroy the evil world—though he did not normally believe that this would in fact involve much burning or killing—but rejected it here and now.

[13] Franz Borkenau, *The Spanish Cockpit* (1937), p. 166ff.
[14] Brenan, *op.cit.*, p. 189.

Everything that made the Andalusian of tradition was to be jettisoned. He would not pronounce the word God or have anything to drink or even to smoke—in the "Bolshevik" period a vegetarian strain entered the movement also—he disapproved of sexual promiscuity though officially committed to free love. Indeed, at times of strike or revolution there is even evidence that he practised absolute chastity, though this was sometimes misinterpreted by outsiders.[15] He was a revolutionary in the most total sense conceivable to Andalusian peasants, condemning everything about the past. He was, in fact, a millenarian.

Fortunately, we possess at least one superb account of the millenarian aspects of village anarchism, as seen by a sympathetic and scholarly local lawyer: F. Diaz del Moral's massive *History of Agrarian Agitation in the Province of Cordoba* which takes the story up to the early 1920's. The sketch which follows is mainly based on Diaz del Moral, and a few other less ambitious sources, supplemented by my own brief study of a single village revolution, that of Casas Viejas (Cadiz') in 1933.[16]

The village anarchist movement may be divided into three sections: the mass of the village population, who were only intermittently active, when the occasion seemed to demand it; the cadre of local preachers, leaders and apostles—the so-called "conscious workers" (*obreros conscientes*), who are today retrospectively called "those who used to have ideas" who were constantly active; and the outsider: national leaders, orators and journalists and similar external influences. In the Spanish anarchist movement the last section was abnormally unimportant. The movement rejected any organization, or at all events any rigidly disciplined organization, and refused to take part in politics; consequently it had few leaders of national standing. Its press consisted of a large number of modest sheets, much of it written by "*obreros conscientes*" from other villages and towns, and intended less to lay down a political line—for the movement, as we have seen, did not believe in politics—but to repeat and amplify the arguments for the Truth, to attack Injustice,

---

[15] *Ibid.*, p. 175; Marvaud, *op.cit.*, p. 43, observes that during the Moron general strike of 1902 marriages were postponed to the day of the *reparto*, but merely puts this down to an excessively naive optimism.

[16] The most reliable source for this is the *Diario de Cadiz* for the period. All national and foreign newspapers and books without exception get the story slightly wrong. I have also spoken to a number of survivors of the revolution in the village itself.

to create that feeling of solidarity which made the village cobbler in a small Andalusian town conscious of having brothers fighting the same fight in Madrid and New York, in Barcelona and Leghorn, in Buenos Aires. The most active of outside forces were the wandering preachers and propagandists who, spurning all but hospitality, went about the country teaching the good word or starting local schools and the great shadowy names of the classics who wrote the standard pamphlets: Kropotkin, Malatesta. But if one or two men might get a national reputation through their oratorical tours, they were not distinct from the village. It was just as likely that a local villager might get such a reputation, for *every* conscious worker regarded incessant propaganda, wherever he went, as his duty. What influenced men was not, they believed, other men, but the truth, and the entire movement was geared to the propagation of the truth by every person who had acquired it. For, having acquired the tremendous revelation that men need no longer be poor and superstitious, how could they do anything but pass it on?

The *obreros conscientes* were therefore educators, propagandists, agitators rather than organizers. Diaz del Moral has given a splendid description of their type—small village craftsmen and smallholders perhaps more often than landless labourers, but we cannot be sure. They read and educated themselves with passionate enthusiasm. (Even today, when one asks the inhabitants of Casas Viejas about their impressions of the former militants, now often dead or dispersed, one is most likely to hear some such phrase as "He was always reading something; always arguing.") They lived in argument. Their greatest pleasure was to write letters to and articles for the anarchist press, often full of high-flown phrases and long words, glorying in the wonders of modern scientific understanding which they had acquired and were passing on. If specially gifted, they clearly developed the sort of popular eloquence which multiplied pamphlets and tracts in 17th-century England. Jose Sanchez Rosa of Grazalema (born 1864) wrote pamphlets and dialogues between the worker and the capitalist, novelettes and orations on the model of the old "dramatic pieces" encouraged by the Spanish friars (but naturally, with a rather different content) which were performed— and indeed partly improvised—in the ranch-houses and labourers' quarters of the large *latifundia* where the men, working away from their villages, spent the week.

Their influence in the village rested on no social position, but primarily on their virtue as apostles. Those who had first brought the good news to their fellows, perhaps by reading out newspapers to their illiterate company, might come to enjoy the almost blind trust of the village, especially if the puritan devotion of their lives testified to their worth. After all, not everyone was strong enough to abandon smoking, drinking and wenching or to resist the pressure of the Church for baptism, church marriage and church burial. Men like M. Vallejo Chinchilla of Bujalance, or Husto Heller of Castro del Rio, says Diaz del Moral, "had the same sort of ascendency over the masses as the great Conquistadors had over their men;" and in Casas Viejas old Curro Cruz ("Six Fingers") who issued the call for revolution and was killed after a twelve hours' gunfight with the troops, seems to have exercised a similar function. In the nature of things the small band of the elect drew together. The case of Casas Viejas, where personal and family relationships linked the leading anarchist cadre, is probably typical: Curro Cruz' granddaughter Maria ("La Libertaria") was engaged to José Cabañas Silva ("The Little Chicken"), the chief of the younger militants, another Silva was secretary to the labourers' union, and the Cruz and Silva families were decimated in the subsequent repression. The *obreros conscientes* provided leadership and continuity.

Normally the village would merely accept them as their most influential citizens, whose word would be taken for anything, from the advisability of attending the visiting circus (travelling showmen soon learned to get a recommendation from the local leader) to making a revolution. But of course revolutions would only be made if in fact the village itself wanted them: for the *obreros conscientes* did not regard it as their function to *plan* political agitation, but merely to make propaganda, so that action in fact occurred only when the peculiar groundswell of village opinion, of which they themselves formed part, made it not only advisable, but virtually inescapable. (The development of anarcho-syndicalism, with rather more organization and trade union policies, began to undermine this reliance on complete spontaneity; but we are not at the moment concerned with the decline and fall of village anarchism, but with its golden age.) In fact we know this happened at about ten year intervals. So far as the village was concerned, however, it normally happened either when something in the local situation made action imperative, or when some impetus from outside fanned the glow of latent revolutionism into a flame. Some piece of news, some portent or comet proving that the time had come, would penetrate into the village. It might be the original arrival of the Bakuninist apostles in the early 1870's; the garbled news of the Russian Revolution; the news that a Republic had been proclaimed, or that an Agrarian Reform Law was under discussion.

> At the beginning of the last autumn (1918, EJH) . . . the conviction seized the minds of the men of the Andalusian countryside, that some thing they called "the new law" had been instituted. They did not know who had decreed it, or when, or where, but everyone talked of it.[17]

Before the rising at Casas Viejas all sorts of rumours had gone round: the time had come, two hundred pueblos had already declared for communism, the land was about to be divided, and so on. (This last rumour may have been due to the news that a large neighbouring *latifundium* was in fact due for land-reform under a recently passed law.)

At such moments endemic anarchism would become epidemic. Diaz del Moral has described it admirably:

> We who lived through that time in 1918-19 will never forget that amazing sight. In the fields, in the shelters and courts, wherever peasants met to talk, for whatever purpose, there was only one topic of conversation, always discussed seriously and fervently; the social question. When men rested from work, during the smoking-breaks in the day and after the evening meal at night, whoever was the most educated would read leaflets and journals out aloud while the others listened with great attention. Then came the perorations, corroborating what had just been read and an unending succession of speeches praising it. They did not understand everything. Some words they did not know. Some interpretations were childish, others malicious, depending on the personality of the man; but at bottom all were agreed. How else? Was not all they had heard the *pure truth* which they had *felt* all their lives, even though they had never been able to express it? Everyone read at all times. There was no limit to the men's curiosity and to their thirst for learning. Even the riders read on their animals, leaving reins and halters trailing. When they packed their lunch, they always put some piece of literature into the wallet . . . Admittedly 70 or 80 per cent were illiterate, but this was not an insuperable obstacle. The enthusiastic literate bought his paper and

[17] C. Bernaldo de Quiros, *El Espartaquismo Agrario Andaluz* (Madrid, 1919), p. 39.

gave it to a comrade to read. He then made him mark the article he liked best. Then he would ask another comrade to read him the marked article and after a few readings he had it by heart and would repeat it to those who had not yet read it. There is only one word to describe it: frenzy. (pp. 190)

Under such conditions the good word would spread from one to the other spontaneously.

In a few weeks the original nucleus of 10 or 12 adepts would .be converted into one of 200s; in a few months practically the entire working population, seized by ardent proselytism, propagated the flaming ideal frenziedly. The few who held out, whether because they were peacable or timid, or afraid of losing public respect, would be set on by groups of the *convinced* on the mountainside, as they ploughed the furrow, in the cottage, the tavern, in the streets and squares. They would be bombarded with reasons, with imprecations, with contempt, with irony, until they agreed. Resistance was impossible. Once the village was *converted*, the agitation spread . . . Everyone was an agitator. Thus the fire spread rapidly to all the combustible villages. In any case the propagandist's job was easy. He had only to read an article from *Tierra y Libertad* or *El Productor* for the hearers to feel themselves to be suddenly illuminated by the new faith.

But how would the great change come about? Nobody knew. At bottom the peasants felt that it must somehow come about if only all men declared themselves for it at the same time. They did so in 1873, and it did not come. They formed the union in 1882 and the girls sang

> All the pretty girls
> Have it written down in their houses
> In letters of gold it says:
> I shall die for a union man.[18]

But the union collapsed. In 1892 they marched on the town of Jerez, took over the town and killed a few people. They were easily scattered. Then around 1900 the news of the international debates on the General Strike which was then convulsing the Socialist movements reached Andalusia, and the general strike seemed the answer. (In fact the discovery of this new patent method of

[18] Todas las ninas bonitas/tienen en casa un letrero/ con letras de oro que dicen/ Por un *asociado* muero. Bernaldo de Quiros, *op. cit.*, p. 10.

achieving the millenium probably roused the villages out of their apathy.) Such strikes were completely spontaneous and solid; even the servant girls and nurses of the gentry left work. The taverns were empty. Nobody formulated any petitions or demands, nobody attempted to negotiate, though sometimes the authorities succeeded in getting the peasants to say that they wanted higher wages and to make some sort of agreement. Such efforts were irrelevant. The village struck for more important things than higher wages. After two weeks or so, when it was clear that the social revolution had not broken out in Andalusia, the strike would end suddenly, as solid on the last day as on the first, and everybody would return to work and wait. In fact, as Diaz del Moral notes acutely, the attempts by anarchist and other leaders to use such strikes for the strengthening of organization or the achievement of limited ends met with opposition or lack of enthusiasm: the peasants wanted "messianic strikes" (p. 358).*

It is not easy to analyse these strikes and the rather similar risings which sometimes took place. They were of course revolutionary: the achievement of a fundamental, overwhelming change was their sole object. They were millenarian in the sense of this discussion, insofar as they were not themselves makers of the revolution: the men and women of Lebrija or Villamartin or Bornos downed tools not so much to overthrow capitalism as to demonstrate that they were ready for its overthrow which must, somehow, occur now that they had demonstrated their readiness. On the other hand what looks like millenarianism may sometimes have been only the reflection of the village anarchists' lack of organization, isolation and relative weakness. They knew enough to be aware that communism could not be introduced in a single village, though they had little doubt that, if it were so introduced, it would work. Casas Viejas tried it in 1933. The men cut the telephone lines, dug ditches across the roads, isolated the police-barracks and then, secure from the outside world, put up the red-and-black flag of anarchy and set about dividing the land. They made no attempt to spread the movement or kill anyone. But when the troops came from outside they knew they had lost, and their leader told them to take to the hills, while he and his immediate companions fought it out in one cottage, and were killed, as they obviously expected to be. Unless the rest of the world acted as the village did, the revolution was

*In Dias del Moral, see ft. Hobsbawn: reference.

doomed; and they were powerless to affect the rest of the world except perhaps by their example. Under the circumstances what looked like a millenarian demonstration might only be the least hopeless among available revolutionary techniques. There is no sign that a village refrained from making a classical revolution—taking power from the local officials, policemen and landlords, when it saw the chance of doing so profitably; for instance in July 1936. And yet, even if we find a functional rather than an historical explanation for the apparently millenarian behaviour of Spanish village anarchism, they would hardly have behaved in quite that way unless their picture of the "great change" had been utopian, millenarian, apocalyptic, as all witnesses agree it to have been. They did not see the revolutionary movement as one engaged in a long war against its enemies, a series of campaigns and battles culminating in the seizure of national power, followed by the construction of a new order. They saw a bad world which must soon end; to be followed by the Day of Change which would initiate the good world, where those who had been at the bottom would be at the top, and the goods of this earth would be shared among all. "Senorito," said a young labourer to a gentleman, "when is the great day coming?" "What great day?" "The day when we shall all be equal and the land will be shared among all." Just because the change would be so complete and apocalyptic, they talked—and once again the witnesses are agreed—so freely about it "publicly, with complete ingenuousness, even in front of the gentry, with a tranquil joy."[19] For the force of the millenium was such that, if it was really coming, even the gentry could not stand out against it. Its achievement would be the result, not so much of a class struggle—for the class struggle belonged, after all, to the old world—as of something inexpressibly bigger and more general.

Spanish agrarian anarchism is perhaps the most impressive example of a modern mass millenarian or quasi-millenarian movement. For this reason its political advantages and disadvantages are also very easily analysed. Its advantages were that it expressed the actual mood of the peasantry perhaps more faithfully and sensitively than any other modern social movement; and consequently, that it could at times secure an effortless, apparently spontaneous unanimity of action which cannot but impress the observer profoundly. But its disadvantages were fatal. Just because modern

[19] Bernaldo de Quiros, *op. cit.*, p. 39; Diaz del Moral, *op. cit.*, p. 207.

social agitation reached the Andalusian peasants in a form which utterly failed to teach them the necessity of organization, strategy, tactics and patience, it wasted their revolutionary energies almost completely. Unrest such as theirs, maintained for some seventy years, spontaneously exploding over large areas of the kingdom every ten years or so, would have sufficed to overthrow regimes several times as strong as the rickety Spanish governments of the time; yet in fact Spanish anarchism, as Brenan has pointed out, never presented more than a routine police problem to the authorities. It could do no more: for spontaneous peasant revolt is in its nature localized, or at best regionalized. If it is to become general, it must encounter conditions in which every village takes action simultaneously on its own initiative, and for specific purposes. The only time when Spanish anarchism came near to doing this was in July 1936, when the Republican government called for resistance against the Fascists; but so far as anarchism was concerned, the call came from a body which the movement had always refused, on principle, to recognize, and had thus never prepared to utilize. Admittedly, the disadvantages of pure spontaneity and messianism had slowly come to be recognized. The substitution of anarcho-syndicalism, which allowed for anarchism, had already meant a halting step towards organization, strategy and tactics, but that was not sufficient to instil discipline, and the readiness to act under direction into a movement constructed on the fundamental assumption that both were undesirable and unnecessary.

Similarly, in defeat anarchism was and is helpless. Nothing is easier than illegal organization in a unanimous village. . . . But when the millenarian frenzy of the anarchist village subsided, nothing remained but the small group of the *obreros conscientes,* the true believers, and a dispirited mass waiting for the next great moment. And if that small group should be dispersed—by death, or emigration, or the systematic attentions of the police, nothing at all remains except a bitter consciousness of defeat. It may be true, as Pitt-Rivers observes, that since the Civil War Andalusian anarchism has ceased to play any active part, what little illegal activity there is being that of the previously unimportant communists.[20] If so, it is

---

[20] *Op. cit.*, p. 223. This may be in part due to the fact that the nuclei of armed resistance in the *sierras* behind Gibraltar, which survived from the civil war, or were revived in 1944-6, seem to have relied in part on the organized supply of arms, equipment and perhaps men, at which communists would be as efficient as Anarchists were bad.

only what we would expect, for a peasants' movement of the anarchist type is incapable of resisting in an organized fashion the sort of genuinely efficient repression and constant control which Spanish governments before Franco never troubled about, preferring to let the occasional outbreaks flare up and die down in isolation.

Classical anarchism is thus a form of peasant movement almost incapable of effective adaptation to modern conditions, though it is their outcome. Had a different ideology penetrated the Andalusian countryside in the 1870s, it might have transformed the spontaneous and unstable rebelliousness of the peasants into something far more formidable, because more disciplined, as communism has sometimes succeeded in doing. This did not happen. And thus the history of anarchism, almost alone among modern social movements, is one of unrelieved failure; and unless some unforeseen historical changes occur, it is likely to go down in the books with the Anabaptists and the rest of the prophets who, though not unarmed, did not know what to do with their arms, and were defeated for ever.

GEORGE L. MOSSE
The Youth Movement

In his study of German Volkish thought in the century before Adolph Hitler, George Mosse is mainly concerned, as is Fritz Stern in a later chapter, with the "roots" of the catastrophe of the 1930's. In the selection which follows, from *The Crisis of German Ideology*, he presents an analysis of the penetration of Volkish ideology into the German Youth Movement, *Die Wandervogel*, in the generation preceding the First World War. In contrast to Thompson's working men and Hobsbawm's peasants, the *Wandervogel* and their leaders were educated and middle class, rebelling from within middle-class industrial society rather than from outside or below. On the other hand, the search for a personalized community, for a liberating creed, and the "idealism of deeds" parallels the transformation of ideas into political and social ideology which occurred among the working men and

peasants—in this case manifesting itself in reaction rather than revolution.

It will be noted that the ideology of the *Wandervogel* is carried
primarily by their adult leaders (the membership was usually between
14 and 18 years of age) whose teachers would have been of the
generation discussed by Stern and Hughes. Thus we have here a
conflict not only of class values, for, as Mosse says, the Youth
Movement "could not discard its class interests and fears," but of
generations—of fathers and sons.

THE DEVELOPMENT and growth of the organized German Youth
Movement was a unique phenomenon in German history. No other
movement produced such spontaneity, filled the young people with
such enthusiasm, or enrolled so many in its ranks. Founded in 1901
as a hiking association for schoolboys in the Berlin suburb of
Steglitz, it soon spread over most of Germany. The organizational
framework was a loose one from the beginning. Each leader
recruited his own followers within a school and led them both on
their excursions and in their singing and talking sessions in their
"den." At first there actually was an over-all organization, and Karl
Fischer became the leader of all the Wandervogel (as the members
of the Youth Movement were called). Yet largely because of the
strong leadership concept which Fischer developed, the movement
soon split into several groups, each with its own leadership structure. These groupings and regroupings need not concern us, for all
shared, to a greater or lesser degree, the basic ideological presuppositions which were essential for the success of the movement as a
whole. From a handful of students at Steglitz the Wandervogel
could claim, by 1911, 15,000 German youths and the movement
continued to grow at an even faster rate. For what was new and
revolutionary about the Wandervogel was the absence of adult
tutelage. The excursions had begun under the slogan "Youth among
itself" and in this way had become symbolic of the revolt of youth
against their elders.

The movement was a conscious effort on the part of the youth to
organize themselves for the purpose of appropriating certain intellectual, cultural, artistic, social, and political ideals opposed to the
manners and outlook of their parents. Or so they thought. This
potential explosiveness of the youth, their inner dynamism—though
it might well have been rooted in disillusionment—was a tempting
target for exploitation by both the left and the right.

Tradition, however, did play a central role in the German Youth Movement. The young people remained faithful to a conservative attitude shared by most German youth throughout the previous century. The movement represented a further turning toward the right on the part of the bourgeois German youth on a scale not equaled until the Nazi harvest of a whole new generation. It is not easy to document at what point it first acquired a definite Volkish allegiance. Nor is it simple to determine to what degree the movement was actually aware of the direction it desired to take and the means to pursue it. During its first, developing years the organization was flexible, and revised its own original declaration of intentions to meet the pragmatic needs of the moment or to follow an especially influential and commanding leader.

But it was firm in its loyalty to the concept of the Volk, myth or reality. Its allegiance to the Volk, Germanic faith, tradition, heroism, nature lore, and its identity with the aesthetic qualities of Nordic man were varied but concrete. Here, among the youth, essentially Volkish aesthetic and ethical values were received with enthusiasm. By 1904, the wave of the Wandervogel had swept Germany with such force that not even Karl Fischer could adequately explain it. Surely we can regard this phenomenon as a radical expression of New Romanticism penetrating the younger generation. It too was a part of the attempt to resolve the crisis in German ideology.

After the inroads made by Volkish thought, a large segment of German youth associated hikes through the countryside with revolution, and identifying with nature was thought equivalent to subverting the existing order. And here alone it functioned as a vital part of the times. Hans Bluher, the movement's first historian, stated that the upsurge was a "protest of youth against the stifling of its spirit." Indeed, it did attempt to liberate itself from the strictures of modernity in the form of school, parents, authoritarianism, and the whole order of bourgeois mores, prejudices, and hypocrisies. But the direction it took immersed youth in a romanticism based upon the native landscape, elemental vitality, and awareness of the German past. The first Wandervogel called themselves "Bacchanten," a name which does not derive from the Greek God Bacchus but from the wandering scholars of the German Middle Ages.

Karl Fischer, the founder of the Wandervogel, regarded the movement as a romantic expression of a vital German character. In view of its sources of inspiration, he was justified in this view. He and his early followers had drawn extensive inspiration from the writings of Lagarde and Langbehn. They also turned to Ludwig Gurlitt for ideological support. Riehl inspired their sense of veneration for the landscape, teaching them how to appropriate the landscape into their souls. And in aesthetics and art Fidus provided them with their favorite depictions of youthful idealism, physical beauty, and the inspiration of nature. Not the least important influence, however, was that of Father Jahn and the patriotism that had been channeled into the youth of his own day remained as a symbol for the youth of modern Germany. The Wandervogel lived up to it, with less patriotism as such, but with a deeper sense of identity with the Volk. "Because the landscape which inspires [the Wandervogel] is the landscape of the German *Heimat,* such love awakens love for Volk and fatherland . . . a national-Germanic background for all their culture and style of life." In these respects, in the context of Wilhelmine society, the movement was radical and viewed itself accordingly.

To dismiss the romanticism of the youth as essentially "unpolitical," as many historians have done, is a grave error. Though it did not present a clear political program or engage in practical politics, its peculiar approach to the nature of the German character clearly presented an alternative way of pursuing the nation's policies and interests. If the political identity of the youth is not recognized, their essential desire to reach a working unity with the Volk through nature and custom is badly misinterpreted. Moreover, their contempt for contemporary politics as "superficial" is mistakenly accepted at its face value.

In defining their patriotism as loyalty to the interests of the Volk, these young people contrasted markedly with their chauvinistic parents and with bourgeois society as a whole. They felt much closer to the ideals of Langbehn than to those of Bismarck. However, during the growth of the movement, its patriotic feeling fluctuated in intensity. As we shall see, its original radical enthusiasm was gradually dissipated, supplanted for a time by an intense patriotism, only to be revived shortly before the war. But this vacillation will be examined in detail in connection with other interrelated issues.

The deep love of fatherland that rises above social class and politics which was stressed in the Wandervogel's manifesto of 1904 presented some difficulty to Hans Bluher, the organization's first historian. He tried to resolve the conflict between the superficially non-political posture of the movement and certain actions which reflected a deep-seated attachment to the fatherland. For example, while the German state did not seem to concern itself with such problems as the morale and aspirations of German nationals in neighboring countries, the Wandervogel took it upon themselves to display an appropriate interest. In his history Bluher describes the journey undertaken by Fischer and his troop in 1902 to visit the German communities in Poland. It was to impress upon their fellow countrymen, settlers in that country, that the youth of Germany were interested in their fate, their aspirations and complaints, and they vowed to communicate their impressions to the people back home. This excursion was supplemented by subsequent trips to other hard-pressed German minorities in the Austrian Empire. How markedly this contrasts with the rest of Bluher's history, which describes the supposedly simple attempt by the organization to join itself with nature and to engage in activities solely on the basis of spontaneity.

The disdain for the patently patriotic, on the one hand, and identity with the Volk, on the other, continued to be exemplified in other practices as well. Instead of celebrating the pompous and popular Wilhelmine festivals, such as the anniversary of the Battle of Sedan, the Wandervogel held rites of Germanic origin. The celebration of the Summer Solstice was especially popular. Here was a ritual that brought forth the aura of heroism, of group participation, of conforming to a natural sublimation in the Volk. A typical celebration began with the lighting of a bonfire in a selected romantic spot. A speaker then would invoke the true spirit of the German people, praise the virtues of Germanic ancestry, and exhort the youth to emulate this great heritage. This was followed by singing, after which each youth, as an act of rededication to Germanic values, jumped through the fire. Their motto, "To maintain oneself in spite of all the powers that be," clearly expressed a revolutionary dynamism which directed itself against the modernity of the bourgeois world and which held forth a vision of a vital union with romantic Germanism.

The identity with the Volk was continued in other fields as well, though in a less spectacular way. Fischer fused the influence of several Volkish thinkers, among them Riehl and Langbehn, with the spirit of adventure found in the fiction of Karl May, a famous German author who concocted tales of American Indians. From these stories Fischer derived a sense of romantic and simultaneously idealistic action, for May's heroes, scouts like "Old Schatter-hand" and noble Indians like "Winnetou," were the epitome of vitality, chivalry, and endurance; they were imbued with a sense of exploration and possessed an individuality that was virile as well as virtuous. Here, perhaps naively, Fischer saw his "idealism of deeds" at work. He aspired to more than adventure; he wanted to create an identity that would lead to deeds, an idealism that would arise spontaneously out of the contact between youth and the landscape. Roaming, wandering through the countryside, was to provide the substructure of such an idealism. It would familiarize the youth with what Riehl had preached so avidly: an intimate knowledge of one's native land, an acquaintance with the customs and aspirations of the simple peasant folk, and the perception of the intimate relationship between the present and tradition. Fischer thought that this would produce a "living contact" with the Volk heritage that would go deeper than anything to be gained from merely looking at national monuments. Here his Wandervogel would find that context in which their idealism of deeds would become operative.

Interestingly enough, the Wandervogel's love of nature sharply contrasted with that depicted in the idyllic scenes which, as children, they must have seen in their homes. For them it was not a pastoral union with a benign force in nature. Rather it was a conquest of, as well as a fusion with, a vital and elemental essence. Only where two comparable energies were at work could a fair merger take place, could the appropriate fusion of individual into the whole be mani-fest. Georg Gotsch, an early Wandervogel leader, aptly described the idea behind this submergence when he stated, in his description of the Siberian landscape, that after his journey there he beheld to the "great unities and encompassing elements" of nature every-where he looked. He was not speaking of the sentimental aspects of a sitting-room nature scene, but of the harshness and inde-pendence of an elemental nature. Both Frank Fischer, one of the movement's most important theoreticians, and Gotsch stressed the idea that hardiness and nature went hand in hand, a concept that was in many ways similar to Fontane's description of the Prussian landscape and its role in the shaping of a stalwart character. This note of physical and emotional toughness permeated the ideals of the Youth Movement and helped shape the concepts of physical beauty which, in turn, were given functional roles in the ideal of German youth.

A further reflection of the young people's desire to achieve unity in a common cause was their love of polyphonic music. The immense popularity of Frank Fischer's collection of German folk songs, first published in 1905, demonstrated that the group function was regarded as more meaningful than the self-awareness of the isolated individual. With their traditional themes, the folk songs enabled the youth to share emotions and values. They described events from the point of view of a group that worked in harmony toward common goals. For their songs the Wandervogel went back to earlier centuries, rejecting contemporary and romantic tunes, which were generally scored for one voice only. As in the fusion of the individual with nature, here too there was a subordination to the virtues of a greater good. The individual was circumscribed by forces that gave him identity—not in the abstract, but in a living community of tradition. Folk songs, like roaming through the countryside, were not merely romantic forms of expression; both stimulated a community of purpose and, through a merging with nature and tradition, a community of the soul.

Though these methods of achieving group identity seem simple and innocent, there was another aspect which became problematical and controversial. Again it was Bluher who pointed to it. In his book *Wandervogel as an Erotic Phenomenon* (1912), which gained notoriety because some thought he was accusing the Youth Movement of encouraging homosexual relations in its ranks, Bluher described the role played in the movement by what he called Eros. While for him Eros certainly meant a sexual attraction between men, these drives did not necessarily lead to an overt display of affection, nor did they culminate in physical sexual relations. Instead, the Eros impulse worked, socially and culturally to deepen friendships between males and to increase the cohesion of a male group. Basing his argument on his own observations and somewhat influenced by the theories of Freud, Bluher claimed that men who stand close in relationship to one another inevitably display homosexual impulses which, however, are sublimated in the form of surplus energy. This vital force, not finding a physical or organic release, eventually finds expression in true creativity which centers on the Mannerbund, the society of men. As evidence, Bluher listed several factors he observed among the Wandervogel. First, there was the *charisma* of the leaders, that captivating quality possessed by the exceptional few, the most imaginative, creative, and attractive personalities. Second, there was the ideal of male beauty, which found expression in the admiration for the muscular and lithe Germanic types. And third, there was the exclusion of women (who nonetheless founded their own organizations).

How serious were Bluher's findings and what connection did they have with the Volkish ideology? . . . . The Wandervogel journals were filled with descriptions of the ideal Germanic man; that given by Carl Bosch, another leader of the movement, may stand as typical. It defined a true Germanic personality as one which possesses an "instinctive" quality linking his soul to nature and the Volk. In addition, he must have that instinct for beauty and form through which he will want to steel his body and make it beautiful. Though this concentration of the physically strong and beautiful was a protest against the bourgeoisie's artificiality and hypocrisy in sexual matters, as indicated by their deep-seated shame of the naked body, it had both an aesthetic and a functional place in the lives of the individual Wandervogel. It became a conscious ideal of male beauty among the youth as portrayed in the paintings of Fidus, which were reproduced in most of the movement's journals. Moreover, this concept of beauty was associated with strength and activism, with the "idealism of deeds." In the hands of Bluher and others, the idea of the Bund, the male society, was elevated to a general principle not only of life but of government as well. As such it will play an important role in our story. The *Bund* was one of the ideals of the Youth Movement, but, in all probability, for the majority of the Wandervogel it was largely devoid of the purely sexual meaning which Bluher alone had superimposed upon it. To be sure, Wilhelm Hansen, who succeeded Fischer as leader, sought to encourage the development of an ideal type through gymnastics and nude bathing ("light and air baths"). He was accused of homosexuality by rival leaders of the movement and expelled. But the physical ideal described by Bosch remained. As late as 1924, a highly respectable Volkish paper praised the love of nudity as the core of the Youth Movement and as a paramount expression of their genuine closeness to nature and the Volk. However, this love of physical form, centered, as it was, upon the male body, in conjunction with the Eros of male membership reflected a negative attitude toward the role of women in society and in the Volk. Even when girls formed their own branch of the Wandervogel they were not readily accepted as an authentic expression of the ideals of youth. Only after the First World War did mixed groups come into existence.

But there was a more significant aspect of the emphasis on male membership and beauty, and that was the effect it had on Volkish principles of organization. The Volkish movement was especially impressed with the Wandervogel's *Bund* formation. Here they saw their own elitist ideas in operation. The *Bund* structure, by means of which the youth were able to organize their members on the basis of strong leadership, while holding them together by ties of Eros and common ideology, appeared as an alternative to both Marxism and capitalist class society. To one leader, writing after the First World War amidst the ruins of the shattered nation, the *Bund* structure seemed to be the only remaining true German form of political organization. It transcended the dichotomy between individualistically oriented capitalist society and the collective emphasis of socialism in that it incorporated the best of both by basing itself on leadership, Volk, and community. The Youth Movement's concept of the *Bund* was to remain a constant inspiration in the Volkish search for a means of organizing society according to their views, a society which was neither capitalist nor socialist.

To be sure, the movement was largely made up of boys between the ages of fourteen and eighteen, and they could hardly be expected to give deep thought to the formulation of a coherent ideology. For them membership in the Wandervogel meant rough adventure, escape from school and home, and status among their classmates. Yet the many talks given by their leaders and the many publications which ascribed a definite purpose to their actions must have had some effect on even the younger members. The ideology was formulated by the young men who led the movement and for them the ideology had far greater meaning than it had for the younger members. Indeed, many came to think that the movement, instead of representing the aspirations, interests, and values of the youth, actually was serving the ideological and personal purposes of the adult leadership. By the First World War a large part of the leadership was composed of adult, mature men whose tutelage and direction dominated the organization to such an extent that many asked whether the movement was still representative of "youth among itself." Indeed, changes of such magnitude had taken place that Bluher accused them of having turned the early romanticism of the movement into a sham artificiality.

But to some extent Bluher's attitude was an unwarranted oversimplification. The New Romantic vision of the Volk was central and remained so. Youth had expressed their love for the fatherland with a fervor and, in their minds, a "genuine" idealism which was far removed from the saber-rattling patriotism of their elders. The German woods and dales, the small towns and villages which nestled within them, and the songs of old made for a union of the individual with the Volk. This was the goal of youth's search for identity and commitment, linked as it was with a shared feeling of Eros springing from such soul experiences, putting before them the "ideal type" of Wandervogel. But, as the movement entered its second decade of existence, much of this had changed. A high school student, writing a speech for a summer-solstice festival in 1914, contrasted the fervor of the movement at its inception with the staid atmosphere of his own time. At the start the Wandervogel had been distinguished by a "flaming romanticism, infinite longing and burning love"; now the soul was dead and even the folk songs had become conventional. The youngster called for a revival of the ideals, but the means were not at hand.

It seems no coincidence that the cooling of the movement's earlier revolutionary ardor paralleled the increasing importance assumed by young teachers in the leadership. They attempted to quell the rebellion of the youth against the society of their elders. One such teacher asserted, in 1913, that a rebellion could not have taken place since the German soul is in complete harmony with order, that it despairs at anarchy and bursting the bounds of discipline. In the same speech he characterized Gurlitt, for his attack on school and religion, as "un-German." The following year another teacher denied that the Wandervogel had ever revolted against the authoritarianism of the schools. The increasingly strident note of conventional patriotism, however, had a longer past. As early as 1906, one of the Wandervogel leaders had exhorted the youth to reformulate their ideas and to direct them toward the interests of the fatherland and the state. He called upon his charges to prepare themselves emotionally and physically to take up arms and fight for their native land.

But the Youth Movement had traditionally been opposed to this kind of saber-rattling patriotism. Their love for the Volk sought a cultural identity, a deepening of true love of fatherland through an understanding of the landscape and the customs and history of the Volk. To them the state was an outward, superficial manifestation of the Volk. The cult of the military, the parades, the outward trappings of what they regarded as bourgeois patriotism, they abhorred. Their allegiance to the Volk, based on a shared culture, tended to be peaceful, and they recognized the validity of other nations' peoplehood. The Youth Movement itself took two steps to reaffirm its own love of fatherland in contrast to that of the "professional and aggressive patriots." By 1913 it was able to go on record for a policy that placed the cultural expression of their allegiance to the Volk above the defense of purely state interests. In that year before the war, the German Youth Movement, meeting on the Meissner Mountain, politely rejected the saber-rattling appeal of their Austrian namesakes to join them in calling for an all-out battle against the encroaching flood of Slavs. Likewise, it dismissed as mere artificial words the exhortation by Gottfried Traub, a young former clergyman and now a member of the Pan-Germans, for youth to enroll themselves as warriors of the German Empire. The movement felt secure in taking such steps because of what it considered to be its own more profound identification with the Volk. To both appeals they replied, in effect, that the patriotism manifest in their "idealism of deeds" was more genuine than any other.

Instead of adopting the state patriotism which men like Traub advocated, the movement deepened its attachment to the nation by building upon its own traditions. Hans Breuer, the principal leader just before the war, did most to propel the ideology in this direction, and with significant results. In 1913, in a famous article, he asserted that the Youth Movement was the only agency capable of restoring Germany to health. The age of science and reason which had done Germany serious injury had to be transformed into an age of culture, which under present conditions could be found only in the precepts of Germanism. Langbehn's prescription for a nation of artists found its echo here. Omitting reference to either Bismarck or Frederick the Great, Breuer cited Kant instead in his appeal for a Volkish commitment. The philosopher's principles of civic duty were read as Volkish cultural imperatives. The Volk was an organic growth basic to any society. The Wandervogel should recognize their duty and become the conscience of the Volk. And this was the Wandervogel's conception of their task when they gave a cool reception to the ultra-patriotic proposals in the debates leading up to the Meissner meeting. It also formed the basis for their attitude toward Jews, and explains as well their soul-searching vacillation with respect to the humanist proposals of Gustav Wyneken.

Though the Meissner resolution of 1913 was vague in all respects, calling only for truth and responsibility, the underlying ideological currents of the Youth Movement became more explicit when faced with questions of immediate relevance. Such an opportunity arose in the framing of the policy on admitting Jews into the Wandervogel and in defining the role of the Jews relative to Germans. It was precisely in this area, in the confrontation with the Jewish question, that the Wandervogel gave expression to the Volkish substance which had underlain their ideological presumptions from the very start.

The exclusion of a Jewish girl from membership in the female branch of the Wandervogel in 1913 thrust the Jewish question into the open. This incident, however, was not the first of its kind. Rather, it served as a catalyst in opening up formal discussions of the issue after a long history of such incidents that had colored the approach of many of the Wandervogel groups. Now all of the Wandervogel chapters were compelled to formulate a definite policy. Essentially four positions were brought forward in the national and local debates that followed in the next few years. Some opted for allowing assimilated Jews to participate in the movement; another faction, vociferous and increasingly popular after 1918 and supported by the Austrians, held that Jews were racially inferior and therefore pariahs; a third point of view, endorsed by many of the leaders, favored recognizing the Jews as an autonomous and separate Volk that had merits similar to those of the German Volk; finally, a smaller group favored granting the Jews essentially unrestricted admittance. But, however the final judgment was rendered, for the many local chapters the confrontation with the Jewish question sharpened the Wandervogel's consciousness of the Volk.

Those who would accept the assimilated Jew nevertheless regarded Jews as a whole as culturally and racially different from Germans. But they granted the possibility that the exceptional Jew might change. One writer emphasized this point when he stated that those Jews who could count several generations in the country could not be excluded *if*, in their appearance and soul, they had shed their "Jewishness." Obviously, the physical qualification here shows that the Germanic criteria were very much in force. This was, indeed, far removed from the liberal idea of a German-Jewish symbiosis. In this respect the Youth Movement clearly reflected the closing of the doors on the Jew as a Jew in Germany. There remained only a slight crack through which Jews who had acclimatized and transformed themselves, who had grasped the uniqueness of the German character, its landscape and tradition, could enter to participate in the revolt of German youth.

The exception made for the Germanized Jews was, however, of some moment, for it meant that a Volkish ideology could exist without a racist outlook that automatically barred Jews from membership in the youth organization or the nation. Along with several local chapters and Wandervogel groups, the Neue Pfadfinder (New Pathfinders), a Volkish youth group established in 1920, adopted the policy of accepting assimilated Jews. Its South German branch admitted Jews on this basis. Nevertheless, it was not all that simple. As a pro-assimilationist Jewish periodical contended, the acceptance of Jews on the basis of Germanization affected "only those Jews . . . who are more Nordic than the Nordic Aryans. Secretly they are made fun of all the same." Since the Neue Pfadfinder also entertained the cult of beautiful Nordic man, Jews who looked "Jewish" were not likely to be accepted. This attitude strongly indicates that the ideology was always determinant in defining the limits of toleration even among those groups that rejected total exclusion of Jews.

The idea that the Jew was racially distinguishable from the German Volk was first presented to the Wandervogel in the years before the First World War. Supported by only a small segment of the movement's leadership, the *Wandervogel Fuhrerzeitung* discussed the Volk and the youth organization in racial terms. This paper was dominated by two of the faction's theoreticians, Friedrich Ludwig Fulda, a young teacher, and Dankwart Gerlach. Gerlach exhorted the youth to become familiar with the work and thought of the racist Lanz von Liebenfels, an intimate member of the Guido von List circle, which maintained the existence of a mystical Aryan race. These racists advocated that the racially different and inferior Jews be refused membership in the Wandervogel, that their own organizations be denied equal status with the German groups, and, in fact, that the Jews be ostracized from the company of youth and the Volk. They based the correctness of their attitude on an instinctively Germanic anti-Jewish prejudice; as one writer put it: "A Jew is an impossibility at the festival of the changing sun." Fulda's and Gerlach's arguments differed little from the general anti-Semitic arguments of the racist element of the Volkish movement and they need not be reiterated here. Suffice it to say, though, that at that time most of the Wandervogel rejected the extremism of their approach. By and large, the Wandervogel settled for a seemingly more harmonious coexistence which they thought would be fair to both peoples.

The third view on the Jewish question had its origins in the social thought of the founder of the Wandervogel, Karl Fischer, who conceived of the Jews as a separate but equal Volk. Consequently, he argued, they had the right and obligation to stand by their nature, heritage, and tradition—in short their peoplehood—just as the Germans did. On these terms he showed respect for the Jews—but not as Germans, as a separate Volk. This point of view prevailed throughout a large section of the Youth Movement and was reflected in the more comprehensive theory which held that humanity consisted of separate Volks, each possessing unique traits.

It was this section of the Youth Movement that for a time displayed a certain sympathy with Zionism, which it recognized as the peculiar expression of the Jews' longing for their own Volk. This attitude was not unique or radical, for it enjoyed some following in Volkish circles at large. For example, Karl Buckmann, a Volkish writer, approvingly cited Martin Buber's *Three Speeches on Judaism*. For Buckmann, Buber's discourse on the Volk and blood ties was sufficient evidence that the Jewish ethos, like that of the Germans, was rooted in the Volk. Within such a conceptual framework the usual anti-Semitic agitation became irrelevant, since the Jewish problem had found its logical solution in Zionism. Jews should be encouraged to draw together around their traditions and beliefs; this would naturally produce a separation of the two peoples. These views do stand in direct and sharp contrast with the low opinion of the Jews held by racial theorists such as Chamberlain. But Buckmann was not alone in his opinion and the question continued to be raised as to whether a clean break between the Germans and the Jews would not put everything in order for both.

Interestingly enough, the argument had its adherents not only among German youth but among Jewish youth as well. Among the latter, Moses Calvary, one of the Jewish Youth Movement's most able spokesmen, asserted in 1916 that Jews would indeed sever themselves from their roots if they adopted a German identity and outlook. To encourage the cultivation of closer ties with the Jewish traditions, which they wanted to transform into national traits, Blau Weiss (Blue and White), the Jewish Youth Movement, was established. It was dedicated to the creation of a Jewish nation, but, singularly enough, not dissimilar to what the German Youth Movement desired for its Volk. Calvary, believing the individual to be inseparably and profoundly tied to the Volk, exhorted the Jews to learn from the German Youth Movement the ways of achieving close identity with the landscape, traditions and beliefs of the Volk. But it was the German landscape they learned to know and identify with—a development that was bound to produce conflicts within those who believed Palestine to be the proper environment for Jews. Moses Calvary drew attention to this ambivalence when he stated, in a remark to a leading Zionist, that his dreams "ripened under pine trees and not under palms." Yet Calvary was a thorough Zionist, and he left Germany for Palestine in the early 1920's. Nonetheless, many Jewish youth experienced similar inner conflicts regardless of their deep Zionist faith, conflicts which arose from an identity with the real and immediate instead of a distant landscape.

Undoubtedly, certain concepts of Jewish nationhood were greatly indebted to the Germanic ideals; what was true for Buber's Speeches was equally valid for the Blau Weiss. One former member, reminiscing about his days in the Blau Weiss, recalled that it was the ideal of the heroic rather than Jewish confraternity that made the Jewish Youth Movement appealing to him. Moreover, the Jewish counterpart of the Wandervogel not only accepted the heroic ideal; its members were also influenced by works such as Conrad Ferdinand Meyer's *Jurg Jenatsch* and even Schulze-Naumburg's works on Nordic beauty. Organizationally the group constituted itself as an "Orden", a "Bund", and replaced its earlier ideas of democracy with the "most efficient and natural" concepts of leadership. Thus, this important movement of Jewish youth, attempting to evolve a deepseated Zionist identity, assimilated certain aspects of the ideology of the German Youth Movement into its theoretical framework. Here we have another instance of German-Jewish symbiosis, but the Zionist solution was rejected by the vast assimilationist liberal Jewish majority.

Admittance without regard to race or creed was the official attitude of the Wandervogel. This policy, however, was supported by only the more liberal faction of the national leadership and a small percentage of the local chapters. The integrationists first presented their arguments in 1916 in a debate on the Jewish question that was carried on in the organ of the Freideutsche Jugend, the university organization which united all former Wandervogel. All points of view received a hearing. Articles opposing anti-Semitism were printed alongside a reprint of Lagarde's views and articles which attacked Jews. In this debate the position of the liberals took shape, especially in the articles of the movement's highly respected Knud Alhorn. He asserted that a healthy and well-run organization with a Volkish emphasis could best be secured by the maintenance of strict standards of selection within the individual groups. These standards were to be defined by the needs of the group and judged by how well they performed; not through the indiscriminate application of racial criteria. Accordingly, these practical standards would be able to provide the best guarantees against infiltration by foreign and divisive influences. Alhorn's argument, in the end, became the basis for the leadership's refusal to demand the outright exclusion of Jews.

Ample evidence exists to show that this debate was essentially a review of decisions which had been implemented locally throughout the early years of the Wandervogel—decisions which were to pursue their set course in the future. Within the individual chapters the picture was not very bright. In fact, according to an inquiry made in 1913-14, 92 per cent of the local chapters reported no Jewish members. Even more revealing was the fact that 84 per cent had specifically adopted resolutions excluding Jews from membership. In the light of this, the leaders' decision not to prevent Jewish membership had little meaning, since they also refused to interfere in the affairs of the local groups. And these local groups, whatever their basis for discrimination—race, autonomy for different Volk identities, or assimilation—set the pattern for future development. Meanwhile, the pressure from the racist-oriented Austrian Youth Movement had steadily increased. The Austrian organization had officially adopted the Aryan paragraph (admitting Aryans only) as early as 1911, and even as late as 1918 they castigated their German brothers for having "foreign blood in their midst."

As the basic Volkish tendencies were reflected in the resolutions of the Jewish question, so they also found expression in the refusal by the Wandervogel to rewrite their ideological creed in a humanist direction. The rebuff received by Gustav Wyneken in his attempt to influence the movement is significant in that it exemplified the integrity of the movement's Volkish roots. After breaking with Lietz and founding his own school at Wickersdorf, Wyneken became interested in the Youth Movement through reading Bluher's books. He believed that his own ideas essentially paralleled those of the youth and that where there were differences they could be resolved in his favor. He too entertained the concept of Eros, of male companionship expressing itself culturally and creatively, and held that the only means of regaining an authentic culture was to break with the contemporary mechanization of life and return to an emphasis on nature. Here the similarity between Wyneken and the movement ceased, for Wyneken had in mind different goals—and different means.

Wyneken spoke at the Meissner meeting. He carefully avoided the blatantly patriotic exhortations employed by other speakers, but, and more significantly, he also rejected the context of the Volk as a frame of reference for deeds, values, and guidance. Calling upon the German youth to refrain from commiting themselves to either nation or Volk, he presented them with a different alternative. He asked them instead to keep their eyes and ideals focused on the concept of freedom, the highest of human values. Freedom, however, was meant here as freedom in an individualistic sense: the development of each person's individuality toward the highest plane of creativity that the human spirit could attain and that the absolute spirit made available. Wyneken thus presented a Hegelian alternative to the ideology of the Volk, an alternative that rejected the Volk not only on its own terms but also as the repository of the *"Geist."* As a Hegelian, Wyneken saw the *"Geist,"* both human and absolute, in terms of never-ending development, furthered through a critical spirit (a point over which he had broken with Lietz) and a creative and artistic education. The movement of a collectivity of individuals toward higher aspirations would develop an ever more profound sense of community in which absolute values and not narrow patriotic considerations centering on the Volk would play central roles.

In his effort to draw the youth into his own ideological camp, Wyneken aligned himself with the editorial policies of the gymnasium student newspaper *Der Anfang* ("The Beginning"). Here he found like-minded youth who agreed on the humanist direction and on discarding the Volkish frame of reference. In its pages, the critic Walter Benjamin, who later in his life moved closer to a Marxist position, called upon youth, under the pseudonym Ardor, to view the present critically and engage themselves in creating a culture commensurate with future needs. Wyneken and the students further supported the development of a truly free community in which Eros could emerge out of the confining darkness. The pages of *Der Anfang* were filled with views reminiscent of the rebellious and idealistic attitude of the early Youth Movement while they also reflected a Nietzschean influence in articles that stressed human effort, will, and aspirations beyond supernatural and irrational forces. In combining Hegelian and Nietzschean ideas, and in pieces

like Otto Braun's poem "Why Should There Be Gods?" the paper
reflected an emphasis on the heroic and willful in man. To a certain
degree, these themes were shared by the Wandervogel, but among
them they were employed in a different service: in the interest of the
Volk, not merely of the individual.

Wyneken and the staff of *Der Anfang* differed with the Youth
Movement in another important area—the role of art in expressing
the human spirit. Whereas the Youth Movement idealized their
stereotypes of the Nordic man, *Der Anfang* welcomed Expressionism from the very start and favorably contrasted it with the crude
colors and vulgarity of the Youth Movement's "primitives," as they
referred to Volkish art. Art for Wyneken and *Der Anfang* was
subject to the Hegelian idea of a necessary development which must
not be blocked by tradition-bound concepts. For Wyneken, Fidus
and his saccharine, sentimental art spoiled the artistic sensibilities of
youth. Even the rejection of realism inherent in Fidus' and the rest
of Volkish art, and the mystical attempt to express nature's soul, did
not satisfy Wyneken. Consequently, he argued, not the existing
Youth Movement, but a reformed one could be linked out of inner
necessity with the revolutionary ethos of Expressionism.

But it was not to be. Regardless of the revolutionary appeal,
the depiction of the ideal landscape and not the portrayal of the
Expressionist search for the essence and chaos of soul, was the
ultimate goal of the Youth Movement. Wyneken had linked his
affinity for Expressionism with his hopes for the movement. He
appealed to youth on the basis of a truly revolutionary dynamic. He
demanded that youth align itself in support of a freely developing
"living community" that was beyond the Volk and that it pursue
individual development through spiritual affinity with the *Geist*,
which, as a force beyond nature, pointed to growth in uncharted
seas. Wyneken summed up his ideas in the slogan "Youth for itself
alone," symbolizing the rejection of bourgeois traditions, parents,
and school for the free development of the unfettered *Geist* of
youth.

At first the movement reacted favorably to his message, but
ultimately it rejected it. Several factors accounted for the initially
favorable reception of his ideas. There was, first of all, his own
charismatic quality. In addition, the movement was eager to retrieve
its anti-bourgeois origins, as reflected in its vacillation, over whether
or not to endorse Expressionism. Wyneken's emphasis on the
revolutionary aspects of the new art form and the freshness of the

style itself did sink into the aesthetic consciousness of the nation. It is interesting to note that after the First World War extreme racists—such as the Geusen, a youth group—regarded Expressionism as a religious experience that penetrated to the depths of the soul. Furthermore, in the 1920's the Volkish movement's emphasis on the mysticism of the soul seemed to provide a congenial climate for Expressionism, while the Nazis, both before and after attaining power, flirted with the idea of endorsing Expressionism as a valid means of depicting the "essence" of Germanic subjects—until Hitler summarily declared that the only authentic art was that based on the Volkish tradition.

The attraction that Expressionism exerted on the Volkish movement was based upon a misunderstanding. The attempt to plumb the depths of the soul seemed to link them together. But that which divided them proved to be more important. Volkish thought could not accept the chaotic individualism which characterized so much of Expressionist art and literature. The soul was tamed and integrated into the Volk. No wonder that Volkish thought only "flirted" with Expressionism, that it always ended up by rejecting it, just as the Youth Movement had rejected Wyneken's dynamic world view which seemed to be beyond the Volk's control.

Wyneken, however, did not fully succumb when the Wandervogel leadership broke off relations in 1914. In 1918 he thought his day had come. In that year he entered the Prussian Ministry of Education as an adviser. He made an attempt to reform the school system and thereby influence the sensibilities of the youth through a series of executive orders which gave students a major voice in the administration of the schools. His most important orders were directed against compulsory religious instruction and called for the creation of school forums where students and teachers could discuss educational problems as equals. Both directives raised a storm of protest, especially among the teachers, and their opposition was instrumental in his dismissal from his post. Looking for support, he appealed to the Freideutsche Jugend. But once more he was repudiated by the Youth Movement. Misfortune now dogged his steps. Charged with sexual offenses against his students, he faced trial . . . , was found guilty, and left public life altogether. Ironically, Wyneken, who had concentrated upon developing his native land, was finally appreciated in the newly constituted Soviet Union, where his work was studied and commented upon. Now, some thirty-seven years later, Wyneken, in looking back on the events and tracing them through recent history, holds conclusions similar to ours. In retrospect, he sees his failure in terms of the triumph of Volkish ideas. Indeed, the ideals of Hermann Lietz, who had dismissed the young Wyneken for differing with him, had triumphed. They proved to be closer to the mainstream of the ideology of the youth than the revolutionary concepts of Wyneken.

This is not surprising. Two thirds of those involved in the Youth Movement came from a middle-class background, at the very least, and the interests of such youth had always been channeled toward national concerns. Throughout the First World War, the youth had wholeheartedly supported the struggle led and rationalized by their elders, whom they had tried to repudiate two decades earlier. Then they failed to rally to the revolution that ushered in prospects of democracy. As one high school student explained to Wyneken, they were merely boys, unfamiliar with freedom, its responsibilities and its application, and therefore unreceptive to his ideas. The older bourgeois youth were outrightly hostile. Like the Volkish movement, these youths did want a revolution, but one oriented toward roots and Germanism, not toward the upheaval of the existing order, not even toward the uncharted seas of the human spirit. They wanted to end their alienation by finding roots, not through a flight forward such as Wyneken advocated.

In short then, the Youth Movement was a bourgeois phenomenon that could not discard its class interests and fears. Though the youth rebelled, theirs was a futile attempt to cast off their essential limitations. Their achievements in the cultural field amounted to only a minor victory that did not alter the alignment of political or economic forces. Their radical turn toward the right only reinforced their anti-modernist position, and in the particular juncture of events and circumstances that made up the Weimar Republic, it placed them in the camp of anti-democratic thought. Thus it is erroneous to absolve the Youth Movement of all and every guilt for the Nazi catastrophe. This has been done, however, by historians who have essentially exonerated the movement. Yet hundreds of thousands of youngsters passed through the Youth Movement, and many of them found it not very difficult to accommodate themselves to the ideological propositions of the Nazis. Their youthful experience, it seems, had not accustomed them to a form of government which was incompatible with the new faith.

That is not to say that the officials of the Wandervogel were on amicable terms with the Nazis, at least not during the 1920's. In fact, during the years of the Republic, most members of the Youth Movement were openly hostile toward National Socialism. The majority of the Wandervogel did not share the racism of the Nazi youth, and the National Socialists, once they geared their drive for power and mass support, frowned upon the *Bund* concept and its Eros and exclusiveness.

Whatever its later relations with National Socialism, there can be little doubt of the Youth Movement's Volkish orientation of thought, which was combined with a rejection of the parliamentary process. Indeed, the youth looked beyond bourgeois representative government, which they considered artificial and lacking the genuineness that their own movement supposedly possessed. Whole generations of German youth regarded the *Bund* of males as a genuine form of political and social organization, in tune with their New Romanticism and Germanic faith, and held the parliamentary process in utter contempt. This was an ominous sign for the Republic and its institutions. For the Volkish movement, however, the ideas were familiar and welcome.

II | Critical Men
and Moments

FRITZ STERN

From Idealism to Nihilism

In recent years a good many books have been devoted to the multiple biography, an analysis and comparison of the lives of several men in a single work. Fritz Stern's study of three German "cultural critics" before the rise of Nazism is an outstanding example of the genre. Plural studies of this sort have some obvious advantages for the intellectual historian over the familiar "Life and Times" biographies: they permit some degree of generalization beyond the unique individual case, they allow for illuminating parallels and contrasts of personality and ideas, and at its best the form has been used to illuminate the deep assumptions and values, the mood, the "Geist," of a generation.

Stern's three subjects fall somewhere between George Mosse's *Wandervogel*, literate but mostly passive assimilators of the Volkish ideology, and H. Stuart Hughes' original system-builders. Paul de Lagarde (1827-1891), Julius Langbehn (1851-1907), and Moeller van den Bruck (1876-1924) were the "terribles simplificateurs," popularizers of the Germanic-Volkish ideology and banal simplifiers of Hegel, Fichte, and Nietzsche. Indeed, Stern locates them as a "bridge" between those frequently abused philosophers of nineteenth-century Germany and the final vulgarization of Nazi activism. As personalities, Stern concludes, they were "midway between the detached philosopher and the uneducated rabble-rouser."

Lagarde, Langbehn, and Moeller thought of themselves as prophets, not as heirs. They were proud of their originality, proud of their intuitive sense of the crisis of their times. In fact, however, they had been much more influenced by past traditions than they realized, and without knowing it they served as cultural middlemen, transmitting old ideas in new combinations to later generations.

They acknowledged no intellectual masters and rarely mentioned earlier thinkers at all. Even in the realm of ideas, they felt lonely. But their silence attested also their distrust of the intellectual life, their unwillingness to wrestle with previous philosophers. They took seriously their own denigration of bookish learning, they were in

From *The Politics of Cultural Despair* (University of California Press, Berkeley, 1961), pp. 326-361. Originally published by the University of California Press; reprinted by permission of The Regents of the University of California.

truth "anti-intellectual intellectuals."[1] What they read, they usually read uncritically, and what was said of one of them—"Lagarde was not a systematic thinker, but a rhapsodist"—was true of all of them.[2] The irrationalism that they preached, they practiced as well.

Still, their thought contained many important themes from past traditions, and their influence was enhanced by the familiar ring of so much of their work. In dealing with their intellectual dependency, we must once more recall that they were essentially uninterested in abstract ideas, that they were more concerned with the moral tone or the idealistic commitment of an author. As a consequence, they were more attracted to men than to ideas, and especially to men whose fate resembled their own—to lonely, suffering, and unfulfilled geniuses. Langbehn, for example, felt an affinity for Novalis, Moeller for Nietzsche. Equally illuminating are their antipathies: they sneered at the "older," successful Goethe, they loathed Heine, and they were indifferent to Kant. From men they liked, they would appropriate certain "key ideas," or tags, which popular memory had fastened to these thinkers. These ideas reappeared in the works of the Germanic critics, as unidentified components of their own ideology. Their indebtedness to past thought was at once vast and insignificant. They were eclectics as well as *terribles simplificateurs*—those whom Burckhardt feared.

They appropriated something from every intellectual tradition of modern Germany, except one. They consistently warred against the ideas of the Enlightenment and of the French Revolution—the so-called ideas of 1789—and hence they were most powerfully influenced by the men who shared this hostility, to wit, the romantics, the cultural nationalists of the late eighteenth century, and the more aggressive nationalists, like Jahn and Arndt, of the Napoleonic period. They illustrated what Nietzsche called "the hostility of the Germans to the Enlightenment," this "obscurantist, enthusiastic, and atavistic spirit" which Nietzsche thought had been overcome, but which a half century later Thomas Mann noted was stronger than ever.

The Germanic critics, following the accepted judgment of their time, condemned the romantics as ineffectual dreamers. Yet theirs

---

[1] On the problem of interpreting "the literature of the unliterary," or the "intellectual anti-intellectualism," see Armin Mohler, *Die Konservative Revolution*, pp., 27-29.

[2] Ludwig Schemann, "Paul de Lagarde. Ein Nachrug," *Bayreuther Blätter*, XV:6 (June, 1892), 202.

was an essentially romantic temper: they exalted energy, will, passion, heroism—the demonic—and they despised the rational, contemplative, and conventional life. Hence they were particularly drawn to the *Stürmer und Dränger,* to the romantic genius as rebel. They further exaggerated the already distorted notion of the romantics concerning the grayness of all theory and the emptiness of all "mechanistic" thought. They also shared the romantics' rejection of what they alleged was the eighteenth-century view of man as an essentially good and rational creature. They thought of man as a volitional and spiritual being, in need of a faith and a community, and they extolled the romantic sense of the tragic and the inexplicable in human fate. In much of this, unknown to themselves, they were remote Rousseauans, and like so many German conservatives they acknowledged their debt only by vilifying Rousseau's democratic thought.

Far greater and more direct, especially on Lagarde and Langbehn, was the impact of Herder. Lagarde's view of language, for example, and Langbehn's emphasis on the primitive, populistic quality of true art seem to be clear adaptations of certain aspects of Herder's cultural nationalism. Herder had been one of the first to associate nationalism with German folk traditions, with the primitive and spontaneous expression of the *Volksseele.* In 1773 appeared the original manifesto of this new nationalism, *Von deutscher Art und Kunst,* to which Goethe and Moser contributed as well. A few years later, Herder exclaimed: "Great Reich, Reich of ten peoples, Germany! You have no Shakespeare, but have you no ancient songs of which you can be proud? . . . Were the Germans from the beginning destined only to translate, only to imitate?"[3] Herder's appeal to national self-consciousness was still subordinated to his cosmopolitan ideal of a common humanity, though he already believed that the German people had a unique calling for the realization of the goals of humanity. Under the impact of the revolutionary wars, later thinkers dissolved this association of nationalism and cosmopolitanism.

The Germanic critics were obviously influenced by the early nationalists, by the patriots who at the time of the French Revolution sought to liberate Germany from the tyranny of foreign rule and fashion. They were particularly attracted to Fichte, who at the

---

[3] J. G. von Herder, "Aehnlichkeit der mittlern englischen und deutschen Dichtkunst," *Sämmtliche Werke*, Carlsruhe 1821, VIII, 58, 55.

moment of German's humiliation sought to exalt the cultural destiny of the nation. Moeller, we know, appeared to his contemporaries— and perhaps to himself—as a latter-day Fichte, who, at a time of still greater disaster, sought to save the nation.

Certainly the "main ideas" of Fichte's *Addresses to the German Nation* reappeared in the works of the Germanic critics. Fichte's famous dictum "to have character and to be German [*Charakter haben und deutsch sein*] undoubtedly mean the same," became a principal tenet of later Germanic nationalism. Likewise his emphasis on *inner* freedom as the sufficient condition of human self-realization, his reconciliation of individualism and authority by means of a *Kulturstaat*, his appeal to youth because its "age lies nearer to the years of childlike innocence and of nature," and his projection of a great future for Germany, his echo of Schiller's "each people has its day in history, but the day of the Germans is the harvest of all times"—all of these were themes of the later ideology as well. . . .

Lagarde, Langbehn, and Moeller shared more with Fichte than the ideas they snatched from his much subtler and more complex philosophic thought. Fichte had inaugurated a new genre of political thinking; as Meinecke said, "among pure thinkers there is no more important example of the invasion of unpolitical ideas into Germany's political life than Fichte's."[4] This metaphysical, moral istic, and thoroughly unempirical manner of dealing with political questions characterized other German romantics as well. Consider, for example, Novalis's poetic approach to politics, his lyrical evocation of a Christian empire, his vision of a Germany reborn, whose faith and spirit would lead and reconcile the warring parties of Europe. Langbehn thought himself inspired by Novalis, as did so many of the new-romantics of the early twentieth century—and yet how remote Langbehn and his followers were from the Novalis who in his *Christendom or Europe* glorified not only the sublimity of the past but also the promise of the new world, which he saw in the "delightful feeling of freedom, the unqualified expectation of vast domains, pleasure in what is new and young, informal context with all fellow citizens, pride in man's universality and joy in personal rights and in the property of the whole, and strong civic sense"![5]

[4] Friedrich Meinecke, *Welbürgertum und Nationalstaat. Studien zur Genesis des deutschen Nationalstaates*, 5th ed., München and Berlin, Oldenbourg, 1919, p. 111.
[5] Novalis, "Die Christenheit oder Europa," *Sämtliche Werke*, ed. by Ernst Kamnitzer, München, Paetel, 1924, III, 25.

The Germanic critics quarried many ideas from the romantics—the organismic view of the state, the idealization of a corporatist and religious organization of society, and finally Schelling's belief in the resolution [*Aufhebung*] of opposites in "higher thirds." More importantly, they emulated the German romantics' esthetic and spiritual interpretation of politics and history, and their disdain for the empirical and material fact. Because of these similarities, Lagarde, Langbehn, and Moeller have often been called romantics, but such a designation overlooks the fact that they were indiscriminate and partial borrowers, who appropriated from incompatible traditions only the elements they happened to know about and that corresponded to their own prejudices.

Lagarde's and Langbehn's primitivist and anti-Semitic notions were foreshadowed by the works of Arndt and Jahn, by their glorification of the German folk, and by the xenophobic spirit of the *Burschenschaften.* Throughout the restoration period, this kind of folk ideology and *Germanomanie* was kept alive by journalists like W. Menzel, and by various artisan groups that blamed their decline on the Jewish exploitation of liberal free-trade principles.[6] . . .

Lagarde's attack on Hegel coincided with the general spirit of anti-Hegelianism that pervaded the second half of the nineteenth century. Hegel's intellectual domination had disintegrated rapidly; his thought was discounted by philosophers and historians, and satirized by Schopenhauer and Nietzsche. Among the educated, some of Hegel's ideas survived in isolation—as slogans and popular generalities—and these we encounter in Langbehn and Moeller. Both of them adopted a vulgarized form of the dialectics, and the "higher thirds" that characterized their writings resembled Schelling's obscure model and Hegel's celebrated but dissimilar method. Even anti-Hegelians found that Hegel's dialectic offered a convenient rhetoric for reconciling or overcoming conflict, and the abolition of conflict was a central aim of Langbehn's and Moeller's. In Moeller's conception of history we find echoes of Hegel's philosophy as well; Moeller's panorama of the history of *The Germans* was filled with world-historical figures that embodied and

---

[6] On this *Germanomanie* and anti-Semitism, see Eleonore Sterling, *Er ist wie Du. Aus der Frühgeschichte des Antisemitismus in Deutschland (1815-1850)*, München 1956, esp. pp. 128-143; on the artisans generally see Theodore S. Hamerow, *Restoration Revolution Reaction. Economics and Politics in Germany, 1815-1871*, Princeton 1958, *passim.*

realized the aim of the World Spirit.[7] His emphasis on these world-historical figures, on the importance of the personality in history, bolstered his antiliberal arguments for a Caesar. The differences between the Germanic critics and Hegel were of course immense; it is especially important to recall that Hegel considered the modern state as the final embodiment of a progressive historical process, while the Germanic critics, anticipating National Socialist usage, sneered at the "mechanistic" state and preferred a kind of folk community.[8]

Lagarde's first essay was written shortly before the rise of Schopenhauer's fame. Both men attacked Hegel's rationalism, but, more importantly, Schopenhauer taught the Germanic critics that the primacy of the human will brought about the irrationality of life and that this, in turn, must fill men with a cosmic pessimism. Beyond the pessimism of his formal philosophy lay Schopenhauer's despair concerning the decline of German culture, and his counsel that only a contemplative, ascetic life offered an escape from the basic evil force in the world, the will. Although accepting Schopenhauer's voluntarism and pessimism, Lagarde and Moeller could not endure his contemplation of the futility of action; rather, they sought an escape into a projected activism, a release through still greater will.

The Germanic critics had reached out to the German romantics and to Fichte and Hegel across the dominant intellectual current of their own day—the empirical, positivist direction in the natural sciences. The growth of science and its institutionalization in the universities constituted one of the most important developments in nineteenth-century Germany, and one that the Germanic critics dreaded. The natural scientists generally avowed their separation from philosophy, but the popularizers of science went even further; Büchner and Haeckel, for example, propagated a mechanistic materialism which denied the possibility of autonomous consciousness. "The idolatry of science" had upset all previous beliefs. Mind

[7] See Charles W. Cole, "The Heavy Hand of Hegel," in *Nationalism and Internationalism. Essays Inscribed to Carlton J. H. Hayes*, ed. by Edward Mead Earle, New York, Columbia University Press, 1950, pp. 64-78, for a discussion of the generally pernicious influence of Hegel's *Philosophy of History* on some modern German interpreters of history.

[8] For "National Socialism versus Hegel," see Herbert Marcuse, *Reason and Revolution. Hegel and the Rise of Social Theory*, New York, Oxford University Press, 1941, pp. 409-419.

was once more banned from a universe whose fundamental reality was conceived to be matter, and after 1850 the claims of eighteenth-century materialistic science were revived, grown more extravagant, by the tangible achievements of the physical sciences of the intervening years.

Darwin's evolutionary theory had an incomparable impact on European culture. After Darwin, the fact of evolution could no longer be denied, and the popular imagination, long prepared for such a theory, extended it to ever new fields. The Germanic critics, despite their hostility to science and materialism, were influenced by the various strands of Darwinism. Moeller . . . believed that the theory of evolution had destroyed all moral absolutes, all truths, all timeless religions. The truth of Darwin, Moeller felt, had swept aside the moral truths of earlier times and thus prepared the way for the triumph of relativism. His own prescription for a new ethics incorporated the evolutionary principle, and he tacitly accepted the belief of the social Darwinists that the laws of nature and of society were identical. Lagarde and Moeller also resorted to the rhetoric of social Darwinism and justified the role of struggle by appealing to the dubious principle of natural selection. The idea of the struggle for survival was transposed by them to the international realm and turned into an exhortation to war, because war would select and ennoble the superior people. Actually social Darwinism was a new and "scientific" guise for their romantic sense of the nobility of struggle and self-conquest, and in this curious mixture of romantic heroism and mechanistic materialism they were once again anticipating the later, and more dangerous, concoctions of the National Socialists.

Darwinism was the last common intellectual experience of the three generations of Germanic critics. Only Moeller felt the full force of Nietzsche's impact on German culture. For Moeller, as for so many of his contemporaries, Nietzsche proved to be of towering importance. The very magnitude of that impact also carried with it the likelihood of terrible misunderstandings. Under no circumstances is a great man's work easily appropriated, but when revolutionary ideas are cast in an irresistible style, as they were in Nietzsche's prose aphorisms, then seduction rather than comprehension is likely to follow. Nietzsche sensed the difficulty, even the obscurity of his thought, for "everything profound loves a mask."

Nietzsche had expected that he would be misunderstood and had demanded university courses of instruction in Zarathustra's philosophy—in vain. There was no academic exegesis of Nietzsche in prewar Germany; everybody had his own sense of "what Nietzsche really meant." Nietzsche's sister tried to create an official—and thoroughly distorted—interpretation. By clever editing and attempted suppression, she sought to convert him, posthumously, into the kind of narrowminded patriot that she herself was.

The terrible dangers of this cultural free-for-all were well exemplified in Moeller's interpretation of Nietzsche. Here we shall see some of the distortions and simplifications that falsified Nietzsche's thought in Germany and that bear out Camus's contention—that few men have suffered so much from posterity: "In the history of the intelligence, with the exception of Marx, Nietzsche's adventure has no equivalent; we shall never finish making reparation for the injustice done to him."[9]

The charge has often been made that Nietzsche fathered Germanic nationalism and the irrational cult of violence. The National Socialists claimed him as one of their distant forerunners, and many of their Western opponents agreed, because they had for a long time regarded Nietzsche as the intellectual source of German nihilism. But the case of the Germanic critics is one instructive illustration of the nature of that "influence." We will see that Nietzsche's thought differed radically from that of the Germanic critics, that the latter were uneasily aware of these differences, and that in essence the Germanic ideology had been formulated before Nietzsche's work was even available. Lagarde, Langbehn, and Moeller were not disciples of Nietzsche—and it is doubtful if anyone ever was a legitimate disciple.

The differences between Nietzsche and these critics were immense. In the first place, Nietzsche was a philosopher, a great and self-critical writer, to whom the search for truth and reality was a measure of his own integrity. Half-truths and the comforts of unreason he loathed. His style was experimental without being precious; witty without being trivial; profound without being ponderous. The reverse held true for the Germanic critics—proof again that style is the man. Nietzsche hoped to learn from his sufferings and weaknesses, in order to understand the condition of man; the Germanic critics succumbed to their weaknesses and sought to

---

[9] Albert Camus, *The Rebel. An Essay on Man in Revolt*, rev. translation by Anthony Bower, New York, Knopf (Vintage Books), 1956, p. 75.

reform the world because of them. In their trivializing and mystify-
ing, the Germanic critics manifested the intellectual qualities that
Nietzsche most despised.

Beyond these differences in style and character were the many
substantive issues on which their positions were antithetical. Nietzsche admired the Enlightenment, the Germanic critics dreaded it.
Joyfully he acknowledged the influence of many earlier thinkers; the
Germanic critics were loath to acknowledge anyone. He started and
ended as the "good European" and tirelessly denounced German
nationalism, anti-Semitism, and other proto-Nazi beliefs. He never
abandoned the individualistic premise of his thought. The individual
could achieve greatness and fulfillment, but only in opposition to
society. Nietzsche loathed every collective tyranny, and he would
have battled the Germanic community as fiercely as he did the
existing state. He never sought to overcome his cultural despair by
facile solutions; there was pride as well as truthfulness in his
oft-repeated assertion that he was the last "unpolitical German."
Truly, Zarathustra's prophet was worlds apart from the parochial
revivers of Wotan.

What appealed to Langbehn and to Moeller, and to their followers, was Nietzsche's relentless denunciation of cultured Philistinism, which could be read as an attack on all learning, and used as
an excuse for intellectual illiteracy. Because he loved wisdom and
integrity, Nietzsche—in this the friend and ally of Burckhardt—
attacked German pedantry and Philistinism, and these attacks
became the ammunition of those who feared wisdom or learning of
any kind. Nietzsche's intermittent brutality, the violence of his
phrases, his glorification of power and the elite—all of these were
echoed as well. Above all, Moeller—and countless other Germans—used Nietzsche's biography, his loneliness, suffering, and
final breakdown, as the validation of their own attacks on German
culture; the severity of Nietzsche's sacrifice was taken as a measure
of Germany's decay. This indecent idolatry of Nietzsche's illness
and death was the epitome of the Nietzsche myth.

In one of his essays, Moeller celebrated Nietzsche as Germany's
greatest cultural critic and as the reviver of metaphysical thought
after the aridity of positivism. He admired Nietzsche's heroic
morality and his individualism, and saw in them the sources of his
own attacks on liberal and Christian humanitarianism. Somewhat
condescendingly he praised Nietzsche's psychological insights and
the political views which he had derived from them. Nietzsche, he
admitted, had destroyed the foundations of a decadent culture—and

for this he deserved the gratitude of his compatriots, but he had built nothing on the ruins of the old world. In short, Nietzsche was "impractical," or, conversely, Moeller was "too practical to be a Nietzschean"—which was precisely what his widow said of him.[10] Moeller was always ready with a formula of reconciliation, with a myth that would promise salvation. Contrast Moeller's insistence that "God himself . . . continues to exist, even if we know that he does not exist," with Nietzsche's comment: "How many people still make the inference: 'one could not stand life if there were no God!' (or as they say in the circles of the Idealists: 'one could not stand life if it lacked the ethical significance of its ground!')—consequently there *must* be a God (or an ethical significance of existence)! . . . what presumption to decree that all that is necessary for my preservation must also really *be there*! As if my preservation were anything necessary!"[11]

The gulf between Nietzsche and Moeller seems widest in their respective interpretations of Darwin. Moeller sought to mediate between Darwin and Nietzsche, and argued that Nietzsche's conception of the superman provided the metaphysical meaning of evolution. Quite aside from Nietzsche's disdain for such mediation—"Anyone who wants to mediate between two resolute thinkers is characterized as mediocre; he does not have the eye for the unique"—we know that Nietzsche's superman was the negation, not the fulfillment, of Darwinian evolution.[12] By self-conquest, by a tremendous effort of the will, superman fashions himself, and thus the elements of purpose and will, which Darwin had banished, were reintroduced. Moeller failed to see that Nietzsche was Darwin's greatest antagonist; more than that, Nietzsche feared the consequences of Darwinism as acutely as Tocqueville had feared the consequences of Gobinism.

Moeller's misreading of Nietzsche emerged clearly in his complaint that Nietzsche did not sufficiently extend the will to power: "It is perhaps obvious that Nietzsche himself should have undertaken the transfer of his principles . . . to the race and to its will to power."[13] Moeller, in short, accused Nietzsche of not being a social Darwinist, of not extending his individualistic morality to the

[10] Interview with Moeller's widow in Berlin, July, 1954.

[11] Moeller van den Bruck, *Die Zeitgenossen*, p. 22. Quoted in Walter A. Kaufmann, *Nietzsche*, p. 312.

[12] *Die fröhliche Wissenschaft*, in *Friedrich Nietzsche, Werke in Drei Bänden*, ed. by Karl Schlaechta, München 1955, II, 152-153.

[13] Moeller van den Bruck, *Führende Deutsche*, Vol. II of *Die Deutschen*, pp. 248ff.

Volk. Nietzsche had, of course, warned against this illicit transfer of the will to power from man to the state. Not so Moeller. He was "practical," and did not hesitate to translate Nietzsche's thoughts to society, to preach a kind of social Nietzscheanism.

Moeller marked an important stage in the vulgarization of Nietzsche. Through him, the authority of a distorted Nietzsche was brought still closer to the antidemocratic movements of Weimar. After the war, as before, Nietzsche's influence was great, and on the surface at least, more evil than good. But this was the work of history rather than of the man; just as Anabaptists followed in Luther's wake, or revolutionary terrorists in Rousseau's, so antidemocrats attached themselves to Nietzsche.

The course and character of Nietzsche's influence were exemplified by his relation to Moeller and the Germanic critics. Though Moeller had appropriated some Nietzschean thoughts, the Germanic ideology as a whole had preceded Nietzsche's works. Lagarde . . . had written his first two essays in 1853, and his third, complete with the important themes of his life's work, in 1873. Also in 1873, but unknown to Lagarde, Nietzsche had published his first explicit criticism of German culture, the incomparable polemic against David Friedrich Strauss. There is no evidence to suggest that Lagarde was influenced by Nietzsche after that date.

Nietzsche, then, had nothing to do with the birth of the Germanic ideology, though he did powerfully affect its historical development—not intellectually, for the contention that Nietzsche and his doctrine of the eternal recurrence "stands at the center" of the conservative revolution greatly overestimates the philosophical foundation of the entire movement.[14] Rather, an uneasy generation, further unsettled by Nietzsche's work, accepted the Germanic critics more readily for their apparent closensss to Nietzsche. Such "disciples" Nietzsche had always feared, and had prophesied: "You had not yet sought yourselves, when you found me."[15]

We have seen how Lagarde, Langbehn, and Moeller appropriated and distorted some of the major intellectual traditions of Germany. Their thought in turn was distorted and usurped; it was distorted by

---

[14] Armin Mohler, *Die Konservative Revolution*, p. 206.
[15] Also *Sprach Zarathustra*, in *Friedrich Nietzsche, Werke in Drei Bänden*, ed. by Karl Schlechta, München 1955, II, 340.

the several generations of "unpolitical" Germans, who shared with our writers a sense of alarm at the direction of German life. Thomas Mann and Ernst Troeltsch, Friedrich Naumann and Christian Morgenstern were deeply affected by Lagarde, and men of equal eminence admired Langbehn and Moeller. These men responded . . . to the "gentle" Lagarde—the Lagarde stripped of what these admirers commonly called his crotchetiness, his anti-Semitism, and imperialism. The National Socialists, on the other hand, usurped the thought of our writers by fastening exclusively on the "tough," nihilistic side; in this way they could claim all three as part of their legacy. In actual fact, Lagarde, Langbehn, and Moeller had a powerful impact on both groups, and thus forged a link between them. The Germanic ideology was one of the traditions that the German elite and the National Socialists shared.

For many years, the Germanic critics were the acknowledged apostles of cultural despair, and their memory was invoked whenever men dreamed of a new Germany, a Germany beyond Philistinism, materialism, and conventional patriotism. There was much genuine idealism in these rumblings of discontent, much danger and much nobility in those German writers who, before and after 1914, refused to see in imperial Germany the perfect society or "the good old days!"

The Youth Movement believed in Lagarde and Langbehn, as did many of the *Bürger* and nationalist reformers who found prewar Germany ugly and unsatisfying. The critics of the republic—who saw in Weimar an enfeebled version of the Wilhelmine Reich—were confirmed in their despair by Moeller and Lagarde. The stronger a certain kind of patriotic discontent, the greater was the popularity of the three writers. The height of their influence, as measured by the circulation of their works, the number of studies about them, and the public references to them, came at the time of the dissolution of Weimar, in the years of Hitler's rise to power. The Germanic critics had predicted the death of liberal society, and when its agony began, they were duly remembered. . . .

The fact that Lagarde, Langbehn, and Moeller were right in so many of their predictions increased their influence, but does not necessarily validate their arguments. Their analysis of Germany's problems . . . was intellectually threadbare; the analysis of many of their liberal and socialist opponents was infinitely subtler—and less accurate. Lagarde, Langbehn, and Moeller anticipated and to some degree created the mood of many Germans, and it was this mood of cultural despair that became a political force which rational thinkers had not reckoned with. Our critics, moreover, had foreshadowed the kind of response that would appeal to this mood: their own despair had prompted their political utopianism, their weariness had inspired their mystique.

After the experiences of war, defeat, and impotent republicanism, this mood of despair and political mysticism had seized both the German right and the National Socialists. Without that pervasive mood, the National Socialists would not have been able to succeed. A thousand teachers in republican Germany who in their youth had read and worshipped Lagarde or Langbehn were just as important to the triumph of National Socialism as all the putative millions of marks that Hitler collected from German tycoons.

The long history of the Germanic ideology throws light on what has been called "the real problem in German history . . ., why so few of the educated, civilized classes recognized Hitler as the embodiment of evil. University professors; army officers; businessmen and bankers—these had a background of culture, and even of respect for law. Yet virtually none of them exclaimed: 'This is anti-Christ!' " A partial answer to this problem is given in this book: long before Hitler, long before Versailles, there appeared in Germany deep national frustrations, galling cultural discontents, which inspired nationalist fantasies and utopias which found ready assent among this German elite. Even without Hitler and without political disasters, the presence of such a force would have had to be reckoned with in an analysis of the political culture of modern Germany.

The educated, civilized classes had been moved by the Germanic ideology when it was only a dream; is it strange that they continued to believe in it when it appeared as a live political reality? By 1930, this generation of Germans clung all the more desperately to the heroic and nationalistic values of men like Lagarde and Moeller; all that they had felt in the Youth Movement, endured in the war, and suffered under Versailles, prepared them to accept—or at least not to reject—Hitler. To them the appeal of the *Führer* was immense, even if the *Führer* adulterated the idealism of his prophets with the nihilism of his brutal followers. The propaganda of the National Socialists, in turn, emphasized the cultural rottenness and political irresponsibility of Weimar—the very themes that Moeller had been driving home as well. The promise of the Third Reich, of the unity of the racial *Volk*, of its aggrandizement, of the resolution of its internal conflicts, the invocation of heroism, of individual exertion and national will—all of these seemed timely echoes of an ideology first disseminated in the days of Bismarck. Finally the National Socialist movement had the elan, the dynamism, the religious tone that our critics, in their lives and thought, had longed for and that their admirers sought as well.

The cultural pessimism which they helped to propagate in German society has been recognized as an important factor in converting men to national socialism. The various attempts to understand the triumph of national socialism have consistently underestimated the deeply rooted spiritual longings which inspired so many of Hitler's followers, and which also restrained members of the German elite from recognizing or resisting the approaching catastrophe. This aspect of the rise of Hitler has been over-looked by Marxist or psychoanalytical explanations of national socialism; it is misunderstood by the "intellectual" approach to national socialism, that is, by those men who blame the ideas of Hitler on every German thinker after Luther. It has found no place in the empirical studies of sociologists who seek to analyze the social base of National Socialist strength.

To some extent, this idealistic element of national socialism was directly derived from Lagarde, Langbehn, and Moeller. We saw how difficult it was to define with precision the relationship of the Germanic critics to earlier movements of thought; similar difficulties obstruct a clear understanding of their relationship to the leaders of national socialism. The question is a particular instance of the larger problem of intellectual influence, of the diffusion and power of ideas. But it is especially delicate because one deals with the effect of confused ideas on irrational men and movements. We are in fact confronted by a mounting process of abstraction and usurpation: the ideas of the romantics, of the critics of democracy, and, above all, the ideas of Nietzsche, were distorted and then appropriated by the Germanic critics and were ultimately vulgarized by men who held thought itself in contempt and regarded ideas as mere weapons in the political fight for power. It is a process which descends from the level of detached contemplation to that of nihilistic activism, from nonpartisanship to fanatical factionalism. As thinkers, the Germanic critics were simultaneously related to European philosophy and to National Socialist ideology; as personalities they stood midway between the detached philosopher and the uneducated rabble rouser.

The National Socialist ideology, in motive, form, and content, resembles the Germanic ideology. Their negative views were indistinguishable. For both, liberalism was the chief enemy, an alien and corrosive force that was devouring the true Germanic spirit and destroying the German Reich. Both demanded the unity and aggrandizement of a folkish Reich, and both insisted that only a Führer could establish and rule such a Reich. Both were embittered critics of the bourgeois way of life, of the spirit of capitalism, and Moeller anticipated the National Socialist belief in a Germanic socialism. Lagarde and Langbehn had emphasized the central place of anti-Semitism in such an ideology, and the Germanic critics as well as the National Socialists believed—with more or less literal-mindedness—in the racial determination of character and history. Lastly, their common thoughts sprang from a common hatred and alienation. We may conclude from this resemblance that the National Socialist leaders were not creating a false ideology with which to manipulate the political will of the masses. The example of the Germanic critics demonstrates that such an ideology has a great intrinsic appeal, and the success of national socialism convinces us that this particular translation of resentment and discontent into political myth offered hope to those who, caught in the throes of economic disaster and social disintegration, craved the certainty of a spiritual redemption.

The two movements then sprang from similar psychological conditions and professed similar ideologies. More, their lines of march often crossed. Abundant evidence attests the direct influence of Lagarde and Langbehn on the most important National Socialist ideologists. Alfred Rosenberg, the chief ideologist of the Hitler movement, considered himself Lagarde's disciple. Ernst Krieck, the National Socialist theorist of education, freely borrowed from and acknowledged the works of Lagarde and Langbehn.[16] The several founders of the Germanic religion based themselves on Lagarde's work.[17] The young idol of National Socialist historians, Christoph Steding, attempted a metahistorical critique of European civilization and placed Langbehn's thought at the center of his own work.[18] The

[16] See Ernst Krieck, *Nationalpolitische Erziehung*, 11th ed., Leipzig, Armanen-Verlag. 1933, *passim*, and George Frederick Kneller, *The Educational Philosophy of National Socialism*, New Haven, Yale University Press, 1941, chapters 4 and 8.

[17] Ernst Bergmann, *Die deutsche Nationalkirche*, Breslau, Hirt, 1933, *passim*.

[18] Christoph Steding, *Das Reich und die Krankheit der europäischen Kultur*, Hamburg 1938.

National Socialists celebrated the older pair as their forebears and, although at one time or another repudiating every other influence, never wavered in their loyalty to these two.

Still more clearly is the junction seen in the person and the work of Moeller. He was the dominant figure of the conservative revolution in the Weimar Republic, and his idea of the Third Reich constituted the most powerful myth of the antirepublican forces. His direct influence on the National Socialists was not very great: when *Das Dritte Reich* appeared, Hitler was already concerned with disengaging himself from the National Socialist program, rather than elaborating it. Goebbels, on the other hand, had been immensely impressed by the book in 1925, and seven years later, on the occasion of a new edition of *Das Dritte Reich*, he enthusiastically endorsed it: "I welcome the dissemination of Moeller's work which is so very important for the history of National Socialist political ideas."[19]

The secondary influence, however, was considerable. Because Moeller's conservative revolution had no means of self-fulfillment, its followers had no path to political power. Despite some misgivings about Hitler's demagogy, many conservative revolutionaries saw in the Fuhrer the sole possibility of achieving their goal. In the sequel, Hitler's triumph shattered the illusioms of most of Moeller's followers, and the twelve years of the Third Reich witnessed the separation of conservative revolution and national socialism again.

This disentanglement was a heartbreaking and heroic experience for the conservative revolutionaries. It is a tribute to the genuine spiritual quality of the conservative revolution that the reality of the Third Reich aroused many of them to opposition, sometimes silent, often open and costly. Some, like Rauschning and Treviranus, sought refuge abroad; others, like Edgar Jung, were killed in the purge of June 30, 1934. In the final plot against Hitler, in July, 1944, a few former conservative revolutionaries risked and lost their lives, martyrs to the genuine idealism of their earlier cause.

For their part, the National Socialists repudiated Moeller and his circle as well. After a few months of adulation in 1933, the National Socialists disavowed Moeller, and Rosenberg formally denied that he had been a forerunner of national socialism. In 1939, the party sponsored an official study of Moeller's work with the avowed

[19] Quoted in Joachim H. Knoll, "Der Autoritäre Staat. Konservative Ideologie und Staatstheorien am Ende der Weimarer Republik," in *Lebendiger Geist*, ed. by Hellmut Diwald, p. 205.

purpose of investigating the relation between Moeller's "unrealistic ideology which has nothing to do with the actual historical developments or with sober *Realpolitik"* and Hitler, "who was *not* Moeller's heir."[20] Moeller was praised for his attacks on the intellectual refuse of the nineteenth century, but the final verdict pronounced that he "never was, and also never wanted to be, the 'spiritual founder' of our National Socialist state."[21]

For us the National Socialist repudiation of Moeller and the opposition of some conservative revolutionaries to the Hitler regime is a partial exoneration of Moeller and of the Germanic critics as a group. Their ideological influence on national socialism was, after all, not decisive, nor did the National Socialists honor *all* aspects of their thought. Above all, Moeller—and the other Germanic critics— did not want *that* Third Reich, and would not have acknowledged the reality of Hitler's Reich as a realization of their dream.

But, we must ask, could there have been any other "Third Reich"? Was there a safe stopping place in this wild leap from political reality? Can one abjure reason, glorify force, prophesy the age of the imperial dictator, can one condemn all existing institutions, without preparing the triumph of irresponsibility? The Germanic critics did all that, thereby demonstrating the terrible dangers of the politics of cultural despair.

MICHAEL CURTIS
Intellectuals and the Need for Action

Like Fritz Stern and Victor Wolfenstein, Michael Curtis examines three "representative" intellectuals who appear to embody a pattern, either a philosophical, psychological, or political mode of thinking which forms a basis for comparison. In the case George Sorel [1847-1922], Maurice Barrès [1862-1923], and Charles Maurras [1868-1952], despite their separation at opposite ends of the political spectrum, the pattern emerges in the violence of their attack on the rationalism, individual-

---

[20] Helmut Rödel, *Moeller van den Bruck*, pp. 3-5.
[21] *Ibid.*, p. 164.

From *Three Against the Third Republic: Sorel, Barrès, and Maurras* (Copyright © 1959 by Princeton University Press). pp. 127-146. Reprinted by permission of Princeton University Press.

ism, and liberalism of the democratic Third Republic. As Curtis points out, the three critics of the Republic were at one in protesting against the idea of the "isolated man" which they saw as inherent in democratic theory and industrial society. The emphasis found in the writings of the three on violence, myth, and the "heroism of the deed" suggests not only the irrationality of which Stern and Hughes speak, but the furious emotion underlying the political thought of this period.

In the selection which follows, Curtis concentrates on Sorel's discovery of the passage from principles to action—the myth. Although the myth in Sorel's vision was to be the General Strike, his understanding of its impelling role in history is evocative both of anarchist millenarianism and, as it is frequently noted, of the more successful mass movements of the Right in the 1920's and 1930's.

THOSE WHO read a great many books," said Anatole France, "are like eaters of hashish . . . books are the opium of the West. We are being devoured by them. A day will come when we shall all be librarians, and that will be the end."[1] There was at the end of the 19th century a climate of opinion which refused to allow itself to be so devoured and was reacting against the tyranny of words. It was a climate in which Bergson and Nietzsche were the principal intellectual influences, and from which Sorel was to draw much in his attack on intellectuals and intellectualism. Barrès, but not Maurras, would support such an attack, and all three, in the attempt to turn back the tide of decadence, would propose the necessity for heroic action and even violence.

SOREL AND THE ATTACK ON INTELLECTUALS

No matter how the political and social views of Sorel varied, his attack on intellectuals and intellectualism was a constant one. Intellectualism he equated with extreme rationalism, which he had attacked as incapable of understanding the complexity of phenomena, and which therefore was based on the conception that science could produce solutions to all problems.[2] History showed that rationalism had led to deplorable results. Through Greek rationalism, philosophy had become dogmatic, incapable of directing experimental research, and responsible for the lack of success in

[1] Anatole France, *On Life and Letters*, New York, 1911, I: xii.
[2] Georges Sorel, *Reflections on Violence* (trans. T. E. Hume), Smith, New York, 1941, p. 154.

the common arts and mechanics. Greek rationalism was responsible for artificial abstractions, verbal analogies, words that ruled things. The deductive spirit of Greek science and geometry was in absolute opposition to the inventive spirit.[3] Its monist superstition had become the vice of most classical philosophers.

In similar fashion, Sorel objected to the popularity and underlying premises of neo-Kantism. He disliked its popularity because Kant and his disciples had introduced into philosophy "a horrible chatter that had noticeably confused problems,"[4] and had thereby greatly contributed to its discrediting. He opposed its subjective and purely moral premises since these were in opposition to the objective certainty of science.[5]

Another objection he raised to rationalism was that of its inevitable optimism. Sorel criticized the optimism of the Sophists which led them both to regard the spectacle of the world as a very interesting panorama, and to conclude that everything had been made for amusement. Pessimism was the indispensable stimulant to creative energy, and every great movement, religious and political, had had a pessimistic conception of life as its basis.

In the contemporary world one could hope to find at most "incomplete developments," traces of fragmentary movements. Even then, observations had to be limited to the economic field. Intellectualism could never fully understand living reality, because it assumed an "invariant structure," a logical movement toward some definite end. In every complex body of knowledge it was possible to distinguish a clear and an obscure region, of which the latter was perhaps the more important. Intellectuals could not deal with the obscure part, the more important part of relationships. In morality, they could deal with problems of justice but not with relations between the sexes; in legislation, with the problem of duties but not of the family; in economics, with the problem of exchange but not of production. A very false idea of revolutions would be obtained if one supposed them made for the reasons that philosophers often attributed to their makers.[6] It was unfortunate that the social reformers of the 19th century had been dominated by intellectualist

[3] Sorel (pseudonym J. David), "L'Idéalisme de M. Brunetière," *Le Devenir social* (June 1896).

[4] Sorel, "Vues sur les problèmes de la philosophie," *Revue de métaphysique et de morale* (1910).

[5] Sorel, "La Science dans l'éducation," *Le Devenir social* (February 1896).

[6] Sorel, *Les Illusions de progrès*, 4th edn., Paris, 1927, p. 135.

conceptions and that for them pure logic had had the value of a social science. The clear, the simple, the distinct—in all these Sorel saw the same metaphysical illusion. Bergson, who was not so deluded, but who, on the contrary, had put mystery in the center of his philosophical preoccupations, was the vigorous tree in the center of the isolated steppes of modern philosophy. Scientific investigation had its honored place, but science was not the only method of knowledge.

The 19th century applications of so-called natural rights had not been happy. Social utopias constituted the clearest manifestation of the aberrations to which the theory of natural rights logically led. However, socialism was not a social science, nor was the revolution a scientific process.[7] Indeed, those revolutions inspired by idealism had been ferocious; the Terror in France had been the work of obstinate theoreticians. Sorel was true to his own maxim: "One dreads bringing too great a rigor into language because it would be in contradiction with the fluid character of reality and the language would be deceptive."[8]

Since intellectualism was incapable of understanding the real world, it was not possible to provide an intelligible exposition of the passage from principles to action without the use of myth. The myth could not be refuted, it was an appeal to a "deeper consciousness." It meant freedom from the "superstition of the book." Though Sorel anticipated the idea of myth in several of his books, in *Le Procès de Socrate, La Ruine de monde antique, Le Système historique de Renan,* and in his *Introduction à l'èconomie moderne,* and applied it to the demon of Socrates, the hysteria of Mahomet, the stigmata of Francis, and even the resurrection of Christ, it was not until the *Reflections on Violence* that he gave a full explanation of what he meant, and defined it as the image held by the participants in a movement of impending action in which their cause will triumph. Sorel paid tribute to those thinkers who had speculated on the general idea of the myth. In *Le Procès de Socrate* he had found Plato to be superior to Aristotle by virtue of the former's appreciation of the value of myths and by the use he made of mythical expositions. He regarded Platonic myths neither as fables, nor as purely poetic inventions for amusement, nor mystic reveries, but as serious and

---

[7] Sorel, "La Crise du socialisme," *Revue politique et parlementaire* (December 1898).

[8] Sorel, *Matériaux d'un théorie du prolétariat,* 3rd edn., Paris, 1929, p. 58.

scientific. He praised Vico's *ricorso*, a poetically creative state characterized by the construction of myths.

Through the teaching of Bergson, he understood that movement explained itself above all by means of images.[9] No philosophic system owed its success to the logical value of its arguments alone. Probably Marx had put forward the conception of a catastrophe only as a myth, illustrating in a very clear way the ideas of class struggles and social revolution.[10]

For Sorel, myths were not descriptions of things, but expressions of the determination to act. It was not reason that had guided and that continued to guide crowds in their passionate actions, but kinds of schematical ideological projections. Active groups were motivated by emotional appeals, which played an important but nonlogical role in history. A myth could not be refuted, since it was fundamentally identical with the convictions of a group, being the expression of these convictions in the language of the movement. In this way, the Knights of the Middle Ages had gone in search of the Holy Grail, and the soldiers of the Convention tramped through Europe. All the major historical movements propelling action had had myths—early Christianity, the Reformation, the French Revolution, militant Catholicism—and the next would be revolutionary syndicalism. While the effect of utopias had always been to direct men's minds toward reforms which could be brought about by patching up existing systems, contemporary myths led men to prepare themselves for a combat that would destroy the existing state of things.[11] Historically, ideologies had been only translation into an abstract form of the myths which impelled to the final destruction. In contemporary France syndicalism was such an ideology, and the idea of the general strike, because it made the concept of socialism more heroic, should be looked upon as having incalculable value, even though, like all myths, it might never come about. The general strike had a character of infinity because it put to one side all discussion of definite reasons and confronted man with a catastrophe.

The manner in which Sorel used the idea of the myth, with its emphasis on the General Strike and on violence, is indicative of the correctness of Cassirer's view that the myth reaches its full force

---

[9] Sorel, *La Décomposition du Marxisme*, 3rd edn., Paris, 1925, p. 60.
[10] Sorel, *Introduction à l'Economie moderne*, 2nd edn., Paris, 1922, p. 396.
[11] *Reflections on Violence*, p. 33.

when man faces an unusual and dangerous situation, that 20th century myths have been a recourse to desperate means, and that myth is not only far remote from empirical reality but is, in a sense, in flagrant contradiction to it.[12] Moreover, Sorel's view of intellectualism was always an extremist one. It was an excessive rationalism which neglected the place of emotions or of instincts in the human situation, which regarded progress as inevitable, which lacked appreciation of reality, and which was exclusively optimistic. It was in fact the same kind of extremist 18th century belief—that all problems could be solved by some simple, uniform method—which had led Graham Wallas in 1908 to warn against the tendency to exaggerate the intellectuality of mankind. Yet the warning Sorel gave of the dangers of excessive rationalism was a salutary one, and it is remarkable that he anticipated, 50 years before it arose, the opposition to what is now called scientism and historicism.

If Sorel was philosophically opposed to intellectualism, he was opposed to intellectuals for a variety of reasons. They were superficial, they were interested only in material benefits or in capturing power, they thought only of their personal interests and never of the general interest, they misunderstood the nature of science, they were interested in politics and in the strengthening of state power, their ideas were basically negative ones, they were attached to the bourgeoisie and to the petty-bourgeoisie and were opposed to the best interests of the proletariat, they were incapable of leadership, they thought an end was definite and foreseeable and that solutions could be found to all problems, they thought of themselves as a sacerdotal caste destined by their superior culture, to impose a new order on the world.

Sorel's personal expressions of distaste for intellectuals, as shown in *Reflections on Violence* and *La Rèvolution Dreyfusienne,* often bordered on the libelous. When "Agathon's" book, *L'Esprit de la nouvelle Sorbonne,* with its attack on the Sorbonne appeared, Sorel gave it a laudatory review under the title "Lyripipii Sorbonici moralisationes."[13] Sorel expanded his attack on intellectuals to cover the whole of recorded history. His first book, *Le Procès de Socrate,* was a bitter attack on Socrates and his disciples. Socrates had created the most deplorable confusion between law, ethics and science, and had introduced probabilism into ethics and lack of

[12] Ernst Cassirer, *The Myth of the State*, New York, 1955, pp. 55, 349-350.
[13] *L'Indépendance*, April 15, 1911.

certainty into politics. His school was to be condemned for its optimism, for its desire to strengthen the state and to transform it into a church, and for its lack of attention to the problem of work. Socrates' chief disciple, Plato, was condemned because of the central place he had given to the philosopher in the ideal city state. In a later work, *Le Système historique de Renan,* Sorel attacked the philosopher-king, Marcus Aurelius, who had attempted to persecute Christians, failed, and thus demonstrated the impotence of official wisdom. Although Christianity had triumphed and had introduced the notion of the sublime, it too would have succumbed because of its theologians and doctors, if it had not been for the mystics.

In the 17th century the humanists, descendants of the Renaissance with its pagan love of life, had replaced the pessimism that had fostered the moral value of Christianity. The Protestants had attempted to conserve the old characteristics of religion, but Protestantism had been vanquished in its turn by intellectualism. In the 18th century, a stupid century,[14] the Philosophes, from Diderot to Voltaire, were "immoral buffoons of a degenerate aristocracy."[15] Only Rousseau escaped partially from this scathing criticism, and that was because he had upheld the dignity of workers. In the 19th century, Sorel criticized the Utopians, Fourier and Saint-Simon, for their desire to impose a strong state, Comte for the authoritarion attitude expressed in his assertion, "There is no liberty of conscience in geometry," which he made analogous to relations in society, and Renan for his intellectual dilettantism, which led to the exploitation of producers.

This historical analysis was significant for Sorel. He argued that one could not read the history of Christianity of the third century without thinking of the present and wondering if the alliance of French intellectuals with politicians could not have consequences very similar to those produced in the third century,[16] with its spectacle of corrupted philosophers and intellectuals who followed their personal interests and allied with those who exploited public credulity. Intellectuals were interested only in material benefits and personal advantages, and would be prepared to sacrifice the general interest to that end. Each of them aspired, like Caesar, to be first in a little group.[17] Unlike workers, they had no spirit of solidarity, they did not form a bloc; they had professional, not class interests.

[14] Sorel, *La Ruine du monde antique,* 3rd edn., Paris, 1924, p. 229.
[15] *Les Illusions du progrès,* p. 133.
[16] Sorel, *Le Système historique de Renan,* Paris, 1906, p. 333.
[17] *Matériaux,* pp. 97-98.

Intellectuals were not thinkers, but men who had adopted the profession of thinking and who expected an aristocratic salary because of the nobility of that profession. It was because of this desire to maintain the level of their salary that so many intellectuals tried to prevent women from becoming members of the liberal professions, since they believed that a profession quickly lost its prestige when women entered it. They made the exploitation of thought and of politics their profession; they had no regard for ideas as such, but appreciated them only for their value in capturing power.[18] They had no industrial aptitude, but tried to persuade the workers that it was in the workers's interest for them to exercise power. The Socratics had asked that government belong to the intellectuals,[19] but could one imagine a more horrible government than that of academicians? It was because of their exploitation of politics that they were capable of adopting attitudes so unexpected and so disturbing to public order. The creative hatred, the ferocious jealousy of the poor intellectual who hoped to send the rich speculator to the guillotine was an evil passion without socialist sentiment. Since rich men had ceased providing their revenues, poor intellectuals had pursued them with fanatical and ferocious hate.[20] Moreover, if intellectuals strove for the conquest of power, they could not want the disappearance of the state, since they would want to use it for their own benefit. Modern intellectuals were like the Socratics and like Calvin who supervised, directed, oppressed public opinion; opponents would be reduced to silence as disturbers of order. The end of intellectual projects like that of Saint-Simonism would be to transform industry according to a unitary, Napoleonic plan.

Intellectuals had more effect as a harmful than a helpful force. History had many examples to bear this out, and the abuse of sophisms that had corrupted socialism was not one of the least examples showing the danger of professional intellectuals. The incommensurable stupidity of M. Homais* was the natural product of the influence of the man of letters on the French bourgeoisie for almost a half century.[21] Intellectuals were not competent to understand great historical movements in general, and their theories had

---

[18] Sorel, *La Révolution Dreyfusienne*, 2nd edn., Paris, 1911, p. 30.
[19] Sorel, *Le Procès de Socrate*, Paris, 1889, pp. 7-8, 183, 237-238.
[20] *La Ruine de monde antique*, p. 273.
* Monsier Homais, the chemist of Flaubert's *MADAME BOVARY* (ed.)
[21] *Les Illusions du progrès*, p. 134.

little relevance to the working-class movement in particular. In fact, there was only an artificial link between socialist theories and the proletarian movement, since the theories were already old and decrepit.[22]

Sorel was concerned both with attacking the supposed superiority of intellectuals and their hold over the proletarian movement, and also with asserting the ability of the workers to take charge of their own movement. The role of the intellectuals was at best an auxiliary one. Some of them, badly paid, discontented, or unemployed, became members of the "intellectual proletariat," but attached themselves to the petty-bourgeoisie, and tried to turn socialism into reaction and utopian socialism. The proletariat, despised by the petty-bourgeoisie, could hope for nothing from the poets, philosophers, and professional do-gooders who lived at its expense and who were interested not in the dictatorship of the proletariat but in the representative dictatorship of the proletariat. Since intellectuals would suffer professionally from a proletarian revolution, those who "had embraced the profession of thinking for the proletariat"[23] must therefore be acting in their own interests. Sorel agreed with Kautsky that "the interests of the proletariat are diametrically opposed to those of the Intellegentsia."

Sorel thought his greatest claim to originality was in having maintained that the proletariat could emancipate itself without the help of middle-class intellectuals. The makers of machines did not need the guidance of theoreticians; the workers had to rely on themselves to ameliorate their conditions of life.[24] The idea of the superiority of intellectuals was false. Qualities of leadership were not exceptional, and were often found among manual workers, perhaps more often than among intellectuals. If the worker accepted control by the intellectuals, he would always remain incapable of governing himself. Theories were born of bourgeois reflection; the task of the proletariat was to march forward without imposing upon itself any ideal plan. "I do not believe," Sorel said, "that one stirs up the masses with writings . . . . It is necessary to galvanize people by an untiring drive, by a struggle that goes beyond manifestos, by the formation of a real army.[25]

[22] Sorel, "Les Syndicats industriels et leur signification," *La Revue socialiste* (August 1902).

[23] *Reflections on Violence*, pp. 37, 151.

[24] *Matériaux*, pp. 65, 307.

[25] Jean Variot, *Propos de Georges Sorel*, Paris, 1935, p. 124.

Like Sorel, Barrès was opposed to the idea that intellectualism could provide an understanding of life, partly because intellect played but a small part in human action, and partly because people were not even masters of the thoughts born in them. The thoughts were inevitably determined by a person's given milieu. In the *Culte du moi* trilogy, Barrès argued that communication takes place mainly through vibrations, by manifestations of sentiment rather than by a process of ratiocination. In the *Romans d'ènergie nationale* trilogy, he asserted that communion with the earth and the dead, the family, the province, and the nation would provide a substitute for reason. There was no liberty to think, for one could live only according to one's ancestors.

Barrès has the dubious distinction of having first used the word "intellectual" as a term of opprobrium. For Barrès, an intellectual was an individual who was deluded by the idea that society must be founded on logic, and who failed to recognize that it rested on prior necessities perhaps foreign to individual reason. Chief among these prior necessities were the ideas of the strengthening of France and restoration to it of the territories lost in 1870. Intellectuals thought of France not for its own sake, but as a means of serving something else.

THE NEED FOR ACTION

Maurras and Barrès joined with Sorel in his insistence of the need for action and in advocacy of the heroic figure who was so lacking in the Republic. Change had to take place through the hero, either as the embodiment of true values, or as the leader of the attack on the contemporary institutions.

The death of French energy, Barrès argued, meant the decadence of the country.[26] The regeneration of its energy, especially as expressed by the hero, would be the means of renaissance for the regime. Barrès was concerned therefore with the hero both in fiction and in history. The artist was great, he said, as he possessed an idea of the hero. In fiction, his leading characters were all concerned with aspiring to heroism and the affirmation of their will. Barrès' leading figure, Sturel, in *Les Dèracinès,* was seeking internal animation through expenditure of energy, presentiment of danger, knowledge of risk, ability to face the unforeseen and to support misfortune. In history, Barrès talked of the common traits of all the heroes of

[26] Maurice Barrès, *Taine et Renan,* ed. V. Girard, Paris, 1922, p. 103.

France, from Vercingetorix to Boulanger and Marchand. "It is possible that in all places Nature is beautiful, but I recognize its temples only on the tombs of great men."[27] The tomb of Napoleon, the professor of energy, was not, for young men, a place of peace; it was the meeting place of all the audacious energies, wills, and appetites. Barrès confessed to loving the man of the 18th Brumaire and along with him, five or six heroes, men who knew how to walk on the waves and, because they had confidence in themselves,[28] were not engulfed.

He was constantly stressing the need for élan. It was, in fact, "less by their doctrines than by their élan that men lead us."[29] It was this more or less tense energy that accounted for the value of an individual or race. In the past, the élan had been expressed in different ways. In the atmosphere of the *Last Supper* of da Vinci, one could see the internal life attaining its greatest intensity, and the human spirit embracing all aspects of reality. In Michelangelo, Barrès saw the effervescence of the man wanting to be God. The Sistine Chapel was one of the immortal reservoirs of energy. Barrès always looked back to the bravery and heroism of the Middle Ages, chronicled in legends, epics, and history. One of the useful ways in which the élan could be developed was through "intercessors," intermediaries between nature and the Infinite. Among these intercessors were Constant and Saint-Beuve, two saints of sensibility who were of great assistance in self-analysis.

In contemporary society, it was socialism that was being organized to utilize the considerable force it had accumulated.[30] Barrès' interest in socialism, in spite of his electoral programs, was less an absorption with economic problems than a passion for self-development. His collaboration in the Socialist movement was one of communion with the soul of the masses, a stimulation of his élan.

Barrès was even willing to allow that cosmopolitans might have as much ability as Catholics to give expression to this élan. He regarded Marie Bashkirtseff as a representative of the eternal force which made heroes emerge in each generation.[31]

But the real contemporary means of inspiring action was the man on horseback, Boulanger. In him, the French people would be able

[27] Barrès, *Mes Cahiers*, 14 vols., Paris, 1929-1957, III:213.
[28] Barrès, "Napoléon, professeur d'énergie," *Le Journal*, April 14, 1893.
[29] Barrès, *Amori et dolori sacrum*, Paris, 1903, p. 64.
[30] Barrès, *Toute Licence sauf contre l'amour*, Paris, 1892, p. 62.
[31] Barrès, *Trois stations de psychothérapie*, Paris, 1891, p. 68.

to envision the modern army, penetrated by the spirit of all classes—an army in which nonprofessional soldiers could play such a large part. Boulanger, in contrast with the old legalist in the Elysée who was incapable of an appeal that could touch the masses, had a brilliance which was always appealing to a warlike nation and was capable of summoning French reserves of energy. It was disillusioning for Barrès later to admit that Boulanger had been for 30 years an official, for three years an agitator, and for one year a melancholic.

In Barrès' demand for action, hate, an emotion that was dominant in the soul, might be a more important sentiment than love in that it could propel the greatest amount of energy in a single direction. The most intense and beautiful hatred was produced by civil wars, and the best of civil wars took place in the corridors of the Palais Bourbon.[32]

Yet Barrès, with his taste for combat—seeing the struggle of Jacob against the angel as one of the most beautiful warlike images, and Jacob as embodying the heart of life—and continually deploring the lack of energy, never reconciled this feeling for action with his attraction to symbols of death and decadence. The writer who so stressed action and élan also thought that the most beautiful thing in the world was "man, falling to pieces." With such complexity of motivation, a temper of moderation becomes impossible, and the emphasis is inevitably placed on destruction.

For Sorel as well as Barrès, the problem was how to produce a renaissance of energy in a society dominated by politicians as empty of ideas as of grandeur of soul, by rhetoricians and money-dealers, a society—interested neither in the sublime nor in eternal glory but only in enduring. Sublimity was dead in the middle class and therefore the bourgeoisie was doomed not to possess any ethic at all. Sorel, who in 1914 had written to Croce that the great problem was to live without religion, was, as his disciple Berth suggested, haunted by the sublime. To introduce the sublime into society meant action, the necessity for tension, the desirability of struggle, the need for the heroic. Movement was the essence of emotional life, and it was in terms of movement that one could speak of creative consciousness. Conscious action was vital because "movements toward greatness are always forced and movements toward decadence always natural."[33] It was unwise to neglect the enormous power of mediocrity in history.

---

[32] Barrès, *Du Sang, de la volupté et de la mort* (New Edition), Paris, 1910, p. 130.
[33] *La Critica* (January 25, 1911); November 14, 1914).

Sorel again drew historical parallels to illustrate his argument. In *Le Procès de Socrate,* he expressed admiration for Xenophon, the man who was an example of heroic behavior and who attacked Socrates, the adversary of the heroes of Marathon. The Socratics were responsible for the fall of Athens because they had destroyed the heroic conception that gave the city its moral basis. "Let us salute the revolutionaries as the Greeks saluted the Spartan heroes who defended Thermopylae and helped to preserve the civilization of the ancient world," urged Sorel.[34] If Christianity had become the master of the Roman world, it was due to the intransigence of those leaders who, like Tertullian, would not admit any conciliation or accept any lessening of antagonism between the Church and the State. Similarly, Calvinism was to be admired. It showed that the enthusiasm accompanying "the will to salvation" would provide the courageous man with sufficient satisfaction to maintain his spirit.

This desirable enthusiasm and spirit was lacking in the French contemporary scene. The bourgeoisie had risen as the auxiliary of the crown, and had benefited from the struggle between the monarchy and the Fronde. A class that had risen in this way could not act as a class of actual rulers would.[35] It was concerned only with the immediate interests of its members. It had lost all idea of the mission of the state or of its own mission as the leading class. Its cowardice showed that it was condemned to death. Only two events could prevent the stultifying of the middle class: a great foreign war which might renew the energy that was lacking, and which in any case would doubtless bring into power men with the will to govern or a great extension of proletarian violence. Since Sorel thought the first was unlikely, it was necessary to have the latter. Employers as well as workers would benefit from the struggle, because the knowledge of the revolutionary tendencies of the proletariat would act on the bourgeoisie as a moral force capable of arousing it from the lethargy to which its too easy prosperity had led it.[36]

Sorel attacked not only the refusal to fight but the very idea of pacifism. It was war above all that explained the juridical genius of Rome. In France the solidity of the Republican regime was due not to reason or some law of progress but to the wars of the Revolution and the Empire which had filled the French with an enthusiasm

[34] *Reflections on Violence,* p. 99.
[35] *Les Illusions du progrès,* p. 80.
[36] *Reflections,* pp. 82-83; *Matériaux,* p. 412.

analogous to that provoked by religion. Sorel approved Proudhon's justification of force, agreeing that war makes man greater.[37] He criticized the prevailing British pacifist feeling which was closely associated with the intellectual decadence there. The trouble was that they did not take war seriously; in the Boer War, they went to war as if they were gentlemen going to a football game.

Sorel was disturbed not only by the pacific nature of the bourgeoisie but also by its preoccupation with the future. Even more unfortunate was middle-class influence on Socialists, who were led to think about future society and to plan utopias. But utopianism was illusionary; to know the present was to be practical. The desired final state was secondary; what was essential was the knowledge of how to act.[38] The question was no longer what society should be like, but what the proletariat could accomplish in the actual class struggle. And for Sorel, it was only the syndicalist movement that studied the Socialist movement from the point of view of the present, not from that of the future.

Sorel ridiculed the "worldly socialism" of the Dreyfusard financiers, the mutualist organizations that fostered social peace, acquired a stake in society, and had a body of officials acting in a bourgeois spirit, consumers' cooperatives which, like all democratic societies, were incompetent, dishonest, and self-seeking, and trade unions that were interested only in arbitration.[39]

Sorel thought Marx was wrong to believe that a democratic regime made revolution more accessible because under it the class struggle became easier to understand. In fact, the exact opposite was the truth, and the workers were led to a trade union mentality. Sorel attacked reformism and rejected social legislation, the eight-hour day, profit-sharing schemes, workers' insurance, and cooperative schemes. All promoters of social reforms were victims of illusions; to believe in reform of bourgeois society was to affirm the principle of private property. Social legislation was useful only if it assisted the progress of revolutionary syndicalism. Sorel broke with his friend and colleague, Lagardelle, because the latter had tried to

[37] Sorel, "Essai sur la philosophie du Proudhon," *Revue philosophique* (July, 1892).

[38] Sorel, "L'Ethique du socialisme," in Georges Sorel, et al., *Morale sociale*, Paris, 1909, p. 135.

[39] Sorel, "Notes additionelles à l'avenir socialiste des syndicats," *Le Mouvement socialiste* (September 1, 1905); *Matériaux*, pp. 11, 154; *Reflections on Violence*, p. 63; *Les Illusions du progrès*, p. 211.

convince himself that they had been associated together in order to surpass, not to destroy, democracy. To preserve democracy would be to perpetuate the omnipotent politician.[40]

The bourgeois conception of life was incapable of giving rise to the vital noble instincts, to heroism, and the sublime, which rested on a pessimistic conception of life. Whereas optimism led to the glorification of passion, the sanctification of cynical individualism, to utilitarianism, a school of moral skepticism, and the formation of utopias, pessimism, with its strong ethics, was necessary for creative activity and the march to deliverance. Sorel's pessimism was not the result of a theory of the world based on original sin, nor was it the romantic pessimism expressed in elegant posturing. Pessimism was valuable as a guide to action: on the one hand because it took account of the obstacles that stood in the way of the satisfaction of human wants, and on the other because of its appreciation of the natural feebleness of man. Sorel's pessimism was in reality the outcome of his belief that the transformation of society was an heroic task requiring heroic qualities. Sorel preferred Corneille to Voltaire because the former created tragic plots whereas the latter, in harmony with his century, knew only success and optimism.

The hidden unity in the theory of Sorel, argued Johannet,[41] was the idea of heroism. It was the pole around which his meditations turned. Sorel's theory seems an excellent illustration of Bergson's belief that heroism is a return to movement and emanates from an emotion akin to the creative act. Yet Sorel made clear his difference on this point from Bergson. In a letter to Berth in February 1911, Sorel said he had never supposed an *èlan vital,* a popular instinct leading humanity toward superior social forms; he had demonstrated that almost all the views proposed by Bergson in reality had their origin in political and economic phenomena.[42]

Although Sorel was always certain of the need for the heroic, he was curiously changeable about the means of deliverance. He had criticized Christianity for its influence on military decadence through the vulgarization of the idea that victory depended on moral, not material, causes.[43] But in 1889 he asserted that the Bible would be the means of regeneration, that it was the only book that

---

[40] Letter to Croce, January 25, 1911, in *La Critica* (September 1928).
[41] René Johannet, *Itinéraires d'intellectuels*, Paris, 1921, p. 193.
[42] Quoted in Pierre Andreu, "Bergson et Sorel," *Les Etudes Bergsoniennes* (1952).
[43] *La Ruine du monde antique*, p. 42.

would instruct the people and initiate them to heroic life. Sorel always paid tribute to the effect of religion on action, as in 1909 when he approved both William James's bemoaning of the feeble part played by heroism in life, and James's demand of religion that it excite heroism.[44] Nor in 1898 could Sorel offer a very heroic solution. The most effective guarantees one could institute against despotism, he wrote in that year,[45] were those provided by working-class associations: cooperatives, *syndicats*, mutual societies. Temporarily he thought that the bourgeoisie might regenerate society, but he quickly turned to the myth of the proletarian revolution, and of the general strike. The renewal of the vital energy would come from the proletariat. It would, unaided by theoreticians or intellectuals, create its own institutions and fight its own class struggles. It was not simply a matter of asking favors, but of profiting from bourgeois cowardice in order to impose the will of the proletarians. The militants of the proletariat were without doubt mystics, if one meant by that disinterested individuals, ready to sacrifice their lives.[46]

With faith in its mission, the proletariat, making use of fighting where necessary, would dedicate itself to the noble role of producer, careful of technical and moral progress, leading society in the direction of economic progress, and directing the free workshop. Sorel, in this argument, was challenging the belief in the natural superiority of the upper class and its automatic assumption that it should rule.

But myth and reality became confused for Sorel. The ideas of a people, he argued, always corresponded to the conditions of existence of a very limited group. During the Napoleonic wars very few soldiers became generals, but all acted as if they had the baton of the marshal in their knapsacks; there were not many Americans who became millionnaires, and yet all American life operated as if each citizen was destined to become head of a great enterprise.[47]

But if, as Sorel argued, an elite is both inevitable in human history and desirable for the successful capture of power, it is difficult to see how the whole proletariat could possess these noble qualities attributed to a minority, unless Sorel, like Barrès, was basically

[44] Sorel, "La Religion d'aujord'hui," *Revue de métaphysique et de morale* (1909).
[45] Sorel, "La Crise du socialisme," p. 609.
[46] *Matériaux*, p. 356.
[47] *Le Système historique de Renan*, pp. 142-143.

concerned with the heightening of sensibility and the moral qualities
of that minority alone. It is in fact noticeable that the qualities Sorel
chose—daring, energy, strength—are the martial qualities of the
aristocracy. The Sorelian hero, chaste and sober producer, admirer
of industrial technique and of law, a kind of ascetic worker, inheritor
of the virtues of artisans, soldiers, and monks,[48] is a figure somewhat withdrawn from reality. Both he and Barrès, in attacking
uniformity, were in effect like John Stuart Mill, pleading for
uniqueness.

Moreover, it is difficult to see how anyone who stressed as much
as did Sorel the necessity for juridical principles which could only
be the outcome of stability could combine this with the desirability
for élan, movement, and revolution. What would be the purpose of
all the violence and activity if it were not to engender a system of
rules; what would be the purpose of the myth stimulating action
unless it were action for the mere sake of action?

For Maurras, force was not, as for Sorel, a method of spiritual or
moral development; it was simply a means of attaining power. "We
did not have to await the ardent oration of Gohier nor even the
curious meditations that Sorel entitled *Reflections on Violence* to say
and write, perhaps the first of our generation, that it might be
necessary to use violence."[49] Maurras was aware that he could not
capture power by constitutional means. The Action Francaise was
neither an electoral bureau, nor a group of spectators, nor a simple
party or political opposition, nor a philosophic school to change
ideas and manners. It was a conspiracy to prepare a state of mind
through which to make a *coup de force*, a coup directed against the
regime that had killed France. The true object of the movement was
the establishment of the monarchy, the act of instituting the royalty,
the royalization, the monarchization of the country.

Maurras, impressed on this occasion by a British example,
believed himself to be writing for Monk, the Monk who awaited the
suitable opportunity that would allow him to arise and make himself
the servant of the needs of his country.[50] A study of the needs of
France and of its confused aspirations dictated, authorized, and
make legitimate the use of force on the making of the monarchy.

---

[48] René Salome, "Le Lyrisme de M. Georges Sorel," *Revue des Jeunes* (January 25,
1923).

[49] *L'Action française*, September 21, 1912.

[50] Charles Maurras, *Enquête sur la monarchie* (Definitive Edition), Paris, 1924, pp.
487-488, 596.

Any Republican, who had lost his faith in the Republic could be Monk: it might be the Minister of the Interior, a prefect of police, or a questor of the Chamber. The task was to prepare and organize a *coup de force* together with the formation and diffusion of a state of mind that would allow that coup to succeed.

Maurras was the defender of order, but only of the right kind of order. His opponents, "those who opposed our street fights,"[51] took for order what was really their stagnant ideas, and the periodical recourse to the "electoral fair."

There was between the extreme Left and Right a remarkable reliance on the conception of the *èlan vital,*[52] and on the idea of violence as the only cure for the evils of a bourgeois civilization. This was the result of a fusion of ideas between the syndicalists, providing a theoretical justification for their small movement, their lack of funds, their minority control, and the Right, with its stress on French strength, on an offensive spirit, and on hierarchical authority and quality. Sorel anticipated the later criticism of the Cartesian world which pointed out that not only was it a mechanical world in which all wants were finitely determined but also a static one. Therefore, since the norm was inertia, the need was for action and heroes. Sorel, argued Guy-Grand, attempted to give to activity a metaphysical value analogous to intuition,[53] but in fact it has not and cannot have such a moral value.

The argument of Sorel, Barrès, and Maurras aptly illustrates what Isaiah Berlin has shown to be the essence of 20th century political thought—finding the process, natural or artificial, whereby the problems are made to vanish altogether.[54] The process attempts to alter the outlook giving rise to the problem, rather than accept the premise of 19th century thought that social and political problems exist and that they can be solved by the conscious application of truths on which all can agree. Philosophies of life of the kind that Sorel, Barrès, and Maurras expounded claim that they indicate the limitations of bourgeois rationalism which is threatening to obscure and devitalize everything that is alive in the world. These philosophies may be useful as a check on absolute rationalism, but, as

[51] Maurras, *La Contre-révolution spontanée*, Paris, 1943, p. 118.

[52] J. Bowditch, "The Concept of the Elan Vital," *Modern France*, ed. E. M. Earle, pp. 32-43.

[53] Georges Guy-Grand, *Le Procès de la démocratic*, Paris, 1911, p. 211.

[54] Isaiah Berlin, "Political Ideas in the Twentieth Century," *Foreign Affairs* (April 1950).

Mannheim has suggested,[55] they constitute a latent opposition to the rationalist world, exalting the idea of "becoming" in the abstract, but severing all connections with the world that is actually coming into existence. The three writers may have suggested that they had a more intimate view of the nature of reality than that possessed by democratic thinkers, but neither the logic of their theories nor the political conclusions they drew from them justify such an opinion.

H. STUART HUGHES

The Decade of the 1920's: The Intellectuals at the Point of Cleavage

The following selection from H. Stuart Hughes' celebrated study of European social thought is one of the best examples of intellectual history written, as the author himself describes it, "from the standpoint of the thought rather than of the deed." In this kind of approach, social history—the "retrospective cultural anthropology" of popular ideas and practices—is treated separately from a clearly delimited category of ideas: those ideas "that have still to win their way."

Hughes' *Consciousness and Society,* from which the selection is taken, is concerned with the last of the long succession of system-builders "descending from Aristotle"—Freud, Croce, Weber, and others whose main period of creativity preceded the First World War. The generation which followed, that of Thomas Mann [1875-1955], Julien Benda [1867-1956], and Karl Mannheim [1893-1947] represents the summing up of an era of broad creativity and innovation in which the limits of consciousness were probed and the opening of an era of specialization in more finite questions of social theory. Thus, in the generation of the 1920's, the intellect was forced to descend from its lofty prospect, where literature, politics, art, and science were one, to the frustrations and dilemmas of commitment, ideology, and mere survival.

---

[55] Karl Mannheim, *Essays on Sociology and Social Psychology,* London, 1953, p. 162.

THE ROLE OF THE INTELLECTUALS:
MANN, BENDA, MANNHEIM

By the mid-twenties . . . two separate and contradictory tendencies . . . had begun . . . to reinforce each other in necessitating a redefinition of the intellectual's role. . . . Both of them implied an impatience with the traditional conception of what the European philosopher or moralist should do. From neither of these standpoints was it possible any longer to maintain that a major writer should concern himself with the whole range of human problems— that he should survey with Olympian calm the social doings of his fellow men and, after a suitable parade of literary and historical learning, and a minimum of reflection on his presuppositions, come to certain rather majestic conclusions about what constituted the true, the beautiful, and the good. This was what the European intellectuals had been doing ever since the species first came into existence, and it was what they had continued to do in the first two decades of the twentieth century. In this sense, philosophers and sociologists such as Croce and Bergson and Weber—even Freud in his more speculative writings—had been in direct descent from Aquinas or Montaigne. And a deviant like Sorel—however much he railed at the intellectualist tradition—had always remained a moralist at heart. Up to about 1920 no sharp division between literature and social science had been drawn, and the intellectual still felt himself as free as Goethe to roam at will throughout the varied domains of human activity.

To the new school of logical positivism, however, such dilettantism was totally unacceptable. And to the advocates of social "commitment" it appeared, for quite different reasons, equally suspect. To the latter, the intellectual's traditional claim to a special status and to the right of suspended judgment seemed an intolerable frivolity in an era of agonizing choices in which each self-conscious individual, without exception, was in duty bound to stand up and be counted. By the mid-twenties, then, there had begun to loom up a vastly altered intellectual prospect in which the old confident generalizing would find no place: the meticulous scientists of words and symbols and the "terrible simplifiers" of Jacob Burckhardt's nineteenth-century nightmare, in their mutually incompatible endeavors, would have the field all to themselves.

Under these circumstances, it is not surprising that in the years 1924 to 1929—the six deceptive years of post-war Europe's apparent stabilization and prosperity—three major works, totally unrelated in character and totally independent of each other, should have sought to redefine in contemporary terms the function and calling of the European *literati*.

The first word came from a novelist. For Thomas Mann the war years had been a period of trial and tragic ambivalence. He had interrupted work on what was to be the second of his major novels, *The Magic Mountain,* and he had felt incapable of sustained creative effort. The one substantial product of this period, the *Betrachtungen eines Unpolitischen (Reflections of an Unpolitical Man),* ranks, by general consent, as the least fortunate of his whole literary output. In writing it, he had felt obligated to assume a propagandist role. He had believed it incumbent on him to make his personal contribution to his nation's war effort by defending the German "cultural" values of hierarchy and inner experience against the merely "civilized" democracy and literary-minded humanitarianism of the West. Yet his own hesitations had penetrated the propagandist surface of his work: in passage after passage, he had been obliged to recognize the extent to which he himself was a *Zivilisationsliterat*—a "civilized" intellectual.

Hence when *The Magic Mountain* finally appeared, six years after the war's end, both its scope and its intellectual emphasis had vastly altered. It had grown from a brief, half-jocular companion piece to "Death in Venice" into an immense *summa* of Mann's recurring interests—the aesthetic, erotic, and destructive function of disease and death, the ambiguous relation of the artist to bourgeois society, the incompatibility between German national values and European democracy, and the dubious ideal of a wider humanity. By the 1920's Mann was ready to grant a respectful and even a sympathetic hearing to the "civilized" values that he had attacked so bitterly in his wartime reflections. In this respect *The Magic Mountain* marked the transition between the early Mann in his self-consciously alienated and unpolitical guise and the later Mann of humanist affirmation.

Thus the book that eventually became the most influential German novel of the inter-war years was a great deal more than a work of imaginative literature. It had a public, political aspect that Mann's contemporaries were quick to recognize. Already in 1922, he had begun to take a more affirmative stand toward his nation's new "Western" institutions in his influential address entitled "The German Republic." Two years later the generally favorable reception of *The Magic Mountain* suggested that the German reading public had found a new and more subtle literary-cosmological breviary to balance Spengler's "narcotic" *Decline of the West.* In fact the publication of his great post-war work established the still hesitant Mann—quite to his own surprise—as a kind of novelist-laureate of the Weimar Republic.

The "public" aspect of *The Magic Mountain* was already apparent in its structure and presentation. Its very locale—a tuberculosis sanitarium high up in the Swiss Alps—gave it a quality of stylization and abstraction, of an artistically imposed isolation from the concerns and relationships of everyday living. "The *milieu* of the sanitarium, which removes its inmates both in time and space from their customary associations, has the advantage of an epic possibility scarcely attainable in other communities—the life of the spirit confronting death." It is a *milieu* in which even an "average" individual, freed from the bonds of practical endeavor, can learn to meditate on ultimate values—a *milieu* in which disease itself becomes the teacher who warns never to take for granted the categories that are simply assumed in the "flatland" down below.[1]

Hence as a novel of education—the form in which it most obviously offered itself to the reading public—*The Magic Mountain* conveyed a rarefied atmosphere, a sense of compression in space and dissolution in time, that were lacking in its picaresque prototype *Wilhelm Meister.* It traced a search for enlightenment through the dialectical method dear to four generations of German thinkers: two self-appointed preceptors were to struggle for the soul of a quite ordinary scion of the upper middle class sent them by accident from the world of practical activity.

Thomas Mann himself has put on record the simplicity of his original conception: "a kind of pedagogical story, in which a young man, cast adrift in a morally dangerous abode, was placed between two equally droll educators, between an Italian *litterateur,* humanist, rhetorician, and disciple of progress, and a somewhat disreputable mystic, reactionary, and advocate of unreason."[2] But in the more than decade-long process of composition, *The Magic Mountain* had changed from a *scherzo* into a novel of a high, if frequently ironical, seriousness. The Italian humanist Settembrini had become far more than the "windbag" or "organ-grinder" that the young protagonist called him in moments of irritation: he was transmuted into a

---

[1] Arnold Bauer: *Thomas Mann und die Krise der bürgerlichen Kultur* (Berlin, 1946), pp. 66-9, 71.

[2] Cited in *ibid.*, p. 70.

pathetic and even dignified figure, who, for all his superficiality and obtuseness of thought, stood for the abiding values of reason, justice, and love of humanity inherited from the Enlightenment. And his antagonist Leo Naphta—combining in his own person the appropriate illogicality of Jewish origin and Jesuit training—had grown through the years from a "disreputable" eccentric into a towering personification of the forces of terroristic orthodoxy unleashed by the war and its aftermath, pointing with uncanny insight to the still more disciplined and pitiless terror of the decade to come. Even the protagonist, the young engineer from Hamburg, Hans Castorp, although still deceptively labeled as "simple," had become an apt pupil qualified to judge in his own right: at the end of the book he had assumed the dominant role, as he sat by Settembrini's bedside, listening to the latter's explanations of the crisis of July 1914 with the tolerant, affectionate respect that one grants to an old teacher to whom one owes much but from whom one can learn nothing further.

In the vast dialectical battles on the *Zauberberg,* it was Naphta who seemed—particularly to Mann's readers of the 1930's and 1940's—to have made the more convincing case. He spoke with the voice of militant irrationalism, and in his triumphant affirmations of the virtues of illogicality, disease, and terror he appeared to epitomize what Jung had called the shadow side of twentieth-century psychology. Yet it was Settembrini who had the last word. After his antagonist's non-logic had reached its inescapable conclusion in the taking of his own life, the Italian humanist had had the pedagogical field all to himself. Failing in strength but buoyant to the end, Settembrini gave the last encouraging counsels that sped Hans Castorp on his way back to the flatland to serve his country in war. "One can only suppose that in allowing the Jesuit to kill himself and Settembrini to live on, Thomas Mann is acknowledging the right to survival of his old enemy, the "Zivilisationsliterat." [3]

The same impression is confirmed in the central passage of the whole book—the sentence that marks the culmination of Castorp's education, and the only sentence in the corpus of Mann's writings printed entirely in italics: *"For the sake of goodness and love, man shall let death have no sovereignty over his thoughts."* [4] The values of

---

[3] J. M. Lindsay: *Thomas Mann* (Oxford, 1954), p. 49.

[4] *Der Zauberberg* (Berlin, 1924), translated by H. T. Lowe-Porter as *The Magic Mountain* (New York, 1927), p. 626.

the Enlightenment, the ethical abstractions that had provided the great European moralists with their *raison d'être*—the values to which Croce and Mosca, Freud and Weber, Durkheim and Bergson had remained faithful—are here endorsed without doubt or qualification.

Yet a final ambiguity remains. Castorp proves unable to hold firm to the vision of truth to which he had attained in a moment of exaltation; the reconciliation of humanism with its necessary foundation of cruelty reveals itself as a synthesis too tenuous to last. Toward the end of the book we find him making a confession—a highly demaging confession from the standpoint of "enlightened" values: "In defiance of Herr Settembrini, I declared myself for the principle of disease, under whose aegis I had already, in reality, stood for a long time back." [5] And the individual to whom the confession is made, Mynheer Peeperkorn, suggests a still more damaging association. For it is quite apparent that Peeperkorn stands for the elemental power of human personality divorced from logic, charity, or the golden mean—for pure charisma, unalloyed by intellect or morality. It is true that this third preceptor, like Naphta, conveniently removes himself as a pedagogical influence by taking his own life. And it is equally true that Castorp is eventually "saved" by his enforced return to the flatland. Yet one cannot help wondering how the author could have resolved his educational dilemma except by the *deus ex machina* of the outbreak of war.

Thus the riddle of Peeperkorn is left in suspense. We are told that in his commanding presence the dialectics of Settembrini and Naphta seemed reduced to mere irrelevancies. "No spark leaped nimbly from pole to pole, no flash of lightning, no current. The intellect which should in its own opinion have neutralized the presence was neutralized by it." [6] The two self constituted educators found their brilliant reasoning collapse before this majestic, essentially stupid personality for whom words were simply compelling sounds that carried no defined meaning.

And so Thomas Mann had revealed something beyond Naphta, beyond the merely intellectual propagation of terror. It was a theme to which he was to return in more specific form in his short story *Mario and the Magician,* published in 1930. A transparent allegory of Italian Fascism, *Mario* took up again in terms of sharp warning

[5] *Ibid.*, p. 760.
[6] *Ibid.*, p. 743.

the dangers of "magic" and personal magnetism. The implication was that the Naphtas of this world, for all the inhumanity of their doctrines, had at least remained within the bounds of conversation and intellectual exchange. The thread of the Enlightenment had been stretched to its farthest limits but not yet entirely broken. With Mynheer Peeperkorn and the magician Cipolla a new species of humanity had appeared. Between them and the European *literati* no sort of understanding was possible.

In the dialectical conflict between Naphta and Settembrini, Thomas Mann had left the issue unresolved. Three years later—in 1927—a French philosopher of the same generation aligned himself unequivocally with the tradition of the Enlightenment. In Julien Benda's *The Betrayal of the Intellectuals* the contestants were not quite identical with those who had battled on the *Zauberberg*: in shifting from a Germanic to a French setting, the argument had lost much of its subtlety. But by the very fact of simplifying the issues, Benda was able to make his polemic cut more sharply. For it was not his intention to give credit to the intellectual innovators of his time or to recognize the nuances that separated one writer from another; he was not interested in the enhancement of understanding that had come from the thirty-year critique of the Enlightenment. He simply wanted to sound an alarm.

For this he was ideally qualified. A Jew by family tradition if not by formal practice, Benda had been born in Paris in 1867: like his co-religionists Bergson and Blum—the former eight years older, the latter five years younger—he remained all his life a Parisian to the marrow. His parents, he felt, had left their temperamental divergences imprinted on his character: in his later years he described himself as the "product of a Jew of the ancient Orient, in love with eternity and scornful of contingence, joined to a petulant Parisian Jewess . . . with the itch for writing."[7] At the same time, their unquestioning love, the atmosphere of warm family affection in which he had grown up, had given him a sense of inner security that never deserted him.

His had been a childhood without problems or painful psychological cleavages. The abstract republicanism of his upbringing—so characteristic of French Jewish families in the last decades of the nineteenth century—was simply confirmed by his schooling; in Benda's case, as opposed to the classic conflict that faced young

[7] *La Jeunesse d'un clerc* (Paris, 1936), p. 36.

Frenchmen of Catholic background, there was no opposition between what was taught in the state school and the values that had
been inculcated at home. Similarly the austere intellectualism of the
lycée found in the adolescent Benda a mind already prepared for
enthusiastic acceptance. Mathematics was his joy; a rhetoric based
on Latin models seemed to respond to the demands of his inmost
being and gave him a bare, muscular style that was to serve him well
in controversy; but the academic philosophy of his day repelled him
by its discursiveness. When still a child he had found the philosopher who was to remain his model for life—need one name
him?—Spinoza.

In the very gaps in his education an older Benda looking back on
the conflicts of his middle years was to discern further explanations
for the tight coherence of his convictions. His family had had small
esteem for non-logical values based on history and religion; energy,
physical courage had been little honored; his ancestors "had never
held functions of command."[8] One could find no sharper contrast
with the ideals that inspired those who were to be the targets of his
future attack—the monarchists, the authoritarians, the apostles of
national dynamism. These might be the socially fashionable doctrines of his mature years—but to the allures of society and
intellectual fashion Benda was singularly unsusceptible. Unlike
Bergson or Blum, he came from relatively modest circumstances
and had not attended one of the famous *lycées* where young
Parisians of promise and prominence struck up intellectual alliances
and came to think of themselves as the leaders of their generation.
For himself Benda had no sense of his generation and was quite
content to stand apart. The "mandarin" aspects of the French
intellectual's existence satisfied him entirely: as in childhood, he
continued "to think . . . that the great human examples are those
who can find joy . . . in remaining quietly in a room with pen and
paper."[9] He enjoyed a personal independence as complete as the
modern world can offer—a comfortable private income, no job, no
wife, no child. And as a man just turning thirty he had experienced
the one decisive event that would dictate for the rest of his life his
notions of political right and wrong—again the reference is obvious—the Dreyfus case. . . .

The events of 1917 and 1922 had given him occasion to think

[8] *Ibid.*, p. 53.
[9] *Ibid.*, p. 73.

through once again his essential convictions about human rationality. It is against this background of the triumph of Lenin and
Mussolini that his *Betrayal of the Intellectuals* needs to be viewed.
Such a book could not have been written before the mid-twenties.
And by that time circumstances so manifestly called for it that it
evoked an immediate response. In brief, Benda's compact, comba-
tive little book warned of the retreat from civilized values that had
already occurred—and in particular ascribed to the European intellectuals a major responsibility for it.

From the early Middle Ages, Benda maintained, the "clerks" or
intellectuals had constituted a class apart, dedicated not to earthly
but to transcendent concerns. Their great "treason of contemporary
times" had arisen from their "*desire to abase the values of knowledge
before the values of action. . . .* About 1890 the men of letters,
especially in France and Italy, realized with astonishing astuteness
that the doctrines of arbitrary authority, discipline, tradition, contempt for the spirit of liberty, assertion of the morality of war and
slavery, were haughty and rigid poses infinitely more likely to strike
the imagination of simple souls than the sentimentalities of Liberalism and Humanitarianism." [10] Hence instead of resisting the popular
drive toward an intensification of racial, class, and national passions,
they had abetted it. Far from constituting themselves as an opposition to the new irrationalism, they had become its spokesmen.

The nineteenth-century Germans had been their precursor. Philosophically they had managed to combine a neo-romantic reliance on
"artistic sensibility" with a positivist insistence that "they consider
only the facts." But this inconsistency had not troubled them: they
prided themselves on their pragmatism. What united them, rather,
was a metaphysics without precedent in history which preached
"adoration for the contingent, and scorn for the eternal." [11]

By this route, then, Benda was led to include in a sweeping
indictment not only such minor and essentially propagandist figures
as D'Annunzio, Barrès, Maurras, and Kipling, and a middle-rank
moralist like Péguy, but also such major intellectual creators as
Sorel and Bergson. The former Benda condemned for his doctrines
of violence and his "glorification of the *homo faber,*" the latter for

---

[10] *La Trahison des clercs* (Paris, 1927), translated as *The Betrayal of the Intellectuals*, Beacon paperback edition (Boston, 1955), pp. 119, 135. See also Robert J. Niess:
Julien Benda (Ann Arbor, Mich., 1956), Chapter 7.
[11] *Betrayal of the Intellectuals*, pp. 78, 94, 137.

his "exhortations to consider everything only as it exists *in time,* that is as it constitutes a succession of particular states, a 'becoming,' a 'history,' and never as it presents a state of permanence beyond time." In the case of Bergson, Benda could attack only the implications of the new metaphysics; it was obvious that the philosopher of the *èlan vital,* unlike Péguy and Sorel, did not personally advocate a warrior ethic. Similarly with Durkheim, Benda could do no more than parenthetically offer reproaches for a neglect of the "notion of good in the heart of eternal and disinterested man." And when he came to William James, Benda confined himself to noting the American philosopher's attitude of approval toward the Spanish-American war and characterizing the "preaching of Pragmatism" in its various forms as the "cult of the strong state and the moral methods which ensure it."[12]

As the foregoing enumeration reveals, *The Betrayal of the Intellectuals* drew most of its examples from contemporary France. Here indeed the lines of intellectual cleavage were almost as sharp as Benda had defined them, and in rough terms corresponded to the political division between authoritarians and republicans. Outside France, however, the situation was quite different. One wonders what Benda would have made of a thinker like Pareto—a prime "traitor," if one considered only the surface of his doctrine, yet rooted in the tradition of the Enlightenment. For the subleties and the ambiguities of German and Italian thought, Benda manifested little concern. His book—despite its constant insistence on eternal values—betrayed a profoundly parochial outlook. It was Parisian-French—classical, formally logical, intellectualist. The mark of the First World War was unmistakably upon it: Benda never thought of apologizing for his distaste and fear of things German. Yet his work had the characteristic strength of the parochial in its simplicity and robust certainty.

At a deeper level of criticism one may suggest that Benda's failure to make his presuppositions explicit gave him an unfair polemical advantage. Essentially what he was doing was taking his stand with the major tradition of Western philosophy from Socrates to Kant. Outside this path, he implied, no firm footing was possible: all around lay the quicksands of relativism and pragmatism. The nobility of such an attitude is unchallengeable. It appears with particular force toward the close of Benda's book, where he warns

[12] *Ibid.,* pp. 39, 74, 79, 98-9, 101.

of the fragility of civilized values as the West has known them. "If humanity loses this jewel, there is not much chance of finding it again . . . . People forget that Hellenic rationalism only really enlightened the world during seven hundred years, that it was then hidden . . . for twelve centuries, and has begun to shine again for barely four centuries." [13]

At the same time, this synopsis of two millennia of intellectual history is staggeringly oversimplified. If Benda had stated his presuppositions more explicitly, it would have been apparent how heavily he was stacking the cards against his adversaries. He was suggesting that salvation—indeed the most elementary intellectual honesty—lay only within the Western rational tradition *as narrowly defined by him.* For the moral dilemmas that practicing intellectuals daily confront in contemporary life, he showed scant sympathy. His ethical rigor and absolutism reflected the serenity of his own career, and the fact that the one great crisis of his life—the Dreyfus case—had been blessedly simple. The Dreyfus case has not repeated itself: its successors in more recent times have been far more ambiguous. And the precept that Benda offered in such emergencies—that the Athenian state was behaving correctly *as state* in presenting Socrates the hemlock, while Socrates *as intellectual* was also correct in making no attempt to escape it—was perhaps sufficient for a man without a family, but for the run of intellectuals offered no adequate guide. [14] (In circumstances similar to Socrates', Galileo had chosen the opposite course.) Had they followed to the letter the advice Benda offered, few European intellectuals would have survived the two decades subsequent to the publication of his book.

Similarly with regard to his more abstract categories. Benda never gave his intellectual adversaries credit for keeping faith with the spirit of the Enlightenment even as they tried to broaden its methods. In the first place, he allowed them no sufficient opportunity to state their case. The greatest of them—Croce, Freud, Weber—are absent from his pages. "This is the weakest point in M. Benda's argument; he compares the minor clerks of our time with the major clerks of other ages." [15] And those of the great who do appear in his book, like Nietzsche and Bergson, figure in travested form. Benda, as he frankly admits, is concerned only with the *tendency* of a man's

[13] *Ibid.,* pp. 156, 158-9.
[14] *Ibid.,* p. 171.
[15] *Ibid.,* Introduction by Herbert Read, p. xxii.

thought ("though I know perfectly well that in reality this teaching is something far more complex"): "Nietzsche as a humanitarian . . . had no influence at all, and my subject is the influence which the 'clerks' have had in the world, and not what they were in themselves . . . Need I say that Nietzsche, who seems to me a bad 'clerk' from the nature of his teaching, seems to me one of the finest from his entire devotion to the passions of the spirit alone?" [16]

But what sort of logic is this? Benda repeatedly asserts his radical opposition to any *practical* criterion. Yet in judging Nietzsche and his like he seems to have fallen into the grossest sort of pragmatism. Was it Bergson's fault that his doctrines gained popularity and were perverted to obscurantist and nationalist ends? The princes of the mind are not always without honor in their own time. If Benda can treat so unjustly two such lofty-spirited intellectuals as Nietzsche and Bergson, is it not possible that there is a deep flaw in his whole argument?

The basic trouble with Benda was that his intellectual range was too narrow. He wore his Cartesian categories and his traditional metaphysics like blinders, and they denied him any sympathetic understanding of the creative achievements of his contemporaries. To him the intuitive approach was anathema without qualification. True to the strict observance of the Enlightenment, he could not imagine how the uses of intuition could possibly be reconciled with it. He saw all too clearly the dangers of intuitive thinking in its destructive, hateful, and irrational guise. He was blind to its potentialities for disinterested investigation and creation. As a moral remonstrance and a call to a long-overdue examination of conscience, *The Betrayal of the Intellectuals* was a major monument of twentieth-century thought. As a summary of past achievement and a guide to the role of intellectuals when the second quarter of the century opened, it was glaringly insufficient.

The last of the three works of intellectual summation that we have singled out as directional signposts for the middle and late 1920's— Karl Mannheim's *Ideology and Utopia*—was less obviously a defense of the Enlightenment than its two predecessors. In fact what it owed to the rationalist tradition was so well concealed under German sociological paraphernalia as frequently to pass unnoticed. Yet the author's intent should have been unmistakable. His book aimed at "inquiring into the prospects of rationality and common

[16] *Ibid.*, pp. 34, 130n, 179.

understanding" in an era that apparently "put a premium upon irrationality and from which the possibilities of mutual understanding" had all but disappeared. [17] And when he came to write of the Enlightenment itself he stressed its "fresh and youthful quality," its "suggestive and stimulating atmosphere," whose "central elements . . . were open to the clear light of day" and which "appealed to the free will" by keeping alive "the feeling of being indeterminate and unconditioned . . . Its abstractness, which was only gradually uncovered by the criticism of the right and left, was never felt by the original exponents of the idea." [18]

Moreover, like Benda, Mannheim was trying to rescue the tradition of abstract, categorized thinking from the shoals of pragmatist method. But he was not proposing to follow his French predecessor in throwing overboard the whole Jamesian and Bergsonian baggage. Rather he was attempting to integrate their notions—and the work of Freud as well—into a grand synthesis that would at last make possible civilized communication among the various competing philosophical and ideological schools. A synthesis it would be—but of a loose and permissive variety. To distinguish his approach from the relativism that he wished to transcend, Mannheim called it "relationism." Viewed from this angle, knowledge would be "by no means an illusory experience"—as it presumably was when viewed relativistically. On the contrary, "all of the elements of meaning in a given situation" would "have reference to one another and derive their significance from this reciprocal interrelationship." The approach would be "dynamic": The observer of society would try to keep all sorts of shifting relationships in uneasy balance. And it would actually be of advantage—in making his thought "flexible and dialectical, rather than rigid and dogmatic"—if he were not to try for an unattainable detachment and were rather to "incorporate into his vision each contradictory and conflicting current." [19]

It was perhaps this frank entertainment of contradictions that gave *Ideology and Utopia* its very special appeal. "Rarely has a sociological study succeeded in arresting the attention of so wide a public. Not only sociologists but economists, historians, philosophers, and theologians, too, participated in the discussion." There was something in it for everybody. Its basic categories of social

[17] Preface by Louis Wirth to *Ideology and Utopia* (expansion and translation of *Ideologie und Utopie* [Bonn, 1929]) (London and New York, 1936), p. xxv.

[18] *Ibid.*, pp. 205-6.

[19] *Ibid.*, pp. 76, 88n.

analysis had been derived from Weber—but to them there had been added Scheler's notion of the collective origin of abstract ideas. And in the process Weber's procedure had been still further relativized. In Weber's work, values alone bore a purely subjective character; scientific knowledge retained a quality of "objectivity." With Mannheim, the order had been reversed. The values themselves possessed a kind of objective stability—it was the criteria of "objective" knowledge that fluctuated.[20] Thus however much Mannheim might protest that his own point of view was not relativistic, it was difficult to detect where the difference lay. As in Weber—but still more clearly than in Weber's case—*Ideology and Utopia* made it apparent that the student of society could never find rest in his quest for certainty.

Or perhaps there was one resting-place that the author himself never specifically mentioned. Like so many German thinkers of the 1920's, Mannheim owed a heavy debt to Marx. A Social Democrat in political sympathy, he was obsessed with Marxist memories. Not that he was dogmatic about them—on the contrary, he repeatedly emphasized the variety of determinants besides class position that went into forming the *Weltanschauungen* of individuals and groups.[21] Yet the social conditioning of human thought remained uppermost in his mind; he had little understanding for the groping toward universals which still characterized thinkers like Freud and Weber and which Benda had just defended with such confident belligerence. A conviction of the ultimate autonomy of man's higher mental processes revealed itself only fitfully in his work—as, for instance, when he wrote of the Enlightenment. Mannheim's effort to absorb into the Marxist tradition the more significant innovations of his contemporaries was only partially successful: in the final amalgam too much of Marx remained.

In retrospect, one can see in the circumstances under which he had written his book the elements of high historical drama. Germany in the late 1920's—deceptively prosperous, deceptively orderly— offered the fitting stage for a last effort to present a progress report on what European social thought had accomplished in the past half-century. Never in European history had there been a population

[20] Hans Speier: "Karl Mannheim's *Ideology and Utopia*," *Social Order and the Risks of War: Papers in Political Sociology* (New York, 1952), pp. 190, 192.

[21] Robert K. Merton: "The Sociology of Knowledge," in Georges Gurvitch and Wilbert E. Moore, editors: *Twentieth Century Sociology* (New York, 1945), pp. 377, 383.

better educated and culturally more aware. Never had the conflict of ideologies been more intense. Weimar Germany offered nearly ideal laboratory conditions for observing a situation in which all values had been called into question and the living "roots from which human thought had hitherto derived its nourishment were exposed." On the edge of a precipice, the more perceptive of the German intellectuals had attained to an intensity of consciousness that recalled the reputed clairvoyance of the dying.

Mannheim himself was aware of the drama of his position. The historical opportunity, he wrote, demanded to be grasped before it was too late:

> At this point in history when all things which concern man and the structure and elements of history itself are suddenly revealed to us in a new light, it behooves us in our scientific thinking to become masters of the situation, for it is not inconceivable that sooner than we suspect, as has often been the case before in history, this vision may disappear, the opportunity may be lost, and the world will once again present a static, uniform, and inflexible countenance. [22]

Hence his book pursued a number of only loosely related goals. The very pluralism of Mannheim's thinking and the form of three virtually free-standing essays in which *Ideology and Utopia* was cast, contributed to its multi-purpose character. Ostensibly—as its title implied—it was a discussion of the conflict of ideologies, or rather, to use Mannheim's own terminology, the interaction among the attitudes of "ruling groups" that were "intensively interest-bound" (i.e., ideologies in the narrower sense) and the viewpoints of "oppressed groups . . . intellectually . . . strongly interested in the destruction and transformation of a given condition of society" (which Mannheim chose to call utopias). The author's method consisted of pushing to its logical conclusion the technique of "radical unmasking" that had originally been a Marxian discovery. [23] If, Mannheim implied, this stripping away of one's adversaries' illusions—and with them one's own—could only be carried out with sufficient rigor, mutual understanding and even, perhaps, reconciliation would be the paradoxical result.

Logically, then, Mannheim did not need to hide his own sympathies. Within the terms of the method that he had devised, it was

[22] *Ideology and Utopia*, pp. 38, 76.
[23] *Ibid.*, pp. 36, 37.

sufficient if he clarified the basis of his preferences and tried to relate them "dynamically" to the prejudices of others. To the careful reader it was readily apparent that the author of *Ideology and Utopia* preferred the vitality of the latter type of world-view to the static repose of the former. His heart went out to the utopias—with the significant exception of "the sombre depths of Chiliastic agitation," whose twentieth-century incarnation was the syndicalist vision that had inspired Sorel. Mannheim's own utopian sympathies were more practical, earth-bound, and optimistic: they lay somewhere between Marx and the Enlightenment. And his fidelity to this type of thinking frequently blinded him to the tenacity of ideologies hostile to it. Fascist movements—to cite the most important case—he underestimated as "transitory formations" emerging during periods when individuals had "lost or forgotten their class orientations."[24]

But we should be very wrong to dismiss Mannheim's utopian attachments as mere sentimentality. His book might offer a maddening alternation between perception and windy verbiage. At its best, however, it shot perspectives into the future which can still bring the reader up short. His concluding vision of a world without utopia is chilling in its contemporary relevance. It is impossible to read today his strictures on the "barrenness" of a society "absorbed by its interest in concrete and isolated details" and a sociology "split up into a series of discrete technical problems of social readjustment" without applying them to the present situation in the United States. For his own generation, Mannheim implied, so "prosaic" an attitude was impossible. "It would require either a callousness which our generation could probably no longer acquire or the unsuspecting naiveté of a generation newly born into the world to be able to live in absolute congruence with the realities of that world, utterly without any transcendent element."[25]

And so by the close of his book Mannheim had been led to a prophetic position almost Spenglerian in its bleakness:

> The complete disappearance of the Utopian element . . . would mean that . . . human development would take on a totally new character . . . We would be faced then with the greatest paradox imaginable, namely, that man, who has achieved the highest degree of rational mastery of existence, left without any ideals, becomes a mere

[24] *Ibid.*, pp. 127, 205-6.
[25] *Ibid.*, pp. 225, 228, 230.

creature of impulses. Thus . . . just at the highest stage of awareness, when history is ceasing to be blind fate, and is becoming more and more man's own creation, with the relinquishment of utopias, man would lose his will to shape history and therewith his ability to understand it.[26]

"And therewith his ability to understand it"—like Dilthey, like Croce, Mannheim believed that the understanding of history could arise only from acting in it. To him, as to his great predecessors of the generation of the 1890's, thought was not a detached and static affair: it was intimately involved in the processes of living. In this view, the intellectual was no mere observer. He represented the conscience of his society—perched perilously between the danger of betraying his trust through failure to give a clear lead, and the opposite "treason" of lending his pen to the purposes of propaganda. Benda—under French conditions—had been more conscious of the latter danger. Mannheim—from a German perspective—saw the greater peril in detachment and apathy. When, four years after the publication of his book, the catastrophe came, the behavior of most German intellectuals proved him right.

Hence when he strove to bind together in tense reconciliation the divergent philosophies and ideologies of his time—to integrate into the rationalist tradition certain of the "irrationalist" tendencies that Benda had refused to countenance—he was as concerned as Benda had been with the role of the intellectual in contemporary society. And—as we have just noticed—he defined this role in similar terms. Like Benda, he traced the sense of special function that still characterized the European intellectuals to their position in the Middle Ages as privileged "clerks." But he differed from his predecessor in stressing the ambiguity as well as the "unexampled intellectual richness" that had resulted from the "disruption of the . . . monopoly of the church." This was a problem that went at least as far back as the sixteenth century. Since the First World War, however, it had grown inordinately acute. The intellectual's relation to the society in which he lived had become dubious in the extreme. For his own part, Mannheim could see only four possible choices—affiliation "with the radical wing of the socialist-communist proletariat"; skepticism "in the name of intellectual integrity" (as in the case of Max Weber and Pareto); seeking "refuge in the past" through "attempts to revive religious feeling, idealism,

[26] *Ibid.*, p. 236.

symbols, and myths"; and a withdrawal from the world and conscious renunciation of "direct participation in the historical process."[27] It was this last possibility that Mannheim had in mind when he traced the outlines of a future without utopia.

Of these, only the second, he believed, held any creative possibilities. Despite its negative features, it possessed the virtue of "frankness," which was perhaps the best that could be expected in an era when utopian hopes were fading. The great advantage of the intellectuals, Mannheim argued, was that they alone constituted "a relatively classless stratum . . . not too firmly situated in the social order . . . . Participation in a common educational heritage progressively tends to suppress differences of birth, status, profession, and wealth, and to unite the individual educated people on the basis of the education they have received." Hence they alone could become the vehicles of "dynamic intellectual mediation"—a last supreme effort to bring about public understanding through entering into a sympathetic internal comprehension of each of the mutually destructive ideologies and utopias that were tearing European society apart. Their intervention offered the only faint hope of arresting the drift toward catastrophe.[28]

An illusion, of course—and yet Mannheim seems to have known it was an illusion even as he wrote. In his many-layered, involuted thinking, the line between intellectual clarity and the partial self-deceptions by which men live was never fixed. Indeed, in the fluid social universe that he had delineated, to draw such a line would appear to be naiveté or nonsense. Similarly the desperate hope that he had vested in the European intellectuals had its own elements of ambiguity: the role he assigned them lay somewhere between the new ethic of "engagement" and the more traditional conception of the "unattached" *(freischwebend)* thinker or writer. On balance, it leaned toward the latter. The final relevance of *Ideology and Utopia* was as a defense and justification of the *Freischwebender* on the brink of disappearance.

The generation of the 1890's had begun their work and completed the major outlines of their thought in a privileged era. Riding the final wave of the century-old faith in progress, they had enjoyed the last great period of peace and security that Europe was to know. Profiting by the comforts, the facilities that modern technology

---

[27] *Ibid.*, pp. 11, 233.
[28] *Ibid.*, pp. 137-8, 168, 231.

offered, they were to witness only in their later years—when their world-view had already been formed—the new face of technology in its destructive guise. They had passed their youth at the climax of the Enlightenment—and simultaneously had inaugurated its most probing critique. Indeed, it was their very certainty of "enlightened" values (however much they might jibe at them) that had enabled them to strip away so mercilessly the illusions with which these values had become encrusted. Their own psychological security— their confidence in such unstated assumptions as humane behavior and intellectual integrity—had given them the inner strength to inaugurate an unprecedented examination of conscience. Perched between two eras of dogmatism—the old dogmas of positivism and Marxism behind them, and the new certainties of "commitment" and exact logic in the future—they could afford the luxury of suspended judgment. The philosophies of urbane doubt— skepticism, pragmatism, pluralism—held no terrors for them.

Hence the quality of serenity, of an untroubled entertainment of contradictions. . . . They led privileged lives of contemplation: never again were intellectuals to be so free from the petty harass- ments that have exasperated the existence of their fellows in most of the eras of European history—financial need, interference by the public authorities, and the sense of personal danger. They were the last of the great *Freischwebende.* Karl Mannheim, a late arrival in their fraternity, might sum up their role and try to redefine it to conform to the vastly altered situation he saw approaching. But he could not revitalize a way of life that was already disappearing. For the next two decades at least, the "unattached intellectual" was to be everywhere on the defensive.

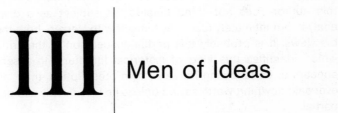

III | Men of Ideas

SIR ISAIAH BERLIN
A Marvelous Decade (Part IV): Alexander Herzen

Among the many methods in which history has been written, biography and autobiography probably come closer to a form of creative literary expression than any other. One thinks of Sandburg's *Lincoln* and Cellini's *Autobiography* more as literature than as history; indeed, biography can often read like a work of fiction. Intellectual biography can also achieve that quality at times, as the following piece by Sir Isaiah Berlin on Alexander Herzen attests. Of course, in this case, the subject was himself an artist and is treated by one of the foremost stylists of historical writing. In contrast to Victor Wolfenstein (on Lenin), this author does not stand outside his subject as a dispassionate analyst, but intimately identifies himself with Herzen, both the man and his views. It is probably this partial suspension of the critical stance which identifies this kind of historical literature. In a sense, Berlin appears to be following Herzen's own prescription, that "nobody has ever said anything worth saying unless he was deeply and passionately partial."

ALEXANDER IVANOVICH HERZEN was born in Moscow in 1812, not long before the capture of the city by Napoleon, the illegitimate son of Ivan Yakovlev, a rich and well-born Russian gentleman, descended from a cadet branch of the Romanoffs, a morose, difficult, possessive, distinguished and civilised man, who bullied his son, loved him deeply, embittered his life, and had an enormous influence upon him both by attraction and repulsion. His mother, Amalia Haag, was a mild German lady from Stuttgart in Wurttemberg, the daughter of a minor official. Ivan Yakovlev had met her while travelling abroad, but never married her. He took her to Moscow, established her as mistress of his household, and called his son Herzen in token, as it were, of the fact that he was the child of his heart, but not legitimately born and therefore not entitled to bear his name.

The fact that Harzen was not born in wedlock probably had a considerable effect on his character, and may have made him more rebellious than he might otherwise have been. He received the

---

From "A Marvellous Decade (Part IV): Alexander Herzen; *Encounter*, Vol. VI, No. 5 (May, 1956), pp. 20-34.

regular education of a rich young nobleman, went to the University of Moscow and there early asserted his vivid, original, impulsive character. He was born (in later years he constantly came back to this) into the generation of what in Russia came to be called *Lishniye Lyudi,* "superfluous men," with whom Turgenev's early novels are so largely concerned.

These young men have a place of their own in the history of European culture in the nineteenth century. They belonged to the class of those who are by birth aristocratic, but who themselves go over to some freer and more radical mode of thought and of action. There is something singularly attractive about men who retained, throughout life, the manners, the texture of being, the habits and style of a civilized and refined milieu. Such men exercise a peculiar kind of personal freedom which combines spontaneity with distinction. Their minds see large and generous horizons, and, above all reveal a unique intellectual gaiety of a kind that aristocratic education tends to produce. At the same time, they are intellectually on the side ofeverything that is new, progressive, rebellious, young, untried, of that which is about to come into being, of the open sea whether or not there is land that lies beyond. To this type belong those intermediate figures, like Mirabeau, Charles James Fox, Franklin Roosevelt, who live near the frontier that divides old from new, between the *douceur de la vie* which is about to pass and the tantalising future, the dangerous new age that they themselves do much to bring into being.

Herzen belonged to this milieu. In his autobiography he has described what it was like to be this kind of man in a suffocating society, where there was no opportunity of putting to use one's natural gifts, what it meant to be excited by novel ideas which came drifting in from all kinds of sources, from classical texts and the old utopias of the West, from French social preachers and German philosophers, from books, journals, casual conversations, only to remember that the milieu in which one lived made it absurd even to begin to dream of creating in one's own country those harmless and moderate institutions which had long become forms of life in the civilised West.

This normally led to one of two results: either the young enthusiast simply subsided, and came to terms with reality, and became a wistful, gently frustrated landowner, who lived on his estate, turned the pages of serious periodicals imported from Petersburg or abroad, and occasionally introduced new pieces of agricultural machinery of some other ingenious device which had caught his fancy in England or in France. Such enthusiasts would endlessly discuss the need for this or that change, but always with the melancholy implication that little or nothing could or would be done; or, alternatively, they would give in entirely and fall into a species of gloom or stupor or violent despair, becoming self-devouring neurotics, destructive personalities slowly poisoning both themselves and the life round them.

Herzen was resolved to escape from both these familiar predicaments. He was determined that of him, at any rate, nobody would say that he had done nothing in the world, that he had offered no resistance and collapsed. When he finally emigrated from Russia in 1847 it was to devote himself to a life of activity. His education was that of a dilettante. Like most young men brought up in an aristocratic milieu, he had been taught to be too many things to too many men, to reflect too many aspects of life, and situations, to be able to concentrate sufficiently upon any one particular activity, any one fixed design.

Herzen was well aware of this. He talks wistfully about the good fortune of those who enter peacefully upon some steady, fixed profession, untroubled by the many countless alternatives open to gifted and often idealistic young men who have been taught too much, are too rich, and are offered altogether too wide an opportunity of doing too many things, and who, consequently, begin, and are bored, and go back and start down a new path, and in the end lose their way and drift aimlessly and achieve nothing. This was a very characteristic piece of self-analysis; filled with the idealism of his generation in Russia that both sprang from and fed the growing sense of guilt towards "the people." Herzen was passionately anxious to do something memorable for himself and his country. This anxiety remained with him all his life. Driven by it he became, as everyone knows who has acquaintance with the modern history of Russia, perhaps the greatest of European publicists of his day, and founded the first free—that is to say, anti-Czarist—Russian press in Europe, thereby laying the foundation of revolutionary agitation in his country.

In his most celebrated periodical, which he called *The Bell*, he dealt with anything that seemed to be of topical interest. He exposed, he denounced, he derided, he preached, he became a kind of Russian Voltaire of the mid-nineteenth century. He was a journalist of genius, and his articles, written with brilliance, gaiety, and passion, although, of course, officially forbidden, circulated in Russia and were read by radicals and conservatives alike. Indeed it was said that the Emperor himself read them; certainly some among his officials did so; during the heyday of his name Herzen exercised a genuine influence within Russia itself—an unheard of phenomenon for an émigré—by exposing abuses, naming names, but, above all, by appealing to liberal sentiment which had not completely died, even at the very heart of the Czarist bureaucracy, at any rate during the fifties and sixties.

Unlike many who find themselves only on paper, or on a public platform, Herzen was an entrancing talker. Probably the best description of him is to be found in the book after which these lectures are named—*The Marvellous Decade*, by his friend Annenkov. It was written some twenty years after the events that it records.

I must own (Annenkov wrote) that I was puzzled and overwhelmed, when I first came to know Herzen—by this extraordinary mind which darted from one topic to another with unbelievable swiftness, with inexhaustible wit and brilliance; which could see in the turn of somebody's talk, in some simple incident, in some abstract idea, that vivid feature which gives expression and life. He had a most astonishing capacity for instantaneous, unexpected juxtaposition of quite dissimilar things, and this gift he had in a very high degree, fed as it was by the powers of the most subtle observation and a very solid fund of encyclopaedic knowledge. He had it to such a degree that, in the end, his listeners were sometimes exhausted by the inextinguishible foreworks of his speech, the inexhaustible fantasy and invention, a kind of prodigal opulence of intellect which astonished and delighted his audience.

After the always ardent but remorselessly severe Belinsky, the glancing, gleaming, perpetually changing and often paradoxical and irritating, always wonderfully clever, talk of Herzen demanded of those who were with him not only interest, but intense concentration, perpetual alertness, because you had always to be prepared to respond instantly. On the other hand, nothing cheap or tawdry could stand even half an hour of contact with him. All pretentiousness, all pompousness, all pedantic self-importance, simply fled from him or melted like wax before a fire. I knew people, many of them what are called serious and practical men, who could not bear Herzen's presence. On the other hand, there were others who gave him the most blind and passionate adoration.

He had a natural gift for criticism—an unparalleled capacity for exposing and denouncing the dark sides of life. And he showed this trait very early, during the Moscow period of his life of which I am speaking. Even then Herzen's mind was in the highest degree rebellious and unmanageable, with a kind of innate, organic, detestation of anything which seemed to him to be an accepted opinion sanctified by general silence about some unverified fact. In such cases the deep, predatory, powers of his intellect would rise up in force and come into the open, sharp, cunning, resourceful.

He lived in Moscow, still unknown to the public, but in his own familiar circle he was already known as a witty and a dangerous observer of his friends. What was not then known (though he could not altogether conceal it), was that he kept secret *dossiers*, secret protocols of his own, about his dearest and most intimate friends within the privacy of his own thoughts. People who stood by his side, all innocence and trustfulness, were invariably amazed, and sometimes extremely annoyed, when they suddenly came on one or other side of this activity—the secret activity—of his mind. Strangely enough, Herzen combined with this the tenderest, most loving relations with his chosen intimates, although even they could never escape his pungent analyses. This is explained by another side of his character. As if to restore the equilibrium of his moral organism, nature took care to place in his soul one unshakable belief, one unconquerable inclination. Herzen believed in the noble instincts of the human heart. His analysis grew silent and reverent before the instinctive impulses of the moral organism as the sole, indubitable truth of existence. He admired anything which he thought to be a noble or passionate impulse, however mistaken; and he never amused himself at its expense.

This ambivalent, as it were, contradictory, play of his nature—suspicion and denial on the one hand and blind faith on the other—often led to perplexity and misunderstandings between him and his friends, and sometimes to quarrels and scenes. But it is precisely in this crucible of argument, in its flames, that up to the very day of his departure for Europe, people's devotion to him used to be tested and strengthened instead of disintegrating. And this is perfectly intelligible. In all that Herzen did and all that Herzen thought at this time there never was the slightest trace of anything false, no malignant feeling nourished in darkness, no calculation, no treachery. On the contrary, the whole of him was always there, in every one of his words and deeds.

And there was another reason which made one sometimes forgive him even insults, a reason which may seem unplausible to people who did not know him. With all this proud, strong, energetic intellect, Herzen had a wholly gentle, amiable, almost feminine character. Beneath the stern outward aspect of the sceptic, the satirist, under the cover of a most unceremonious, and exceedingly unreticent humour there dwelt the heart of a child. He had a curious, angular kind of charm, angular kind of delicacy, but it was given particularly to those who were beginning, who were seeking after something, people who were trying out their powers. They found a source of strength and confidence in his advice. He took them into the most intimate communion with himself and with his ideas—which, nevertheless, did not stop him, at times, from using his full destructive, analytic powers, from performing exceedingly painful, psychological experiments on these very same people at the very same time.

This vivid and sympathetic vignette tallies with the descriptions left to us by Turgenev, Belinsky and others of Herzen's friends. It is borne out, above all, by the impression which the reader gains if he reads his own prose, his essays or the autobiographical memoirs collected under the title *My Past and Reflections*. The impression that it leaves is not conveyed even by Annenkov's devoted words.

The chief influence on Herzen as a young man in Moscow University, as upon all the young Russian intellectuals of his time, was of course that of Hegel. But although he was a fairly orthodox Hegelian in his early years, he turned his Hegelianism into something peculiar, personal to himself, very dissimilar from the theoretical conclusions which the more serious-minded and pedantic of his contemporaries deduced from that celebrated doctrine.

The chief effect upon him of Hegelianism seems to have been the belief that no specific theory or single doctrine, no one interpretation of life, above all, no simple, coherent, well-constructed schema—neither the great French mechanistic models of the eighteenth century, nor the romantic German edifices of the nineteenth, nor the visions of the great utopians Saint-Simon, Fourier, Owen, nor the socialist programmes of Cabet or Leroux or Louis Blanc—could conceivably be true solutions to real problems, at least not in the form in which they were preached.

He was sceptical if only because he believed (whether or not he derived this view from Hegel) that there could not in principle be any simple or final answer to any genuine human problem; that if a question was serious and indeed agonising, the answer could never be clear cut and neat. Above all, it could never consist in some symmetrical set of conclusions, drawn by deductive means from a collection of self-evident axioms.

This disbelief begins in Herzen's early, forgotten essays which he wrote at the beginning of the forties, on what he called dilletantism and Buddhism in science; where he distinguishes two kinds of intellectual personality, against both of which he inveighs. One is that of the casual amateur who never sees the trees for the woods; who is terrified, Herzen tells us, of losing his own precious individuality in too much pedantic preoccupation with actual, detailed facts, and, therefore, always skims over the surface without developing a capacity for real knowledge; who looks at the facts, as it were, through a kind of telescope, with the result that nothing ever gets articulated save enormous, sonorous generalisations floating at random like so many balloons.

The other kind of student—the Buddhist—is the person who escapes from the wood by frantic absorption in the trees; who becomes an intense student of some tiny set of isolated facts, which he views through more and more powerful microscopes. Although such a man might be deeply learned in some particular branch of knowledge, almost invariably—and particularly if he is a German (and almost all Herzen's gibes and insults are always directed against the hated Germans, and that despite the fact that he was half German himself)—he becomes intolerably tedious, pompous and blindly philistine; above all, always repellent as a human being.

Between these poles it is necessary to find some compromise, and Herzen believed that if one studied life in a sober, detached, and objective manner, one might perhaps be able to create some kind of tension, a sort of dialectical compromise, between these opposite ideals; for if neither of them can be realised fully and equally, neither of them should be altogether deserted; only thus could human beings be made capable of understanding life in some profounder fashion that if they committed themselves recklessly to one or the other of the two extremes.

This ideal of detachment, moderation, compromise, dispassionate objectivity which Herzen at this early period of his life was preaching, was something deeply incompatible with his temperament. And indeed, not long after, he bursts forth with a great paean to partiality. "I know," he writes, "that it will not be well received. I know that there are certain concepts which simply are not received in good society—rather like people who have been in gaol or have disgraced themselves in some appalling way. I know that partiality is not something which is well thought of. Nevertheless, nobody has ever said anything worth saying unless he was deeply and passionately partial."

There follows a long and typically Russian diatribe against the chilliness, meanness, impossibility and undesirability of remaining objective, of being detached, of not committing oneself, of not plunging into the stream of life. The passionate voice of his friend Belinsky is suddenly audible in Herzen's writings in this phase of his development.

But the fundamental belief which emerges at this time, and is then developed throughout his later life with marvellous poetry and imagination (I say poetry advisedly; for a Dostoevsky in later years very truly said, whatever else might be said about Herzen, he was certainly a Russian poet; which saved him in the eyes of this jaundiced but, at times, uncannily penetrating critic: Herzen's views or mode of life naturally found little favour in his eyes).

The thesis which Herzen offered to the world comes to this: that any attempt to explain human conduct in terms of, or to dedicate human beings to the service of, any abstraction, be it never so noble—justice, progress, nationality—even if preached by impeccable altruists like Mazzini or Louis Blanc or Mill, always leads in the end to victimisation and human sacrifice. Men are not simple enough, human lives and relationships are too complex for standard formulae and neat solutions, and attempts to adapt individuals and fit them into a rational scheme, conceived in terms of a theoretical ideal, be the motives for doing it never so lofty, always lead in the end to a terrible maiming of human beings, to political vivisection on an ever increasing scale. The process culminates in the liberation of some only at the price of enslavement of others, and the replacing of an old tyranny with a new and sometimes far more hideous one—by the imposition of the slavery of universal socialism, for example, as a remedy for the slavery of the universal Roman church.

There is a typical piece of dialogue between Herzen and Louis Blanc, the French socialist (whom he respected greatly), which Herzen quotes, and which shows the kind of levity with which Herzen sometimes expressed his deepest convictions. The conversation is described as having taken place in London somewhere in the early fifties. One day Louis Blanc observed to Herzen that human life was a great social duty, that man must always sacrifice himself to society.

> "Why?" I asked suddenly. "How do you mean, why?" said Louis Blanc. "Surely the whole purpose and the whole mission of man is the well-being of society?" "Oh, but it will never be attained if everybody makes sacrifices and nobody ever enjoys himself." "You are playing with words." "Only the muddle-headedness of a barbarian," I said laughing.

In this gay and apparently casual passage, Herzen embodies his central principle—that the goal of life is life itself, that to sacrifice the present to some vague and unpredictable future is a form of delusion which leads to the destruction of all that alone is valuable in men and societies—to the gratuitous sacrifice of the flesh and blood of live human beings upon the altar of idealised abstractions.

Herzen is revolted by the central substance of what was being preached by some of the best and purest-hearted men of his time, particularly by socialists and utilitarians, namely, that vast suffering in the present must be undergone for the sake of an ineffable felicity in the future, that thousands of innocent men may be forced to die that millions might be happy—battle cries that were common even in those days, and of which a great deal more has been heard since. The notion that there is a splendid future in store for humanity, that it is guaranteed by history, and that it justifies the most appalling cruelties in the present—this familiar piece of political eschatology based on belief in inevitable progress seemed to him a fatal doctrine directed against human life.

The profoundest and most sustained—and the most brilliantly written—of all Herzen's statements of this topic is to be found in the volume of essays which he called *From the Other Shore,* and wrote as a memorial to his disillusionment with the European revolutions of 1848 and 1849. This great polemical masterpiece is Herzen's profession of faith and his political testament. Its tone and content is well conveyed in the characteristic (and celebrated) passage in which he asks:

> If progress is the goal, for whom then are we working? Who is this Moloch who, as the toilers approach him, instead of rewarding them, draws back, and as a consolation to the exhausted and doomed multitudes shouting, "We, who are about to die, salute thee!", can

only give the mocking answer that after their death all will be beautiful on earth. Do you really wish to condemn human beings alive today to the mere sad role of caryatids supporting a floor for others one day to dance upon? Of wretched galley slaves who, up to their knees in mud, drag a barge with the humble words "Future Progress" on its flag? A goal which is infinitely remote is not a goal at all, it is a deception. A goal must be closer—at the very least the labourer's wage or pleasure in work performed. Each epoch, each generation, each life has had, has, its own experience, and en route new demands grow, new methods.

He continues:

The end of each generation must be itself. Nature not only never makes one generation the means for the attainment of some future goal; she does not concern herself with the future at all. Like Cleopatra, she is ready to dissolve the pearl in wine for a second's pleasure. If humanity marched straight towards some result, there would be no history, only logic. One has to arrange life as best one can because there is no libretto. If history followed a set libretto, it would lose all interest, it would become unnecessary, boring, ludicrous. Great men would be simply so many heroes strutting on a stage. History is all improvisation, all will, all extemporised. There are no frontiers, there are no timetables, no itineraries. All that exists is specific conditions, and sacred discontent, the flow of life and its endless challenge to the fighters to try their strength, to go where they will, where there is a road; and when there is no road, there genius will blast a path.

But what if someone were to ask, "Supposing all this is suddenly brought to an end? Supposing a comet strikes us and brings to an end life on earth? Will history not be meaningless? Will all this talk suddenly end in nothing? Will it not be a cruel mockery of all our efforts, all our blood and sweat and tears, if it all ends in some sudden, unexplained brute fashion by some mysterious, totally unexplained event?" Herzen replies that to think in these terms is a great vulgarity, the vulgarity of mere numbers. The death of a single human being is no less absurd and unintelligible than the death of the entire race; it is a mystery we accept; merely to multiply it enormously and ask, "Supposing millions of human beings die?" does not make it more mysterious or more frightening.

In nature, as in the souls of men, there slumber endless possibilities and forces, and in suitable conditions they develop, they develop furiously. They may fill a world, or they may fall by the roadside. They may take a new direction. They may stop. They may collapse. Nature is perfectly indifferent to what happens. But then, you may ask, What is all this for? The life of people becomes a pointless game. Men build something with pebbles and grass and sand only to see it all collapse again; and human creatures crawl out from underneath the ruins and again start clearing spaces and build huts of moss and planks and broken capitals and, after centuries of endless labour, it all collapses again. Not in vain did Shakespeare say that history was a tale told by an idiot.

To this I reply that you are like those very sensitive people who shed a tear whenever they recollect that man is born but to die. To look at the end and not at the action itself is a cardinal error. Of what use to the flower is its bright magnificent bloom? Or its intoxicating scent, since it will only pass away? None at all. But nature is not so miserly. She does not disdain what is transient, what is only in the present. At every point she achieves all she can achieve. Who will find fault with nature because flowers bloom in the morning and die at night, because she has not given the rose of the lily the hardness of flint? And this miserable pedestrian principle *we* wish to transfer to world history. Life has no obligation to realise the fantasies and ideas of civilisation. Life loves novelty. She seldom repeats herself. She uses every accident, simultaneously knocks at a thousand doors, some of which may open—who can tell?

And again:

Human beings have an instinctive passion to preserve anything they like. Man is born and therefore wishes to live for ever. Man falls in love and wishes to be loved, and loved for ever as in the very first moment of his avowal. But life gives no guarantees. Life does not ensure existence, nor pleasure; she does not answer for their continuance. Every historical moment is full and is beautiful, is self-contained in its own fashion. Every year has its own spring and its own summer, its own winter and autumn, its own storms and fair weather. Every period is new, fresh, filled with its own hopes and carries within itself its own joys and sorrows. The present belongs to it. But human beings are not content with this, they must needs own the future too.

What is the purpose of the song the singer sings? If you look beyond your pleasure in it for something else, for some other goal, the moment will come when the singer stops and then you will only have memories and vain regrets because, instead of listening, you were waiting for something else. You must not be misled by categories that are not fitted to catch the flow of life. What is this goal for which you (he means Mazzini and the liberals and the socialists) are seeking, this permanent goal? A programme? An order? Who conceived it? To whom was the order given? Is it something inevitable? If it is, we are simply puppets. Are we morally free or are we wheels within a machine? I would rather think of life, and therefore history, as a goal attained, not as a means to something else.

And:

Is it really the purpose of a child to grow up simply because it does grow up? No. The purpose of a child is to play, to enjoy itself, to be a child; because, if we follow the other line of reasoning, then the purpose of all life is death.

This is Herzen's central political and social thesis, and it enters henceforth into the stream of Russian radical thought as an antidote to the exaggerated utilitarianism of which its adversaries have so often accused it. The purpose of the singer is the song, and the purpose of life is to be lived. Everything passes, but what passes may sometimes reward the pilgrim for all his sufferings. Goethe has told us that there can be no guarantee, no security. Man could be content with the present. But he is not. He rejects beauty, he rejects fulfillment to-day, because he must own the future also. That is Herzen's answer to all those who, like Mazzini, or the socialists of his time, called for supreme sacrifices and sufferings for the sake of nationality, or human civilisation, or socialism, or justice, or humanity—if not in the present, then in the future.

Herzen rejects this violently. The purpose of the struggle for liberty is not liberty tomorrow, it is liberty today, the liberty of living individuals with their own individual ends, the ends for which they move and fight and perhaps die, ends which are sacred to them. To crush their freedom, their pursuits, to ruin their ends for the sake of some vague felicity in the future which cannot be guaranteed, about which we know nothing, which is simply the product of some enormous metaphysical construction that itself rests upon sand, for which there is no logical, or empirical or any other rational guarantee—to do that is in the first place blind, because the future is uncertain; and in the second place vicious because it offends against the only moral values we know; because it tramples on human demands in the name of abstractions—freedom, happiness, justice—fanatical generalisations, mystical sounds, idolised sets of words.

> Why is liberty valuable? Because it is an end in itself, because it is what it is. To bring it as a sacrifice to something else is simply to perform an act of human sacrifice.

This is Herzen's ultimate sermon, and from this he develops the corollary that one of the deepest of modern disasters is to be caught up in abstractions instead of realities. And this he maintains not merely against the Western socialists and liberals among whom he lived (let alone the enemy—priests or conservatives) but even more against his own close friend Bakunin who persisted in trying to stir up violent rebellion, involving torture and martyrdom, for the sake of dim, confused and distant goals. For Herzen, one of the greatest of sins that any human being can perpetrate is to seek to transfer moral responsibility from his own shoulders to those of an unpredictable future order, and, in the name of something which may never happen, perpetrate crimes today which no one would deny to be monstrous if they were performed for some egoistic purpose, and do not seem so only because they are sanctified by faith in some remote and intangible utopia.

For all his hatred of despotism, and particular of the Russian régime, Herzen was all his life convinced that equally fatal dangers threatened from his own socialist and revolutionary allies. He believed this because there was a time when, with his friend, the critic Belinsky, he too had believed that a simple solution was feasible; that some great system—a world adumbrated by Saint-Simon or by Proudhon—did provide it: that if one regulated social life rationally and put it in order, and created a clear and tidy organisation, human problems could be finally resolved. Dostoevsky once said of Belinsky that his socialism was nothing but a simple belief in a marvelous life of "rich and unbelievable splendour, built on new, adamantine foundations." Because Herzen had himself once believed in these foundations (although never with simple and absolute faith) and because this belief came toppling down and was utterly destroyed in the fearful cataclysms of 1848 and 1849 in which almost every one of his idols proved to have feet of clay, he denounces his own past with peculiarly intense indignation:

> We call upon the masses to rise and crush the tyrants. The masses! The masses are indifferent to individual freedom . . . . They want a government which will rule for them, not against them. But they do not dream of governing themselves. . . . It is not enough to despise the Crown; one must not be filled with awe before the Phrygian cap either.

He speaks with bitter scorn about monolithic, oppressive communist idylls, about the barbarous "equality of the gallows," about "the slave labour camps" of socialists like Cabet, about barbarians marching to destroy.

> Who will finish us off? The senile barbarism of the sceptre or the wild barbarism of communism; the bloody sabre, or the red flag? . . .- Communism will sweep across the world in a violent tempest— dreadful, bloody, unjust, swift. Our institutions, as Proudhon so politely put it, will be liquidated. I am very sorry for the death of civilisation, but the masses are not sorry; the masses to whom it brings nothing but tears, ignorance, suffering, humiliation.

He is terrified of the oppressors, but he is terrified of the liberators too. He is terrified of them because for him they are the secular heirs of the religious bigots of the ages of faith; because anybody who has a cut-and-dried scheme, a strait-jacket which he wishes to impose on humanity as the sole possible remedy for all human ills, is ultimately bound to create a situation intolerable for free human beings, for men like himself who want to express themselves, who want to have some area in which to develop their own resources, and are prepared to respect the originality, the spontaneity, the natural impulse towards self-expression on the part of other human beings too. He calls this Petrograndism—the methods of Peter the Great. He admires Peter because he did at least overthrow the feudal rigidity, the dark night, as he thinks of it, of medieval Russia. He admires the Jacobins because the Jacobins dared to do something instead of nothing. Yet he is clearly aware, and became more and more so the longer he lived (he says all this with arresting clarity in his open letter to "An Old Comrade"—Bakunin—written in the late sixties), that Petrograndism, the behavior of Attila, the behavior of the Committee of Public Safety in 1792—the use of methods which presuppose the possibility of simple and radical solutions—always in the end lead to oppression, bloodshed, and collapse. He declares that whatever the justification in earlier and more innocent ages of acts inspired by fanatical faith, nobody has any right to act in this fashion who has lived through the nineteenth century and has seen what human beings are really made of—the complex, crooked texture of men and institutions. Progress must adjust itself to the actual pace of historical change, to the actual economic and social needs of society, because to suppress the bourgeoisie by violent revolution—and there was nothing he despised more than the bourgeoisie, and the mean, grasping, philistine financial bourgeoisie of Paris most of all—before its historical role has been played out, would merely mean that the bourgeois spirit and bourgeois forms would persist into the new social order. "It is not possible to build houses for free men out of materials designed for prisons." And who shall say that history has proved that Herzen was mistaken?

His loathing of the bourgeoisie is frantic, yet he does not want a violent cataclysm. He thinks that it may be inevitable, that it may come, but he is frightened of it. The bourgeoisie seems to him like a collection of Figaros grown fat and prosperous. He declares that, in the eighteenth century, Figaro wore a livery, a mark of servitude to be sure, but still something different from, detachable from, his skin; the skin, at least, was that of a palpitating, rebellious human being. But today Figaro has won. Figaro has become a millionaire. He is judge, commander-in-chief, president of the republic. Figaro now dominates the world, and, alas, the livery is no longer a mere livery. It has become part of his skin. It cannot be taken off; it has become part of his living flesh.

Everything that was repellent and degrading in the eighteenth century, against which the noble revolutionaries had protested, has grown into the intrinsic texture of the mean middle class beings who now dominate us. And yet we must wait. Simply to cut off their heads, as Bakunin wanted, can only lead to a new tyranny and a new slavery, to the rule of the revolted minorities over majorities, or worse still, the rule of majorities—monolithic majorities—over minorities, the rule of what John Stuart Mill, in Herzen's view with justice, called conglomerated mediocrity.

Herzen's values are undisguised: he likes only the style of free beings, only what is large, generous, uncalculating. He admires pride, independence, resistance to tyrants; he admires Pushkin because he was defiant; he admires Lermontov because he dared to

suffer and to hate; he even approves of the Slavophils, his reactionary opponents, because at least they detested authority, at least they
would not let the Germans in. He admires Belinsky because he was
incorruptible, and told the truth in the face of the arrayed battalions
of German academic or political authority. The dogmata of socialism seem to him no less stifling than those of capitalism or of the
Middle Ages or of the early Christians.

What he hated most of all was the despotism of formulae—the
submission of human beings to arrangements arrived at by deduc-
tion from some kind of *a priori* principles which had no foundation
in actual experience. That is why he feared the new liberators so
deeply. "If only people wanted," he says, "instead of liberating
humanity, to liberate themselves, they would do a very great deal for
human freedom." He knew that his own perpetual plea for more
individual freedom contained the seeds of social atomization, that a
compromise had to be found between the two great social needs—
for organization and for individual freedom—some unstable equilibrium that would preserve a minimal area within which the
individual could express himself and not be utterly pulverized, and
he utters a great appeal for what he calls the value of egoism. He
declares that one of the great dangers to our society is that
individuals will be tamed and suppressed disinterestedly by idealists
in the name of altruism, in the name of measures designed to make
the majority happy. The new liberators may well resemble the
inquisitors of the past, who drove herds of innocent Spaniards,
Dutchmen, Belgians, Frenchmen, Italians to the *autos-da-fé*, and
"then went home peacefully with a quiet conscience, with the
feeling that they had done their duty, with the smell of roasting
human flesh still in their nostrils," and slept—the sleep of the
innocent after a day's work well done.

Let us encourage egoism instead of trying to suppress it, which is
anyhow impossible. Egoism is not a vice. Egoism gleams in the eye of
an animal. It is wild, self-centred and salutary. Moralists bravely
thunder against it, instead of building on it. What moralists try and
deny is the great, inner citadel of human dignity. They want to make
men tearful, sentimental, feeble, kindly creatures asking to be made
slaves. But to tear egoism from a man's heart is to rob him of his living
principles, of the yeast and the salt of his whole personality. Fortunately this is impossible. Of course it is sometimes suicidal to try to
assert oneself. One cannot try and go up a staircase down which an

army is trying to march. That is done by tyrants, conservatives, fools and criminals. Without altruism we are orang-outangs, but without egoism we are nothing but tame monkeys.

Human problems are too complex to demand simple solutions. Even the peasant commune in Russia, in which Herzen believed so deeply as a "lightning conductor," because he believed that peasants in Russia at least had not been infected by the distorting, urban vices of the European proletariat and the European bourgeoisie—even the peasant commune did not, after all, as he points out, preserve Russia from slavery. Liberty is not to the taste of the majority—only of the educated. There are no guaranteed methods, no sure paths to social welfare. We must try and do our best; and it is always possible that we shall fail.

The heart of his thought is the notion that the basic problems are perhaps not soluble at all, that all one can do is to try to solve them, but that there is no guarantee, either in socialist nostrums or in any other human construction, no guarantee that happiness or a rational life can be attained, in private or in public life. This curious combination of idealism and skepticism—not unlike, for all his vehemence, the outlook of Erasmus, Montaigne, Montesquieu—runs through all his writings.

Herzen wrote novels, but they have not survived because he was not a born novelist. His stories are greatly inferior to those of his friend, Turgenev, but they have something in common with them. For in Turgenev's novels, too, you will find that human problems are not treated as if they were soluble. Bazarov in *Fathers and Children* suffers and dies; Lavretsky in *A House of Gentlefolk* is left in melancholy uncertainty at the end of the novel, not because something had not been done which could have been done, not because there is a solution round the corner which someone simply had not thought of, or had refused to apply, but because, as Kant once said, "from the crooked timber of humanity no straight thing was ever made." Everything is partly the fault of circumstance, partly the fault of the individual character, partly in the nature of life itself. This must be faced, it must be stated, and it is a vulgarity and, at times, a crime to believe that permanent solutions are always possible.

Herzen wrote a novel called *Who Is To Blame?* about a typical tragic triangle in which one of the "superfluous men" of whom I spoke earlier falls in love with a lady in a provincial town who is married to a virtuous, idealistic, but dull and naive husband. It is not a good novel, and its plot is not worth recounting, but the main point, and what is most characteristic of Herzen, is that the situation possesses, in principle, no solution. The lover is left broken-hearted, the wife falls ill and probably dies, the husband contemplates suicide. It sounds like a typically gloomy, morbidly self-centered, caricature of the Russian novel. But it is not. It rests on an exceedingly delicate, precise, and at times profound description of an emotional and psychological situation to which the theories of a Stendhal, the method of a Flaubert, the depth and moral insight of George Eliot are inapplicable because they are seen to be too literary, derived from obsessive ideas, ethical doctrines not fitted to the chaos of life.

. . . His irreverence and the irony, the disbelief in final solutions, the conviction that human beings are complex and fragile, and that there is value in the very irregularity of their structure which is violated by attempts to force it into patterns or strait-jackets—this and the irrepressible pleasure in exploding all cut-and-dried social and political schemata which serious-minded and pedantic saviours of mankind, both radical and conservative, were perpetually manufacturing, inevitably made Herzen unpopular among the earnest and the devout of all camps. In this respect he resembled his skeptical friend Turgenev, who could not, and had no wish to, resist the desire to tell the truth however "unscientific"—to say something psychologically telling, even though it might not fit in with some generally accepted, enlightened system of ideas. Neither accepted the view that because he was on the side of progress or revolution he was under a sacred obligation to suppress the truth, or to pretend to think that it was simpler than it was, or that certain solutions would work although it seemed patently improbable that they could, simply because to speak otherwise might give aid and comfort to the enemy.

This detachment from party and doctrine, and the tendency to utter independent and sometimes disconcerting judgments, brought violent criticism on both Herzen and Turgenev, and made their position difficult. When Turgenev wrote *Fathers and Children*, he was duly attacked both from the right and from the left, because neither was clear which side he was supporting. This indeterminate quality particularly irritated the "new" young men in Russia, who assailed him bitterly for being too liberal, too civilized, too ironical, too skeptical, for undermining noble idealism by the perpetual oscillation of political feelings, by excessive self-examination, by not engaging himself and declaring war upon the enemy, and perpetrating instead what amounted to a succession of evasions and minor treacheries. Their hostility was directed at all the "men of the forties," and in particular at Herzen who was rightly looked on as their most brilliant and most formidable representative. His answer to the stern, brutal young terrorists of the sixties is exceedingly characteristic. The new revolutionaries had attacked him for nostalgic love of an older style of life, for being a gentleman, for being rich, for living in comfort, for sitting in London and observing the Russian revolutionary struggle from afar, for being a member of a generation which had merely talked in the *salons*, and speculated and philosophized, when all round them was squalor and misery, bitterness and injustice; for not seeking salvation in some serious, manual labour—in cutting down a tree, or making a pair of boots or doing something "concrete" and real in order to identify himself with the suffering masses, instead of endless brave talk in the drawing-rooms of wealthy ladies with other well-educated, nobly-born, equally feckless young men—self-indulgence and escapism, deliberate blindness to the horrors and agonies of their world.

Herzen understood his opponents, and declined to compromise. He admits that he cannot help preferring cleanliness to dirt; decency, elegance, beauty, comfort, to violence and austerity, good literature to bad, poetry to prose. Despite his alleged cynicism and "aestheticism," he declines to admit that only scoundrels can achieve things, that in order to achieve a revolution that will liberate mankind and create a new and nobler form of life on earth one must be unkempt, dirty, brutal and violent, and trample with hob-nailed boots on civilization and the rights of men. He does not believe this, and sees no reason why he should believe it.

As for the new generation of revolutionaries, they are not sprung from nothing:

> They are our fault. We begat them, by our idle talk in the forties. These are men who come to avenge the world against us . . . the syphilis of our revolutionary passions . . . The new generation will say to the old: "You were hypocrites, we are cynics; you spoke like moralists; we shall speak like scoundrels; you were civil to your superiors, rude to your inferiors; we shall be rude to everyone. You bowed and felt no respect, we shall push and jostle and make no apologies."

He says in effect: Organized hooliganism can solve nothing. Unless civilization—the recognition of the difference of good and bad, noble and ignoble, worthy and unworthy—is preserved, unless there are some people who are both fastidious and fearless, and are free to say what they want to say, and do not sacrifice their lives upon some large, nameless altar, and sink themselves into a vast impersonal, grey mass of barbarians marching to destroy, what is the point of the revolution? It may come whether we like it or not. But why should we welcome, still less work for, the victory of the barbarians who will sweep away the wicked old world only to leave ruins and misery on which nothing but a new despotism can be built? The "great case for the prosecution which Russian literature has been drafting against Russian life" does not demand a new philistinism in place of the old. "Sorrow, skepticism, irony, the three strings of the Russian lyre" are closer to reality than the crude and vulgar optimism of the new materialists.

Herzen's most constant goal is the preservation of individual liberty. That is the purpose of the guerrilla war which, as he once wrote to Mazzini, he had fought from his earliest youth. What made him unique in the nineteenth century is the complexity of his vision, the degree to which he understood the causes and nature of conflicting ideals simpler and more fundamental than his own. He understood what made—and what in a measure justified—radicals and revolutionaries: and at the same time he grasped the frightening consequences of their doctrines. He was in full sympathy with, and had a profound psychological understanding of, what it was that gave the Jacobins their severe and noble grandeur, and endowed them with a moral magnificence which raised them above the horizon of that older world which he found so attractive and which they had ruthlessly crushed. He understood only too well the misery, the oppression, the suffocation, the appalling inhumanity, the bitter cries for justice on the part of the crushed elements of the population under the *ancien régime*, and at the same time he knew that the new world which had risen to avenge these wrongs, must, if it was given its head, create its own excesses and drive millions of human beings to useless mutual extermination. Herzen's sense of reality—in particular of the need for, and the price of, revolution, is unique in his own, and perhaps in any age. His sense of the critical moral and political issues of his time is a good deal more specific and concrete than that of the majority of the professional philosophers of the nineteenth century, who tended to try to derive general principles from observation of their society, and to recommend solutions which are deduced by rational methods from premises formulated in terms of the tidy categories in which they sought to arrange opinions, principles and forms of conduct. Herzen was a publicist and an essayist whom his early Hegelian training had not ruined: he had acquired no taste for academic classifications: he had a unique insight into the "inner feel" of social and political predicaments: and with it a remarkable power of analysis and exposition. Consequently he understood and stated the case, both emotional and intellectual, for violent revolution, for saying that a pair of boots were of more value than all the plays of Shakespeare (as the "nihilistic" critic Pisarev once said in a rhetorical moment), for denouncing liberalism and parliamentarism which offered the masses votes and slogans, when what they needed was food, shelter, clothing; and understood no less vividly and clearly the aesthetic and even moral value of civilizations which rest upon slavery, where a minority produces divine masterpieces, and only a small number of persons have the freedom and the self-confidence, the imagination and the gifts to be able to produce forms of life that endure, works which can be shored up against the ruin of our time.

This curious ambivalence, the alternation of indignant championship of revolution and democracy against the smug denunciation of them by liberals and conservatives, with no less passionate attacks upon revolutionaries in the name of free individuals; the defense of the claims of life and art, human decency, equality and dignity, with the advocacy of a society in which human beings shall not exploit or trample on one another even in the name of justice or progress or civilization or democracy or other abstractions—this war on two, and often more, fronts, wherever and whoever the enemies of freedom might turn out to be—makes Herzen the most realistic, sensitive, penetrating, and convincing witness to the social life and the social issues of his own time. His greatest gift is that of untrammelled understanding: he understood the value of the so-called "superfluous" Russian idealists of the forties because they were exceptionally free, and morally attractive, and formed the most imaginative, spontaneous, gifted, civilised and interesting society which he had ever known. At the same time he understands the protest against it of the exasperated, deeply earnest, *révolté* young radicals, repelled by what seemed to them gay and irresponsible chatter among a group of aristocratic *flâneurs,* unaware of the mounting resentment of the sullen mass of the oppressed peasants and lower officials that would one day sweep them and their world away in a tidal wave of violent, blind, but justified hatred which it is the business of true revolutionaries to foment and direct. Herzen understood this conflict, and his autobiography conveys the tension between individuals and classes, personalities and opinions both in Russia and in the West, with marvelous vividness and precision.

The Past and Reflections is dominated by no single clear purpose, it is not committed to a thesis; its author was not enslaved by any formula or any political doctrine, and for this reason, it remains a profound and living masterpiece, and Herzen's greatest title to immortality. He possesses other claims: his political and social views were arrestingly original, if only because he was among the very few thinkers of his time who in principle rejected all general solutions, and grasped, as very few thinkers have ever done, the crucial distinction between words that are about words, and words that are about persons or things in the real world. Nevertheless it is as a writer that he survives. His autobiography is one of the great monuments to Russian literary and psychological genius, worthy to stand beside the great novels of Turgenev and Tolstoy. Like *War and Peace*, like *Fathers and Children*, it is wonderfully readable, and, save in inferior translation, not dated, not Victorian, still astonishingly contemporary in feeling.

One of the elements in political genius is a sensibility to characteristics and processes in society while they are still in embryo and invisible to the naked eye. Herzen possessed this capacity to a high degree, but he viewed the approaching cataclysm neither with the savage exultation of Marx or Bakunin nor with the pessimistic detachment of Burckhardt or Tocqueville. Like Proudhon he believed the destruction of individual freedom to be neither desirable nor inevitable, but, unlike him, as being highly probable, unless it was averted by deliberate human effort. The strong tradition of libertarian humanism in Russian socialism, defeated only in October 1917, derives from his writings. His analysis of the forces at work in his day, of the individuals in whom they were embodied, of the moral presupposition of their creeds and words, and of his own principles, remains to this day one of the most penetrating, moving, and morally formidable indictments of the great evils which have grown to maturity in our own time.

J. P. NETTL
Rosa Luxemburg—Who, What, and Why

In Rosa Luxemburg we have the case of the "intellectual in politics" *par excellence.* A founder of the German Communist Party, a leader of the Polish Communist Party, a Marxist theoretician of international stature approaching that of Lenin or Trotsky, and the premier martyred heroine of the revolutionary Left, she embodies an extraordinary fusion of idea and action, that consonance which has so often eluded the modern intellectual. The late Peter Nettl's acclaimed biography also makes a persuasive case for her status as an "autonomous political thinker" whose contributions override the narrow Marxist polemics to which her writings have usually been relegated. Whether that claim is finally confirmed or not, the bold confrontation of this electric little woman with the mandarins of the Second International and her precocious advocacy of revolutionary "participation" has immediate interest and relevance for the study of ideas in politics. Nettl's treatment of Rosa Luxemburg is both partisan and analytical; he combines the best characteristics of the biographer and social scientist. It is the happy resolution of the typical and the unique which has so bedevilled and divided sociology and history.

MANY PEOPLE actually know Rosa Luxemburg's name, but its associations are vague—German, Jewish, and revolutionary; that is as far as it goes. To those who are interested in the history of Socialism she emerges in clearer focus, as the spokeswoman and theoretician of the German Left, and one of the founders of the German Communist Party. Two aspects of her life seem to stand out: her death—which retrospectively creates a special, if slightly sentimental, interest in a woman revolutionary brutally murdered by the soldiery; and her disputes with Lenin in which she appears to represent democracy against Russian Communism. The translator and editor of her works in America has seen fit to put out an edition of her polemics against Lenin under the title *Marxism or Leninism,* presumably because he too thinks this neatly sums up her position.[1] To many casual readers in the West she has therefore come to

From *Rosa Luxemburg* by J. P. Nettl published by Oxford University Press, 1966.

[1] Bertram D. Wolfe (ed.): Rosa Luxemburg, *The Russian Revolution* and *Leninism or Marxism?*, Ann Arbor (Michigan) 1961.

represent the most incisive defender of the democratic tradition in Marxism against the growing shadow of its misuse by the Bolsheviks. In so far as revolutionary Marxism can be democratic, Rosa Luxemburg stands at its apex. She has become the intellectual sheet-anchor of all those old, but ever young, radicals who think that Communism could have been the combination of violence and extreme democracy. In their frequent moments of nostalgia it is the name Rosa Luxemburg that they utter.[2] Her death in action ended any possibility of giving effective battle to the Bolsheviks and also sanctified her views with the glow of martyrdom. But the difficulty is that these same Bolsheviks and their followers, whose ascendancy she is supposed to have resisted, have also claimed her for their own. In spite of her alleged mistakes and misinterpretations they see her ultimately committed to Communism in its struggle against Social Democracy; had she lived she would have made the choice even more decisively than in the confusion of 1918. Once again the date of her death is crucial—as well as its form. Communist tradition can no more afford to ignore a martyr than any other embattled faith—and so someone who later might well have been buried with all the obloquy of a renegade, today still retains her place in the official pantheon, by dying early and by dying hard.

So the first reason for Rosa Luxemburg's importance in the history of political Marxism is the unique moment of her death. She and Karl Liebknecht were perhaps the only Marxists who committed themselves to the Bolshevik revolution in spite of fundamental criticisms, which are as old as that revolution itself. What makes Rosa Luxemburg's case especially interesting is that her debates with Lenin on certain fundamental Marxist problems date back to 1903—they are central to her philosophy. Others in Russia had

---

[2] Sometimes in the most improbable places. 'I remember sitting up [with some girls in Los Angeles who had a "strange set-up with some football players" from College] one night and trying to explain patiently, I mean without patronizing them or anything, how the Third International might never have gone off the tracks if only they had listened to Rosa Luxemburg. I would have liked to have known, for instance, just what Radek and Bukharin felt when Rosa said her piece about over-centralization. . . . [The girl] seemed to think about [all] this at least as seriously as when one of the USC football boys asked her whether she preferred the quick-kick punt or a quarter-back sneak. . . .' (Clancy Segal, *Going Away* (2nd edition), New York 1963, p. 46.)

Quite a number of English and American poets and painters find a continuing source of artistic protest in Rosa's life.

departed from or quarrelled with Bolshevism long before 1917—quite apart from those who were never within sight or sound of sympathy with Lenin. These had nothing to contribute to orthodox revolutionary Marxism after 1917. . . . . Rosa Luxemburg, however, could neither be brushed aside as irrelevant before 1917 nor denounced as a traitor afterwards. When she died she was a critical supporter; in her own words, 'Enthusiasm coupled with the spirit of revolutionary criticism—what more can people want from us?'[3] She too would no doubt have had to make a more concrete choice had she lived. But death is final, it freezes into perpetuity the views, however tentative, held at the time. The most that could be done was to speak of Rosa Luxemburg's 'errors'—and to avoid any detailed analysis of her contribution and attitude in their historical context. . . .

The whole problem of revising Marx—which is none other than the problem of capturing the only authoritative interpretation of Marxism—was of great concern to Rosa Luxemburg. She expended some of her most important political analysis on the difference between Marxism and revisionism and on the consequences of the attempts to revise Marx. The contrast between *postulating* revolution and *being* revolutionary, which today agitates the Russians as much as the Chinese, was precisely the central issue which Rosa Luxemburg tried to emphasize for the first time in her much neglected polemics against Kautsky in 1910. In addition, the inevitable confrontation, not of alternative philosophies but of the two different worlds of socialism and capitalism, was central to Rosa Luxemburg's thesis just as it is the mainspring of the Chinese attack on the Soviet Union. Placid and well-fed capitalism leading to an equally placid and well-fed socialism was as much Rosa Luxemburg's bogey as it is that of the Central Committee of the Chinese Communist Party. If Lenin's works are now being used in this controversy as the main arsenal of ammunition for both sides, Rosa Luxemburg's writings could just as well serve for this purpose—except that the Chinese could find better and more systematic weapons in Rosa Luxemburg's armoury than in Stalin's. ⨪ . .

Rosa Luxemburg was not alone, out of her time, in the expression of ideas. Some things she said were exclusive to her, the emphasis often particular; but there was a whole consensus of similar views and aspirations. The relevance Rosa Luxemburg has re-acquired

[3] Adolf Warski, *Rosa Luxemburgs Stellung zu den taktischen Problemen der Revolution*, Hamburg 1922, pp. 6-7.

with recent changes in the complexion and emphasis of Communism applies equally to others. But few covered the ground as thoroughly and vivaciously, as totally as she. Before we look at those of her merits which are justifiably unique we must be clear about the present-day importance of a wider trend in Marxist thinking of which she was but a part, albeit an important one.

For a start, the cyclical revival of particular ideas should not be exaggerated. Many of the concepts advocated by Rosa Luxemburg are still anathema to present-day Communism. Her disregard, even contempt, for the problems and techniques of organization can have no place in a society as highly organized as the Soviet Union or China. Those societies that have become Communist since the Second World War are also preoccupied with 'correct' organization and to that extent Rosa Luxemburg has no place in them. As in other areas of stark disagreement—between Lenin and herself, between the German Left and the Bolsheviks—the debate has simply become out of date. It refers to problems which have no more bearing on existing Communist societies, even though they might once have altered the course of history. To extrapolate views specifically concerned with past issues into a totally different present or future is an exercise on which we shall not waste any time.

Thus I do not claim complete relevance or justification for all her work today. The most that can be said is that some neglected aspects are coming into their own. Surely it is already a mark of greatness for part of a political writer's work to have retained even partial relevance for fifty years, particularly when that writer was not concerned with general philosophy but with analysis of and in-fluence on contemporary events. Yet even so, Rosa Luxemburg's importance does not end here. While history has decided some of the issues against her, a substantial part of her so-called errors prove on closer examination to be based not on what Rosa Luxemburg said or meant but on later interpretation of her work—hammered out in the course of political controversy. She is relevant because of, as well as in spite of, these interpretations. We shall have to disentangle them. But both matter. As long as Marxism exists politically, no contributor can ever become irrelevant. Marxist writers may be deliberately annihilated, but they never die or fade away.

This is, in a very special sense, true of Rosa Luxemburg. The refined implications of her ideas fade into a colorless background compared with the freshness of their presentation. She had much of that vital quality of immediate relevance which she praised so highly in Marx himself—often to the detriment of his actual arguments. She made Marxism real and important in a way which neither Lenin nor Kautsky nor any other contemporary was able to achieve—even more so than Marx himself, for his most attractive writing was also the most dated. She was total where Lenin was selective, practical where Kautsky was formal, human against Plekhanov's abstraction. Only Trotsky had the same vitality, but—as far as his pre-war writing was concerned—only in retrospect, a belated attribute of his post-revolutionary stature. Though there are hardly any Luxemburgists, in the way that there were Stalinists and still are Trotskyites, it is almost certainly true that more people at the time found their early way to revolutionary Marxism through *Social Reform or Revolution* and other writings of Rosa Luxemburg than through any other writer. And justly so. The very notion of Luxemburgism would have been abhorrent to her. What makes her writing so seductive is that the seduction is incidental; she was not writing to convert, but to convince.

Not only the quality of her ideas, then, but the manner of their expression: the way she said it as much as what she said. The bitter tug-of-war for Rosa Luxemburg's heritage was a struggle for the legitimacy bequeathed by an important Marxist and in even more outstanding exponent of revolutionary Marxism. Social Democracy of the 1920's, particularly the German Social-Democratic Party (SPD), thought that it could see in her an ardent advocate of democracy who sooner or later was bound to come into conflict with oligarchical and arbitrary Bolshevism. Such an interpretation was cherished particularly by the many ex-Communists who left the party in the course of the next thirty years. They found in Rosa Luxemburg's undoubted revolutionary Marxism, combined with the frequent use of the words 'masses', 'majority,' and 'democracy', a congenial lifebelt—to keep them afloat either alone or at least on the unimportant left fringe of official Social Democracy. Nearly every dissident group from official Communism—German, French, or Russian—at once laid special and exclusive claim to the possession of Rosa Luxemburg's spirit, and it is significant that Trotsky, whose relationship with Rosa Luxemburg had been impersonal and hostile for a decade, claimed her spiritual approval for the Fourth International from the day of its foundation.[4]

---

[4] L. Trotsky, *Rosa Luxemburg et la quatrième Internationale*, Paris 1933.

The Communists were in no way prepared to let her go. However, to answer Social Democracy and their own dissidents it became necessary to interpret her work in such a way that those items and quotations on which the enemy based its case could be knitted together into a whole system of error. It no longer sufficed to shrug these off as so many isolated mistakes, and in due course Communist theorists constructed for and on behalf of Rosa Luxemburg a system called Luxemburgism—compounded from just those errors on which Social Democracy relied. The person became increasingly separated from the doctrine—rather like the English notion that the Crown can do no wrong. The fiercer the Communist struggle against Luxemburgism, the greater the attachment to the revolutionary personality of Luxemburg, stripped of its errors. As we have seen, this delicate surgery made Rosa Luxemburg unique in Communist history. Though the result of later political controversy, the fact that the operation was worth doing at all is striking evidence of the continuing importance of the victim—or beneficiary. . . .

Beneath the caricature of 'Luxemburgism' and its 'spontaneity' there can be seen a consistent set of principles with which Rosa Luxemburg hoped to arm nascent Communism in Germany. She never set out to produce a comprehensive or even logically cohesive system. Almost invariably her ideas found expression in the form of criticisms or polemics against what she considered to be errors. Out of this negative aspect of her own correction (and often over-correction, like Lenin's 'bent stick' of orthodoxy), we have to construct the positive content of her intentions. To do this it is sometimes necessary to postulate a neutral no-man's-land, arbitrarily empty except for the clear and present conflict—as though each dispute were new and unique. Why? Because the later Communist construction of a Luxemburgist system for the sole purpose of demolishing it in public showed that what Rosa Luxemburg imparted to the German Labour movement was sufficiently powerful and pervasive to require systematic demolition. No one else in Germany, not even Kautsky, was elevated to a Communist-created, proprietary 'ism'. In Russia only Lenin and Stalin on one side, Trotsky and the Mensheviks on the other, were given such an honor. While it would therefore be wrong to construct a 'true' system in place of the false one—and no such attempt will be made—certain dominant ideas remain and these must be examined with all their 'true' implications. The strong emphasis on action as a prophylactic as well as a progressive social impulse is deeply rooted in Communism today—deeply enough for its specific reincarnation in China because of its allegedly formal abstraction in Russia—and this was Rosa Luxemburg's most important contribution to practical Marxism. What has usually been ascribed to Lenin's peculiar genius for action, asserting itself against the bureaucratic and cautious hesitations of his closest supporters in 1917, was no more than the specific and longstanding recommendation of the German Left, most ably expounded in Rosa Luxemburg's writings. For most of her life revolution was as close and real to her as to Lenin. Above all, she sensed and hammered home the difference between theoretical and real revolutionary attitudes long before Lenin was aware that such differences could exist in the SPD. Modern revolutionary Marxism is thus peculiarly her contribution even though the debt may not be acknowledged. . . .

Finally, and perhaps most important of all, there is Rosa Luxemburg's position as an autonomous political thinker—irrespective of whether one believes in, repudiates, or is simply indifferent to Marxism. Her ideas belong wherever the history of political ideas is seriously taught. Though she herself was fully committed to Marxism, the validity of her ideas transcends the Marxist framework. For hers was an essentially moral doctrine which saw in social revolution—and socialist revolutionary activity—not merely the fulfillment of the laws of dialectical materialism but the liberation and progress of humanity. Rosa Luxemburg preached participation above all, not merely the passive reward of benefits from the hands of a conquering élite. And participation is the problem that still occupies most political analysts today, Marxist and bourgeois alike. Rosa Luxemburg's controlling doctrine was not democracy, individual freedom, or spontaneity, but participation—friction leading to revolutionary energy leading in turn to the maturity of class-consciousness and revolution. Though it is undesirable and meaningless to try and lift her writings one by one out of the context of Marxism (to which they most emphatically belong), the significance of her life's work and thought is not confined to Marxists alone— just like Marx's own achievements. The value of the few really original political thinkers cannot be tagged with the artificial label of any school or group. Even the most orthodox disciples can become a burden; like barnacles they have to be painfully scraped away. The claim of universal validity beyond context is precisely what distinguishes the great from the merely partisan. . . .

What sort of person was Rosa Luxemburg? Small, extremely

neat—self-consciously a woman. No one ever saw her in disarray, early in the morning or late at night; her long hair was carefully but simply combed upwards to add to her height. She had not been a pretty child and was never a beautiful woman: strong, sharp features with a slight twist of mouth and nose to indicate tension. Her appearance always commanded respect, even before she opened her mouth. Her dark eyes set the mood of the moment, flashing in combat or introspectively withdrawn, or—if she had had enough— overcast with anger or boredom.

The fastidiousness extended to her clothes right down to her polished shoes: plain but expensive, simple yet carefully chosen clothes, based on a precise evaluation of the image which she wanted to create; clothes that were obtrusive or claimed an existence in their own right; accompaniment not theme. A hip defect acquired in early childhood was overcome completely in all postures but walking—and Rosa Luxemburg was a substantial walker precisely because of the difficulties of this exercise. She judged people—though with admitted humour—in accordance with their ability and willingness to walk; Karl Kautsky's physical laziness was one of the first black marks chalked up against him.

Her own appearance she viewed with slightly mocking contempt which never for an instant approached masochism or self-hatred. The imperceptible border between humor and bitterness was never crossed. Her long nose, which preceded her physical presence like an ambassador on permanent attachment, her large head which soured the lives of several milliners, all were captured in brief and flashing images of literary self-caricature. She called her self-portrait in oils, presented to Hans Diefenbach, *ein Klumpen von Lumpen* (an assortment of lumps). But such comments were reserved for intimates. In public her appearance was neutral; she did not use it to achieve any effect but was never inhibited by it either. The long imprisonment and the spells of ill-health during the war turned her hair white and lined her face, but it is only from the evidence of friends who saw her in prison or after November 1918 that we know it. In moments of crisis her body became an anonymous vehicle to achieve her purposes.

The only aspect of which she was always consciously aware was the fact that she was small. She admitted a penchant for tall and big-boned maids and housekeepers—'I would not like anyone to think that they had entered a doll's house'. Her domestic staff was subjected to the same demands of fastidiousness both in their personal appearance and in their work; breakages roused Rosa Luxemburg to fury and hatred. These were feudal relationships. Though she half-humorously complained to her friends about her involvement in the uninteresting private lives of her staff, she took on this task as manfully as any party assignment. There was a succession of such persons. The one to whom she was most attached was Gertrud Zlottko, who left for other jobs intermittently but somehow always returned. When her household had for all intents and purposes to be liquidated after her second arrest in 1916, a part of her personality went with it.

Her apartment was a faithful reproduction of her person: books carefully stacked in cases, manuscripts put away tidily in a desk, ornaments, paintings, and botanical collections all neatly labelled and instantly to hand. From 1903 onwards she had her own neatly embossed notepaper—for special occasions. Rosa Luxemburg could write for a book from province or prison, and secretary, housekeeper, or friend were able to lay their hands on it instantly. The favorite apartment was at 58 Cranachstrasse in Berlin—the red room and the green room, the old but well-preserved furniture, the carpets, the collection of gifts large and small which, once they had passed her critical taste in the first instance, were treasured for ever. She gave up this apartment in 1911, ostensibly because the city and its growing traffic had engulfed it. More probably its associations had become too painful—the years of gregarious optimism. She then moved to the outskirts of the city at Südende, where she remained until 1916, and nominally to the end of her life. Her home, her privacy, were always sacred. Already in Switzerland her rooms near the University of Zürich had fulfilled an overpowering need for refuge and escape for those hours which so many of her contemporaries argued away in smoke-filled cafés. The closing of doors against all comers was always one of the pleasantest moments of her day. Though many people stayed with her, sometimes for long periods, it was always *her* home: her guests were welcome but the extent to which they could make themselves at home was carefully circumscribed. She entertained often but fastidiously. Unlike so many emigres from Poland and Russia, there was nothing easy-going about her hospitality, and those who abused it were quickly shown the door. The English phrase 'make yourself at home' was unknown to her. In every respect she was as houseproud as any middle-class German; the German mania for cleanliness which as a symptom she held in such contempt was none the less discharged meticulously *chez* Rosa Luxemburg. Instead of making it a major subject of conversation, she employed others to carry out the work unobtrusively. No wonder that those of her students from the party school who were privileged with a Sunday invitation would sit hesitantly on the edge of the sofa and clutch the proffered plate of cake to their bosom for fear of dropping crumbs!

Such an establishment needed money and Rosa Luxemburg's problems in this regard were precisely those of any middle class career woman, whose appetite for minor luxury constantly exceeds the supply of funds with which to meet it. Her private bank account—strictly to be distinguished from the party funds—was delicately balanced between credit and debit; most of the time projected income had already been pledged, if not actually spent. Apart from extraordinary sums needed to help close friends in trouble, an annual crisis centered round her summer holiday; Rosa Luxemburg always planned a year in advance and began to consider the possibilities the day after she returned from the current year's excursion. These holidays were mostly in the south—Switzerland in the early days to see friends, and particularly Leo Jogiches; later Italy whenever she could afford it. Always there was the mirage of a long trip farther afield—Corsica, Africa, the East. None of it—except Corsica—ever happened.

Among her closer friends she had the reputation of a spendthrift. Hans Diefenbach left her money in his will—strictly in trust: "Her management of her personal economy is less sound than her knowledge of political economy." Rosa's *fata morgana* of ready cash was something of a joke with her German friends but a harmless one, since she was punctiliously correct about repayment and refused to borrow money from anyone if she sensed the slightest danger of distorting a relationship. When she went on holiday her funds were available to those who accompanied her. Again and again Konstantin Zetkin's pleas of penury were dismissed by the assurance that she would have enough for them both. There were periods when her journalistic work was largely inspired by the need to earn; the sense of urgency in her writing, which always suggested that she had not the slightest notion what to say until she actually sat down to write it. Touchy, then as ever, for fear of letting money dominate her relationships, generous to a fault with friends, unable by nature to save and quite uninterested in trying, she was one of those secure in the knowledge that, if not God, at least her own abilities would always provide. The only evidence of meanness was in her dealings with shopkeepers and printers. To her these were a special class of twisters whose every account had to be carefully checked and with whom negotiation and much oriental bargaining, though she would never entertain it in other spheres, was a necessary and sensible proceeding. Rather than be cheated, she was prepared to engage in endless guerrilla warfare; her staff was taught—sometimes tearfully—to do the same. She would bow only to the ultimate deterrent of legal action. "In the last resort," she wrote to her housekeeper, "it doesn't suit me to have a court case over a baker's bill—even though I am bound to win."[5]

The whole problem of money, the need to relate earning in some way to spending, was something that, as an objective aspect of the human condition, came to Rosa Luxemburg relatively late in life. As long as she was living with Leo Jogiches in Switzerland, his own substantial remittances from home—he came from a wealthy family—were enough for them both. But money played a curiously symbolic role in their relationship right from the start. Rosa Luxemburg, who in the last resort would not defer judgement about her own opinions and actions even to Leo Jogiches, almost eagerly seized on money as a symbol of total deference. Whenever she was away from him she accounted at length and in detail for every penny, and craved indulgence for her often imaginery extravagance—while he in turn played out his part in the mannered comedy by scolding her soundly. On this subject his word was law; to borrow or not to borrow, to take from the German executive or to ask for support from home—he developed an absurd stinginess as part of the role of comptroller. And Rosa, who would circuitously but firmly reject his criticisms of her policy in Germany after 1898, when she went to live in Berlin, who berated him for his clumsy proof-reading of her doctoral thesis and much besides, none the less beat her breast under his financial strictures. This continued as long as their personal relationship itself.

Rosa Luxemburg was never an easy person to get on with. Her passionate temperament, of which she was aware and very proud, generated a capacity for quick attachment but also an unpredictable touchiness which acted like tripwire to unsuspecting invaders. Her rigid standards of behavior were partly the moral superstructure of

[5] Rosa Luxemburg to Gertrud Zlottko, 1913, *International Institute of Social History at Amsterdam.*

her philosophy of life. But, though rigid, they were not constant; she deliberately adjusted them to what she thought was the capacity of the other person. A man like Parvus, who had a strong temperament himself, was granted more latitude than most run-of-the-mill members of the German party. Devotion and a willingness to please were no use by themselves. Anyone servile or self-pitying, anything routine, above all anything *mechanical* started at a disadvantage; so did self-satisfaction and a display of public virtue—German qualities all, but English too; Rosa Luxemburg's private hell was Anglo-German. Other Nordic nations suffered too, more by ethnic generalization than personal dislike since she had few Dutch or Swedish acquaintances. Henriette Roland-Holst, a close friend for a time, was specifically exempted; 'Rosa's blonde madonna' was the exception to prove the rule. In private at least there was no doubt that Rosa sometimes used the collective over-simplifications of a racist—but in her dislike more than her approval. The Russians came off best. There was always an innate sympathy for Russians—in a German context; against their own background they were at once judged more severely. Her friends in the Russian and Polish movements always appeared much more attractive among Germans than they were when compared with their own compatriots. One aspect of Rosa's internationalism was always to prefer the foreign.

To make things more difficult, her standards rose the closer people were to her; her demands for privacy became more exacting. Those admitted to the inner circle of friends were always in danger of trespassing on areas which were totally 'off limits'. . . . Close friends also had to have some measure of intellectual strength—she was incapable of intimacy with a stupid person. In spite of her close attachment to Clara Zetkin, the disparity of their intellectual capacities obstructed the friendship. It was only Clara Zetkin's acceptance of Rosa's primacy and her agreement with nearly every view propounded by Rosa on important questions that enabled the latter to put up with Clara's personal obstinacies and her political sentimentality.

There were a few people whom Rosa Luxemburg disliked beyond all reason. This was connected only marginally with politics. Kurt Eisner, an intelligent, sensitive, and kind-hearted person, was anathema to her. The few letters she wrote to him were couched in a tone of outstanding pettiness. 'Oh, anxious ethical colleague,' she began an epistle in 1905, 'may you drown in the moral absolutes of your beloved *Critique of Pure Reason*.'[6] Similarly Trotsky, whose intellectual and personal characteristics were very similar to her own, was always referred to like an enemy in whom she could find nothing creditable. Where personal dislike cut across political alliance, dislike predominated: one of the most curious examples of Rosa Luxemburg's personal attitudes in the German party was her ferocious dislike of Karl Radek and her refusal to accept or even notice the contribution he was making to her cause—and this at a time when she badly needed allies, particularly intelligent ones who shared her views on imperialism.

One type that Rosa Luxemburg always disliked was the 'great man'. She resented Plekhanov's authority even before she attacked his views; as she wrote to Jogiches, one looked for opportunities to put out one's tongue at him. Much of her resentment against Kautsky was generated by his unchallenged supremacy in all matters of theory—a position she did not automatically accept even in 1898. Authority was a matter of present performance, not the capitalized glories of the past. Thus she denied Plekhanov, Kautsky, and Wilhelm Liebknecht, but never begrudged Bebel; even after they had fallen out openly in 1911 Rosa Luxemburg never attempted to belittle his role in the SPD. On the whole she was uncharitable in her personal judgements. Her letters to the few people with whom she was really intimate—Leo Jogiches and later Konstantin Zetkin—show that even those who considered themselves close friends or allies were not immune from sarcastic epigrams which played up their faults and gave them small credit for their virtues. The letters to Leo Jogiches from Germany shortly after her arrival in 1898 present the SPD leadership as a cabaret turn of caricatures. Of course she felt an outsider and to a large extent chose to remain one; she proudly differentiated her own attitude to life from that of the Germans. None the less, her judgements were far too specific for a mere culture-clash. She despised those whose opposition was merely the product of resentment, and had an unerring eye for *personal* weakness—just as Lenin could usually spot *political* weakness however well hidden or camouflaged.

But these judgements are not only evidence of her particular personality: they show a rare self-confidence which was not only psychological but also social, a product of the secure political group

---

[6] From a private collection of letters in Israel.

in which she was firmly anchored from 1893 until after the first Russian revolution. All those who have written about Rosa Luxemburg have seen only the personal aspect and have ignored the social one. Without it no portrait of these thirteen years can be complete; and even afterwards, when the original close-knit group began to disintegrate, its influence lingered on. The Polish Social Democrats (SDKPiL), that small body of intellectual activists who broke out of the main Polish Socialist Party (PPS) in 1893, a year after it had been founded, was much more than a mere doctrinaire sect. This Social Democracy of Poland and Lithuania was a group of intellectual peers long before it became a political party. It provided its members with all the attributes of a primary group, an association which all the other emigrés lacked—a family, an ideology, a discipline, in short a constant and reliable source of strength . . . in some respects as conspiratorial and tight a group as Lenin's Bolsheviks, but open and outward-looking in others. The discipline was largely voluntary and was confined to public action; for the rest, it left large areas of freedom and choice to the participants, even room for profound intellectual disagreements. That is why the comparison with the Bolsheviks is instructive and at the same time meaningless. Trotsky, with all his friends, admirers, and disciples, never had the benefit of a peer group; hence his difficulty in building a following before the revolution and the fragility of his political support after 1923.[7]

Nowhere in the Second International was a small group so brilliantly led; nowhere for that matter was any leadership shared between such brilliant individuals. Unlike the Bolsheviks who, by the end of 1911, had submitted completely to the powerful personality of their leader, the SDKPiL was not the party to submit to anyone—and split in two because Jogiches attempted to emulate the personal ascendancy of Lenin. The strength and importance of this social group cannot be sufficiently stressed. We tend to consider the members too much as individuals without giving sufficient regard to

---

[7] A peer group is a sociological term denoting a latent relationship among a group of people of roughly similar age and outlook, whose opinion is of particular importance with reference to one's own. Thus it is intended to express both the concept of reference group as well as convey a group source of ideological and moral strength, but not to imply a sense of conformity strong enough to subsume self-made decisions; other-directedness as opposed to inner-directedness as used by David Riesman, *The Lonely Crowd*, New Haven 1950, or Winston White, *Beyond Conformity*, New York 1961, pp. 16ff.

the additional strength which they derived from their association. On the one hand there is the structure, and on the other hand there are individuals. The connection between them and above all the *mutual* augmentation of strength have been overlooked.

Rosa Luxemburg's relations with the rest of this group are a fascinating study in themselves. With the significant exception of Jogiches, she was not especially close to any of them. She criticized them all severely on occasions; both their views and their persons. But all the same she was attached far more profoundly to this group than ever to the German party. Her criticisms and comments are part of the intellectual elbow-room which the SDKPiIL permitted, indeed almost forced on its members. In so far as the old-fashioned word 'companion' has any political meaning in a modern context, it applies to this relationship—more than ally yet less than friend: a connection more secure than personal sympathy but at the same time more colourful than any purely functional, political relationship.

Naturally Rosa Luxemburg's role in the SDKPiL cannot be understood except in terms of her special relationship with Leo Jogiches. In the eyes of the world they *were* for many years the SDKPiL. It is rare for an intimate personal relationship to be matched by a political one without one dominating the other. Yet here no political concessions were made for personal reasons, nor personal allowances for the sake of political harmony; there was no question of either one leading the other. In her letters the varied strands of their lives were so completely intertwined that the very distinction between personal and political lost all meaning. Only with Leo Jogiches did she ever achieve such fusion. This woman, whose personality was built out of concentric, increasingly impenetrable rings of which the last and innermost was the loneliness of absolute privacy, always needed one and only one person with complete access, someone from whom nothing must be hidden. Precisely because further access became proportionately more difficult for friends once they had passed from the antechamber of acquaintance into the living-room of friendship, precisely because Rosa Luxemburg found it so difficult to open the last doors of frankness and intimacy, she made a point of stripping herself almost ritually naked before the one person whom she loved. This was the meaning of love. Far from the usual diffuse glow, from the see-saw agony of ecstasy and despair, love was something clinical and precise to Rosa—complete frankness. Again and again she demanded ruthless honesty in return—it was the one quality of which her love would not permit the slightest diminution. To a man like Leo Jogiches—closely compartmented, secretive and reserved by nature, unwilling to commit and reluctant to communicate—Rosa Luxemburg's insistent demand for frankness posed a constant challenge. He was jealous, both of her success and of her person. The required frankness thus forced his jealousy out into the open—with the result that Rosa had often to make difficult choices and flout the wishes she had forced him to express. They clashed often and hard, especially during her early months in Germany, when her judgement was pitted against his remote control. But comments and instructions were anyhow not the full measure of frankness she demanded. He was open enough about her—it was with regard to himself that she had to insist on communication, often simply on scraps of information. 'Why have you not written?' was her constant complaint. By 1905 she suspected that some of the doors of access to him, which she had so painfully forced open for many years, were being closed against her once more; she rushed to Cracow in September of that year just to 'look straight into his eyes', and the fear of losing him may well have been a contributory reason for her going to Warsaw in December 1905, in the middle of the revolution.

Her devotion to Jogiches ended brutally fourteen months later when she heard that some of the doors closed to her had been opened to someone else. Rosa Luxemburg saw only black and white in personal matters; the strain of maintaining constant political contact with someone whom she was now determined to shut out of her personal life proved enormous. None the less the relationship survived, fossilized for a time in the iron clamp of sheer political necessity. In the midst of the spiritual desert of the First World War, with many of her old friendships brutally broken off, the resurrection of the old comradeship with Leo Jogiches must have helped them both to survive. But it was furtive and unspoken—and has left almost no trace for historians. Touchingly, Jogiches spent valuable time in ensuring that she was supplied with the right food for her increasingly delicate and nervous stomach. During the last few months of their lives he was constantly at her side, advising, guiding, cheering. This man, who had set his sights at the personal leadership of both the Polish and the Russian parties, whom his opponents thought ambitious to the point of madness, was finally content to accept a subordinate role to the brilliant woman who had for all practical purposes been his wife. After her death he concentrated his own last months' efforts on the identification and punishment of her murderers, and on ensuring that her ideas should survive.

When she learnt of his betrayal in 1907 it was Rosa herself who insisted on her freedom. For a long time Jogiches would not let her go—and beneath the hectic political activities from 1906 to 1909 a dark and grotesque comedy was played. From those who knew of their relationship—and this was already a privileged minority—the carefully preserved front of political collaboration hid the vacuum that was now between them. The role of Rosa's unique confidant was transferred to another man—a young, sensitive, talented, and unhappy boy whose mother was one of Rosa Luxemburg's closest friends. This touching interlude, which Rosa herself described as straight from the pages of Stendhal's *Le Rouge et le Noir*, is totally unknown. Rebound, loneliness, disappointment—all the scientific claptrap of psychology—no doubt played their part. But there was more. Rosa Luxemburg's temperament was capable, in her own words, of setting the prairie on fire, her passion for life more than enough for two; one wonders how the young man's frail shoulders were able to bear the torrents of intellectual and emotional discharge which Rosa Luxemburg unleashed on those she loved. In the end it was too much: twice she sensed a restiveness which immediately made her withdraw the extended antennae of her personality as rapidly as she had at first extended them. Twice she released him and yet on each occasion she felt his need for her to be greater than his revolt. It was not until the war that she finally recognized the frailty of the vessel into which she had poured so much of herself. But the need in her which he had filled was still as constant and real as ever. So she promoted her devoted Hans Diefenbach to the privileged place instead. Her letters to him mark a tragic but profoundly moving inflation of a small personality into the needed image of a big one—yet shot through with flashes of sad irony at this very process of self-delusion. Again one wonders how uncomfortable she must have made pale, precise, fastidious, and reserved Hans Diefenbach, who worshipped Rosa Luxemburg and her exotic temperament with fear and trembling. He died in the war, and then there was no one left. The errant, irrepressible warmth had to be shared out between faithful and deserving friends like Luise Kautsky and Marta Rosenbaum. No lover, no intimate confidant waited for Rosa Luxemburg to come out of prison. And when she did emerge there was no more time for the exquisite business of love and living.

'Civilized'—the epitome of Rosa Luxemburg's attitude to life. She was as tight in her personal relationships as with the arrangement of her possessions. Everyone had an allotted place which could not be exceeded except by invitation—and then only to advance a step at a time. Yet there was nothing dry or formal about her relationships. She inspired enormous loyalty and devotion in her immediate circle which, had she permitted it, would have itself become a form of love. People like Mathilde Jacob and Fanny Jezierska, themselves basically unpolitical or only on the fringe of politics, were largely inspired by loyalty to Rosa Luxemburg. After Rosa's death Mathilde Jacob soon put active politics behind her. Her bewildered plea in the pages of *Freiheit* in answer to the Communist charge of absconding with Rosa Luxemburg's literary remains speaks volumes for Rosa's personal magnetism. This capacity to inspire purely personal devotion was one of the complications in the later struggle for Rosa Luxemburg's heritage; to many it seemed inconceivable that someone so free and 'unpolitical' could really have carried her allegiance to incipient Communism through to the bitter and unforeseeable end.

The same problem was raised by Rosa Luxemburg's approach to art. Once more she appeared above all as a civilized person, very much the product of her age and time, scion of a cultured international optimistic bourgeoisie which sat appreciatively at the pinnacle of many centuries of artistic achievement. Rosa Luxemburg did not so much deny the existence of a valid proletarian culture; even the notion of such a thing was utterly incomprehensible to her. She was quite oblivious of the self-conscious efforts in the SPD to produce workers' songs and poems, to create a deliberately 'popular' art. At the same time, however, the revolutionary new forms of expression that were breaking through in painting and music were lost on her. She went to a few of the exhibitions—when Diefenbach succeeded in dragging her along—but she did not enjoy them. The other Russian revolution of the first decade of the twentieth century, that of the painters Kandinsky and Jawlensky, the movements of the *Blaue Reiter* and the Brücke, were as remote to her as the realities of the 1905 upheaval in Russia were to the German bourgeoisie.

Her tastes were conservative and classical. She liked the same music as any cultured *fin de siècle* citizen of Berlin—or, better, of

Vienna. She had neither the pioneering disdain for convention of an aristocrat nor the selfsatisfied and rather squat certainties of working-class realism; her sole demands were clarity and honesty of purpose, and a harmony of means. Imperceptibly, her judgement advanced from a basic series of 'doubts' to a selective approval of such art as stood her severe tests, an *agrégation* of merit. There was little instinctive about it. Any 'clever' appeal to the intellect, any romantic invasion of the emotions, any too obvious *purpose* in art—even social—meant automatic disqualification. Art was *sui generis*. It had above all to reflect the realities of its time, at most foreshadow the immediate future but never extrapolate into the distance; what made art timeless was not vision but quality. As a means of social change she preferred direct political activity. Yet in speaking of 'art' in general we are already doing Rosa Luxemburg a major injustice. She hardly used the word, and never generalized about it. It was as private and individual a sphere as politics were public—and as such not susceptible to systematic analysis. Rosa strenuously resisted the many attempts of her friends to get her to indulge in literary criticism, and only wrote an introduction to her translation of Korolenko with great reluctance at the insistence of her publisher. All the generalizations made here are therefore no more than my perhaps impermissible interpretation of Rosa Luxemburg's individual comments.[8] . . .

Undoubtedly the most important aspect of Rosa's interest in literature was her profound feeling for the Russian nineteenth-century writers. She was not the person to experience the sudden all-engulfing whirlpool of empathy which Lenin felt when he first read Chernyshevsky's *What is to be done?* No single literary figure blazed her moral trail. Instead a whole tradition, a discipline, had captured her admiration; not what they said but how they said it.

---

[8] Yet Rosa Luxemburg's standards of classification appear very similar to the much more specific doctrine put forward by the great Marxist literary critic, Georg Lukacs, in, e.g., *Der russische Realismus in der Weltliteratur* (Berlin (East) 1940) and, more generally, in his *Studies in European Realism* (London 1950) and *Probleme des Realismus* (Berlin 1955). But she always insisted on remaining a recipient rather than a critic; she never systematized and rarely argued about her opinions. Thus her assumptions resemble those of Lukács's great antithesis of realism—naturalism, though she never formulated it in such conceptual or general terms. (See Georg Lukacs, 'Erzählen oder Beschreiben?' [Narrate or depict?] in *Probleme des Realismus,* pp. 103-46.) Significantly it is as a literary critic only that Rosa Luxemburg has recently (1961) been reprinted and commented on in Russia—the first for forty years that her views have appeared in Russian.

Year in year out she preached the importance of the Russian novelists into German Socialist ears that were intermittently attuned but more often blocked—a philistinism which roused her to a grotesque fury.

In prison during the war she tackled a full-scale translation of Korolenko's *History of My Contemporary* and wrote a preface in which for once her views on literature in general and the Russian writers in particular were systematically set down. Almost unconsciously she established a general classification of merit which is most revealing. Among other things it underlined the acute Russian-German dichotomy which played such a significant part in Rosa Luxemburg's life. For her this was the central axis of contemporary civilization—the achievements of western bourgeois culture tempered with the emerging Socialist future in the East. Just because Rosa Luxemburg made no artistic concessions to politics, it would be a mistake to suppose that art and politics were not related on the highest level of personal consciousness. There was no conflict here—conflict was only created by self-conscious attempts to manipulate art for political purposes instead of letting it play its own autonomous, possibly even superior, role. The greater the art, the more important its ultimate political effect—that of heightening civilization.

It is in this context that the fascinating interplay of German and Russian influences must be viewed. When Rosa first went to Germany in 1898 the political quality of German Socialism dominated her thinking. Much as she disliked the place and people right from the start, this was on account of personal, psychological faults; the German contribution to political civilization was still predominant and the task of spanning West and East consisted in emphasizing German unity and self-discipline to the disorganized and inchoate Russians. In course of time all this changed. Closer acquaintance with Russian writers—in her home, self-consciously permeated with western *Kultur*, they had been relatively neglected—now opened up vistas of civilization from the East which made the German contribution look increasingly formal and unreal. Participation in the Russian revolution of 1905 accelerated the process. Not that she appreciated masters like Goethe less; it was rather their irrelevance to the German present when compared with the immediacy of writers like Dostoievsky and Tolstoy which obsessed her. More and more the particular German virtues became so much debris in a torrent of social confrontation. The real hope of cultural as well as political salvation now seemed to lie in the East. A touch of the conscious Slavophil was there, though it did not come to the surface. The official criterion of excellence was the relationship of art to society, the inescapable concern for social questions in Russia which seemed so strongly to contrast with the dead weight of formal *Kultur* in Germany.

In the last resort Rosa Luxemburg shared the common misunderstanding about the real nature of the German virtues. It still exists today; understandable as they are, these misconceptions none the less carry a great share of responsibility for the tragedies of the last fifty years. And in a way the Socialists are most to blame. For it was they who took up the great cry against the patriarchal discipline, the authoritarian tradition of obedience in the Prussian-German empire—and in attacking these only reproduced them *chez eux*. But what they pilloried (and copied) as public 'virtues' were in fact poor compensations for a lack of them. German virtues were and are essentially private, lonely ones, a tradition of *Einsamkeit*, of deprivation, of seeking to compensate for loneliness. The real home of public virtue is England, with its team games, its group loyalties, its tradition of different faces in public and in private. *Kadavergehorsam*, or *Friedhofsdisziplin*, and all the other emanations of the German tradition on which Rosa Luxemburg laid such sarcastic emphasis, were in fact vices derived from a lack of public virtues, rather than consequences of public virtues themselves. She would have been astonished to think of the sheep-like obedient Germans as lonely and lost.

Throughout her life in Germany she remained a self-conscious Easterner. It was a difficult situation and she never tried to make it any easier. Germany was in no sense a refuge to be grateful for. Rather it was the duty of any progressive and advanced Socialist party to welcome foreign participants, while *their* duty, far from abstaining, was to involve themselves in the new domestic environment as thoroughly as possible. Rosa Luxemburg's allegiance was not to Germany but to the SPD. The frequent references to a fatherland were not merely a sarcastic caricature of a sentimental and chauvinistic phrase but a positive acknowledgement to the only real fatherland she knew or wanted—the proletariat in general and German Social Democracy in particular. She was not alone in this. It was an allegiance shared by many of the intellectual émigrés, mostly Jews, who deliberately renounced the attempt to find refuge in any particular nationalism of the present or future. The fight against Polish national self-determination carried out by a ferocious and highly articulate group in the Second International, for whom Rosa Luxemburg was the most prominent spokesman, cannot be understood merely in terms of a negation, but by the superimposition of nationalist sentiment on to political and class ideology. The only attainable fatherland was the working class—or, more correctly, the proletarian revolution. This concept was not just a political abstraction or even an inspired tactical expedient; it had all the hidden strength of patriotic attachment. Most of the protagonists were Jews, who found even in the limited 'national' articulation of the Jewish *Bund* an echo of the more rigid geographical patriotism of the PPS. But there were others, like Marchlewski and Dzierzyński, whose anti-nationalism was obviously not due merely to the neurosis of national dispersion and oppression. Their presence and strength within the group proves more clearly than anything else that, far from being a mere negation, the onslaught on national self-determination was a positive substitution of one fatherland for another. Why, after all, should the notion of patriotism be confined to arbitrary political or ethnic frontiers, and be based on the artifact of a nation state?[9]

This deeply shared attitude was one of the main links which bound our peer group and provided a cohesive factor for people who were otherwise individualist and often very egocentric. Some historians have been puzzled by their rejection of any form of national self-expression but have not understood the substitution function of Socialism in this regard. Yet without it the whole history of the SDKPiL makes little sense. From 1907 to 1914 the political differences between the PPS-Left, which had broken away from the open nationalism of Pilsudski, and the SDKPiL appear increasingly irrelevant to the historian. Apart from ventilation of personal spleen the polemics are incomprehensible—except that the difference between *playing down* existing nationalist sentiment and acknowledging a totally *different* fatherland is somehow enormous. Rosa Luxemburg's whole career in the SPD, the fact that she put up with the strongly anti-Semitic and anti-Eastern tinge of the criticisms levelled against her from within and without the SPD, was due to her

[9] J. L. Talmon claims to have 'discovered' the significance of Rosa Luxemburg's anti-nationalism and to see in it a peculiarly Jewish quality. The attempt to rescue Rosa Luxemburg for Jewish causes is not new, though it is lamentably absurd. In deference to his 'discovery', passing reference should therefore be made to this third Jewish force tugging at the essential Rosa, alongside the 'democratic' Marxists and orthodox Communism.

insulation: she was genuinely impervious to anti-Semitism and the charge of national vagrancy. Why, after all, stay in a country that you admittedly dislike, and insist on participation in its political affairs, unless you deny the very basis of the opposition which your presence creates?

People like Rosa Luxemburg, Parvus, and Marchlewski brought into German politics a quality hitherto unknown. It was not a matter of different policy or original views, but was what Trotsky himself called 'the Russian method'—the idea that action was of a superior order to any other facet of political life, and that it was the one and only cure for social rheumatism. For those who felt like this, the ability to align themselves with German methods became a measure of their patience. Parvus, the most impatient and untrammelled of them all, gave up after fifteen years of intermittent attempts to galvanize the SPD and went to amass a fortune in Turkey until the war opened up new possibilities of action for him. Rosa Luxemburg was more self-disciplined. In spite of intense frustration, she pursued her efforts to influence events in Germany, though even she retired for lengthy periods. Besides, Rosa was more closely involved with Germany than any of the others—Parvus, Radek, Marchlewski, Jogiches; and her contribution as a revolutionary in Germany is therefore unique.

Behavioural scientists have a yearning to create types, while historians study and seek comfort in the unique—this is the greatest difference between them. This divergence of approach becomes relevant here as soon as we confront the history of Rosa Luxemburg with the general problem of the intellectual in politics, which has fascinated modern sociology. That we may have been approaching the possibility of some such generalization may well have become obvious. Yet the surface appearance of felicity in applying the general concept is deceptive. Everyone who has analysed the intellectual has seen his participation in politics as something which perverts his natural functions. Thus 'absence of direct responsibility for practical affairs' is the intellectual's hallmark—and so the intellectual is defined as a deviant product of modern capitalist industrialization, with all its emphasis on achievement and role-differentiation.[10] How does someone like Rosa Luxemburg, whose primary interest was the analysis and amendment of these capitalist

---

[10] See Josef Schumpeter, *Capitalism, Socialism and Democracy*, New York 1950, p. 147.

processes, fit into the category of unpractical? Schumpeter's definition clearly accents the cultural preoccupation of the intellectual. More recent analysis, specifically concerned with the intellectual in politics, provides little more help. He is either the propagator of chiliasm—the millennium on earth—or the apologist for hard-boiled and practical conspirators—*le trahison des clercs*—the scribbling admirer of Leninism seeking sublimation.[11] Perhaps the most accurate characterization is the purely negative one: 'he who innovates is not heard; he who is heard does not innovate'—though this sad verdict is the product of research into the limited and specific problem of modern bureaucracy.[12] . . . Rosa Luxemburg's tentative participation in the 'modern' bureaucracy of the SPD ended in failure and contempt—so far the analogy holds. Similarly the SDKPiL—Rosa's 'ideal' party—was deliberately orientated towards correct theoretical formulations, and practical problems were not, before 1905, allowed to restrict the preferred intellectual activity of the leading elite. But Rosa Luxemburg's reluctance to participate in practical work was limited to the most obvious manifestations of bureaucracy; far from abstaining from practical affairs, she not only kept her writing strictly aligned to political immediacies but also participated in the highly practical events of revolution whenever the opportunity presented itself. To this extent the abstentional definition of intellectuals applies much less to her than to people like Plekhanov and Kautsky. Rosa Luxemburg accepted politics at their face value; she never self-consciously promoted culture in opposition to politics and only occasionally tried to subordinate political activity to considerations of conceptual neatness. Politics are analysed, not beautified; there is no apology for mud and blood. She recognized that revolutionary politics brought confusion and much personal unpleasantness; violence was necessary, an instrument—yet not a proper subject for cult worship as it was for Sorel, and even for the Bolsheviks, with their specific dialectical 'theory' of terror, alias the dictatorship of the proletariat. Either we must create a special sub-category of intellectuals for her and her peers—and run the risk that it will still prove neither exhaustive nor exclusive—or we must handle the 'type' with care and reservations. The

[11] See the collection of writings in G. B. de Huszar, *The Intellectuals: A controversial portrait*, Glencoe (Illinois) 1959.

[12] See R. K. Merton, 'The Intellectual and Modern Public Bureaucracy' *Social Theory and Social Structure*, Glencoe (Illinois) 1957.

contrast between influence and power which Rosa Luxemburg raised to a unique relevance, is not quite the same as that between practical politicians and intellectuals. The latter are rarely front-line casualties in battle.

The politics of influence failed in the Second International— together with the whole International itself; power was still the centerpiece of all politics, whether reactionary, reformist, or revolutionary. The question was, who should wield it, and Leninism's most enduring lesson was that it should, and could, be wielded by intellectuals—not of course scribblers or apologists, but those political intellectuals like Rosa Luxemburg and himself whose choice lay between influencing those with power and displacing them. It is here that both Mao and the leaders of the new Afro-Asian countries trace their legitimate ancestry back to Lenin, and that Khrushchev's impressive bureaucracy had less to offer. Subversion is one thing, but positive revolution requires the fusion of ideology and power.

Rosa Luxemburg was primarily a journalist, a pamphleteer. She wrote fast and with few corrections; as with any good practitioner, her work was selfgenerating so that she did not always know at the beginning fo the article what she would say at the end. This is why so many of the really interesting flashes of insight come not in the main argument but are incidental illustrations. Her style was demanding: long sentences with a logic of their own which often have to be read two or three times to do full justice to her intentions. She was much misquoted—her critics found it all too easy to pick out gaudy daubs from the composition of a balanced whole. Though she could write simply and popularly—more so in Polish than in German—the elaborate use of classical illusions, metaphors, and even quotations, typical of the period and abounding also in the writings of Franz Mehring and Karl Liebknecht, necessarily limited her faithful circle of readers to the party intellectuals. But she reached a wider audience through her speeches, and it is on these that her best prose was expended—and on the letters; she was a better communicant in private than in public, to one person rather than to the lowest common factor of the crowd.

Unlike Kautsky, she had no interest in expounding Marxism for its own sake—not even with a view to making it popular. The only object of quotations from Marx was to illustrate a particular political point. But here again she differed from people like Lenin, who constantly searched the works of the master for concrete evidence in support of a current view of a political argument. She treated

Marxism and Marx much as Trotsky did—as a view of life, a technique, and the great man himself primarily as a superb publicist. What she admired in Marx was not so much his intellectual achievement—which she took for granted as a *necessary* even more than an *excellent* analysis of reality—but the forcefulness of his style. Though she never produced any *over-all* comment or criticism of Marx, she repeatedly asserted that many of his practical conclusions were limited in value as merely the product of his period. Thus she was able to fly in the face of specific doctrine from time to time. On the national question she brought Marx up to date; by using his own techniques she arrived at precisely the opposite conclusion. In *The Accumulation of Capital*, too, though she did not reverse his analysis, she altered both the method and the impact. And in her private correspondence she readily recommended her friends to read Marx for the 'freshness of his style and the daring of his thoughts, the refusal to take anything for granted', rather than for the value of his conclusions. His mistakes in political analysis were self-evident, indeed inevitable; that was why she never bothered to engage in any lengthy critique.

The analyst of political theory comes up against a major difficulty here—one that is usually abstracted or played down. Comparing ideas is difficult enough *in vacuo*—even when they are specifically related through deliberate comment on or criticism of each other. When it comes to differences of personality and method, the difficulty of confrontation is greatly enhanced. Nor is it solved by explaining these differences extraneously; they have to be borne in mind and used continuously as an organic part of the comparison. Let us take Rosa Luxemburg, Kautsky, and Lenin. The last was a disciplined thinker, acute rather than profound, who used theory and system sparingly—enough to 'prove' his points and no more: not a word, not a thought wasted; disciplined combat with just the right application of ideas and analysis to make what was generally a simple, political point. That is why Lenin's theories have been so useful—imperialism, organization, the state. In contrast to Lenin, Kautsky was a theorist by disposition, who could hardly handle discrete facts without at once knitting them into a theory. Thus he produced a theory for every occasion—and in the process vulgarized theory into a convenient and respectable cloak for every tactical adjustment, objective or subjective. Rosa Luxemburg was more original than either. She always overshot her limited political objective; her argument bursts with assumptions, ideas, and hints, sometimes supporting it but occasionally running far beyond and contrary to her intentions. Her mind was a complicated machine; once stimulated, it generated its own energy and ranged way beyond the original problem. Consequently we find things in unexpected places. Like Lenin, her basic theories were few; like Kautsky, however, she subordinated tactics to basic theoretical propositions. Comparing Rosa with Kautsky is like comparing a compound equation with a host of simple ones; compared with Lenin she was atomic fission instead of fusion—releasing energy rather than compressing it. A three-way comparison (or four, or five) thus becomes almost impossible.

But this did not mean that she was a Marxist only *in partibus.* To her what we call Marxism—the combination of history, economics, sociology, and philosophy into one over-all process of analysis—was unchallengeable reality, and Marx merely the best interpreter of reality of them all. She used the word 'Marxism' rarely; in many ways it was a meaningless term. This was in the tradition of the Second International, where Social Democracy was the modern term for the contemporary and political application of the laws first postulated by Marx.[13]

[13] The exclusive identification of revolutionary Socialism with Marx and Marxism and the consequent re-establishment of Marx's pre-eminence was really a short-circuit process created by the Bolshevik revolution. It happened that Lenin was particularly faithful to the works of Marx. In Germany, too, the foundation of the Communist Part in December 1918 was seen as a reconnection to a tradition that had been broken in the Second International. (The analogy is actually Rosa Luxemburg's.) But this deliberate attempt to reconnect directly to Marx was only a reaction to the failure of the Second International. In 1914 such a need was still unthinkable. In the Second International those who preached and popularized specific Marxism were few and isolated—Plekhanov, Kautsky, Mehring, and some others. Plekhanov particularly complained again and again of the reluctance of his fellow Socialists to take an interest in philosophy. For the rest, the relationship between Social-Democratic policy and Marxism was tenuous and purely historical; a debt that only needed formal acknowledgement on a few solemn occasions.

According to this view, therefore, the enthronement of Marx on the Left after 1918 was at first an incidental part of the formal act of negating the immediate past. The notion of textually confronting pre-war Social Democracy with Marxism and evaluating the former in accordance with the extent to which it departed from the latter, was not really a contemporary exercise but the later contribution of Communist history *as a form of* current political combat. The revisionist controversy was perhaps the one significant exception, when a contemporary confrontation was undertaken. Perhaps *this* is why the revisionist controversy has been continuously invested with such excessive importance. It would be interesting to pursue this point with further research. It is, for instance, striking that from the whole range of Marx's work certain parts only were widely read and quoted over and over again in the period before the war, while other important works remained entirely neglected.

Here, too, Rosa Luxemburg was the product of her times—the optimistic pre-war world of peace and progress. Her personality as much as her political ideas made her the champion of active revolution. Imperialism, with all its overtones of violence and inescapable confrontation of classes, was the hand-maiden of her obsession with the self-satisfaction and immobility of German Social Democracy. War was objectively inevitable but subjectively beyond imagination—and no one, except perhaps Lenin, was more surprised than she when one day it broke out and engulfed pre-war Social Democracy. For her, peace and progress were not the usual bourgeois notions of economic development and a growing liberalism, but a Socialism strong enough to withstand the impact of international war and reassert the fundamental necessity of class conflict against it. Thus before 1914 wars no longer had their primeval overriding power of pre-emption; their impact was now limited by the requirements of the class struggle. All this of course proved an illusion, in 1914 as in 1939; and when the illusion was exposed the basis of her world collapsed. Unlike Kautsky, Rosa Luxemburg was acute and revolutionary enough to realize that the collapse was final. She drew the consequences. But she herself had been too much part of this world. She survived the political collapse of Social Democracy, but the revolutionary requirements of the future, the kind of personality that built the modern Soviet Union, that created twelve years of the thousand-year Third Reich, even the socially inclined conservatives of England, France, and America—these were alien monsters to Rosa Luxemburg. Her brilliant and devoted efforts during the German revolution were still no more than an attempt to deal with the problems of a new world by using the best tools and precepts of the old. In the last resort the relevance of her ideas to the world of today must mean a return to the basically optimistic enthusiasms of the Second International.

Probably Lenin's single most remarkable achievement was his confrontation of the Socialist collapse of 1914. He saw it as a constructive beginning, not a sad end. In this he was alone. It does not make him very lovable, but it certainly made him great. He never had to look back, either in sorrow or in (genuine) anger.

E. VICTOR WOLFENSTEIN

Young Manhood of the Revolutionary Personality

Victor Wolfenstein's well-known study of Lenin, Trotsky, and Gandhi (*The Revolutionary Personality,* 1967) is a recent and controversial addition to a type of analysis, sometimes called "psycho-politics," laid out earlier by Harold D. Lasswell and Erik H. Erikson. The principal method employed derives from the techniques of Freudian psychoanalysis which distinguish Erikson's *Young Man Luther* and Lasswell's *World Politics and Personal Insecurity.* The purpose of this sort of study, Wolfenstein is careful to point out, is not to achieve a "definitive" clinical portrait of the three revolutionists, but merely to form hypotheses about the revolutionary personality, why some men revolt, how the intellectual rationale of the revolutionist is affected by his psychological history, in short, about how his political behavior is shaped by his mind, one of the central problems of intellectual history.

In the following chapter on Lenin as a young man Wolfenstein throws considerable light not only on why revolutionary doctrine and action satisfied certain emotional needs in the man (that is, how Marxism affected Lenin) but also on how Lenin's distinct personality tended to transform the doctrine, and thereby shape the character of the revolution in Russia.

LENIN DID not react to Sasha's death† by immediately taking up the revolutionary banner. Although he was deeply disturbed by his brother's death—and appalled by the behavior of the local "liberals" who deserted the Ulyanovs now that they were tainted with treason [1]—he enrolled in the University of Kazan in the fall of 1887. He entered the faculty of law and political science, for reasons not known. [2] In any case, his tenure at the university was very short—he was expelled in December. The students of the

---

From *The Revolutionary Personality: Lenin, Trotsky, Gandhi* (Copyright © 1967 by Princeton University Press): pp. 103-124. Reprinted by permission of Princeton University Press.

† Alexander Llyich Ulyanov, Lenin's older brother, hanged for the attempted assassination of Tsar Alexander III in 1887.

[1] N. K. Krupskaya, Lenin's wife, notes that the liberal's "widespread cowardice made a very profound impression upon him at that time." See *Memories of Lenin* (New York, 1930), I, 4.

[2] See Bertram Wolfe, *Three Who Made a Revolution* (New York, 1964), p. 71.

university had assembled to present a petition of grievances to the provincial inspector, and Ulyanov, for reasons which are again unknown, was among them, standing in the front row.[3] As the group disbanded, registration cards were checked and Vladimir's bore the name which his brother had made known. That night he was arrested and subsequently ordered to leave the city of Kazan.

He was ordered to go to Kukushkino, in the province of Kazan, where his elder sister Anna had already been exiled as a result of her innocent contact with Sasha during the period of his revolutionary activity. There he remained until the autumn of 1888. Lenin was undoubtedly bored at Kukushkino, and highly uncertain about his future.[4] He and his mother made repeated efforts to get him readmitted to the university, but to no avail. Neither he nor his mother had any intention of letting him remain idle, but tsarist authority was making it difficult for him to take up the life of a peaceful citizen.

On the whole, Lenin passed the time productively, unlike many men in similar situations who, when removed from the stimulus of active life, allow themselves to sink into despondency and inactivity. He read avidly but somewhat unsystematically, digging out what he could from dated liberal periodicals he found in the area and the books he was allowed to borrow from the University of Kazan. By this time he was certainly trying to piece together his brother's orientations towards political action, but his orderly mind could find no coherent argument in the materials with which he was able to come in contact.[5] During the months in Kukushkino, or perhaps even somewhat earlier, he did read Chernyshevsky's *What Is To Be Done?* This had been one of his brother's favorite books and in it he found an appraisal of the social situation in terms of Hegelian dialectics and a call to tough, vigorous action.[6] The revolutionary

---

[3] Although we do not know specifically why Lenin was involved in this protest, it probably was connected with his brother's death. His position in the front row, however, does not seem to have been connected with his leadership of the activity; apparently he was little more than an observer. *Ibid.*, p. 78.

[4] *Ibid.*, p. 81.

[5] Adam B. Ulam, *The Bolsheviks* (New York, 1965), p. 99.

[6] Leopold Haimson, *The Russian Marxists and the Origins of Bolshevism* (Cambridge, Mass., 1955), pp. 97-103. In particular, Lenin must have been attracted to the character Rakhmetov, who is an apt representation of what was to become the famous Bolshevik hardness. Cf. N. G. Chernyshevsky, *What Is To Be Done?*, trans. Benjamin R. Tucker (New York, 1909), especially pp. 207-22.

message of *What Is To Be Done?* became part of Lenin's orientation to politics; it was firmly implanted before he turned to Marxism and was never really displaced by Marxism. Its emphasis on coming to grips with facts, however, undoubtedly helped to make him receptive to Marxism, while its voluntaristic leanings and approval of violence as a political tool gave him an activist perspective that was not quite Marxist. . . . But it did not provide him with a system of thought adequate for guiding action. It provided a leaning, a direction, not a tool of analysis or basis of justification.

Psychologically *What Is To Be Done?* was part of Lenin's image of his brother. As he later told a friend:

> After my brother's execution, . . . knowing that Chernyshevsky's novel had been one of his favorite works, I started to read it in earnest and spent on it, not days, but weeks on end. Only then did I understand its depth. It is the kind of book that influences you for your whole life.[7]

Thus in his effort to understand *What Is To Be Done?* Lenin was seeking an understanding of what had guided and motivated Sasha in his sudden and violent action. His abiding admiration for the book is hence one sign of his identification with Sasha, of his attempt to play a revolutionary role "like Sasha." . . . [He] was inclined to caution from a very young age, and the disastrous consequences of his brother's sudden action (whether it was impulsive or not in fact, it would have appeared so to Lenin, who only learned about it after it was brought to light by the authorities) made him more apprehensive than ever about the probable consequences of precipitous action. Thus Sasha's way was too dangerous; until some other course of action could be found, Lenin would remain torn between the desire to relieve his guilt through identification with his dead brother and a fear that such identification would result in danger, if not death, to himself.

To relieve the tension and reduce boredom Lenin lost himself in chess, physical activity, and helping other members of the family with their studies.[8] Later, when back in Kazan, he even took up smoking, but at his mother's request gave it up. He maintained his self-discipline, but the strain was obviously great.

---

[7] Cited in Haimson, p. 98.
[8] His mother had brought the rest of the family to Kukushkino shortly after Lenin was ordered to reside there.

In the autumn of 1888 Lenin was allowed to return to Kazan but not to enter the University. He spent the winter reading and playing chess and, according to his sister Anna, reading the first volume of Marx's *Capital*.[9] In the spring of 1889 his mother, despairing of getting her son back into a university, bought a farm in Alakaevka in the Samara *Gubernya*. There Lenin was to try his hand at running an estate but, as he told Krupskaya, his "relations with the muzhiks got to be abnormal."[10] Luckily his mother finally secured permission for him to take the law examination at the University of St. Petersburg in the summer of 1890, so that he was relieved of the burden of landowning after a short tenure. Lenin took his examinations in the spring and fall of 1891 as an external student (that is, he was not admitted to a university but was allowed to study on his own for the degree), passing with the highest possible grade—and this despite having to compress a four-year course into one year. In January 1892 he was licensed to practice law and enrolled with an old chess foe, A. N. Khardin, as a junior attorney in the town of Samara, not far from the ill-fated farm. Here he was to remain until the end of 1893, so that Samara was his home for four years in all.

Lenin spent a year and a half of the Samara period as a junior attorney, during which time he participated as the defense attorney in ten clear-cut cases of petty theft, wife-beating, and the like. Not unexpectedly he secured no acquittals.[11] There was one case, however, which he undertook on his own initiative and which he did win. Lenin and a relative were taking a trip, during which a river had to be crossed.[12] The ferrying privileges across the river were held by a man named Arefeev, who by might rather than right allowed no other boats to ferry passengers across but his own. When Lenin and his companion arrived at the river, they discovered that there would be some wait for the ferry, so Lenin persuaded one of the local boatmen to take them over. Arefeev, as was his custom, had the boat turned back and made them wait for his ferry. Lenin was incensed and brought charges against Arefeev and, despite all kinds of tricks by the latter and inconveniences resulting from his influence with the local authorities, won the case.[13]

[9] *Reminiscences of Lenin by His Relatives* (Moscow, 1956), p. 30.

[10] Quoted in Wolfe, p. 85.

[11] *Ibid.*, p. 86.

[12] Dmitry Ulyanov in *Reminiscences of Lenin*, says that Lenin's brother-in-law accompanied him (p. 122); Wolfe claims that it was a sister (p. 87).

[13] *Reminiscences of Lenin*, pp. 122-29.

Here, then, for the first time in his own experience, Lenin came in contact with an authoritative figure who was in the wrong, against whom, by practically any standards, one could fight with a clear conscience. The incident took place in the summer of 1892 and was pursued well into the winter. By this time Lenin was already getting impatient to leave Samara, to try out his Marxist wings. The fight against Arefeev was a temporary substitute for the larger battle he was longing to enter. Several years later, when he was exiled in Siberia, he would use legal defense, although in this case on other people's behalf, as a means of using up some of the energy he longed to devote to revolutionary activity.

Living in Samara were many members of *Narodnaya Volya,* the revolutionary organization of which Sasha and his friends had considered themselves a part. The police had placed them here to rusticate and grow old after their prison terms had expired. From them Lenin tried to learn of his brother's cause, but he found them vague and imprecise.[14] He did learn from them a number of technical skills, like the chemical basis of invisible inks and the ways of getting false passports. Aside from the bias towards terror and voluntarism developed earlier, however, he found little in what these old revolutionists said that was useful. He was looking for two things which Narodism could not supply: first, a justification of rebellion that would be total, that would define all relationships of man to man. Intense problems such as those Lenin was dealing with demand strongly formulated solutions. When the problem is one of ambivalence, of a mixture of feelings that keep getting in the way of each other, a system of justification is needed which precludes ambivalence, which reduces conflict to simpler and more manageable terms. Russian populism was not such a system of thought. It dealt with a set of special relationships, such as the people to the Tsar, and justified action relevant to such relationships; it did not suffice for Lenin's more encompassing needs.

Second, Lenin was looking for some assurance that revolutionary activity would not lead to disaster. The remnants of men he found in Samara did nothing to increase his confidence in the possible success of *Narodnik* activity. With his basic mistrust and the lesson learned from his brother's fate, Lenin needed mighty assurance of ultimate success. Marxism, which in the early 1890's was growing in popularity as a result of industrial unrest and the talented pen of G.

[14] Cf. Ulam's discussion of the Samara period, *The Bolsheviks*, pp. 96-110.

V. Plekhanov, met both needs; it was a total explanatory and justificatory system and it promised inevitable success. Marxists even claimed that the victory of the working class was a scientifically demonstrable fact. Here was the hardheaded realism and the instrument of analysis and justification Lenin needed, all rolled up into one and brilliantly expounded.

Lenin learned his Marxism and rejected Narodism quietly. He tried out his growing ideas only on members of the family and a few intimates.[15] He did not rush into activity based on what he was learning or attempt to refute others who were inclined to populism until he felt he had really mastered Marxist analysis. Not until his last months in Samara did he write his views in such a form as to make them accessible to others and not until the fall of 1893 did he leave Samara for St. Petersburg where participation in quasi-revolutionary activity was possible. Gandhi and Trotsky would immediately act upon the truth as they saw it. Lenin took the time to thoroughly convince himself before he sought to convince others. Similarly Lenin would never debate just for the enjoyment of intellectual engagement and the fruits of verbal victory. As early as the Samara period he did not attempt to refute the exiled populists of the area; he simply turned away (although not without some personal pain in creating the rupture).[16] Trotsky and Gandhi, by contrast, would argue their cause before anyone who would listen.

Another implication of Lenin's "silent" development as a Marxist is that he would not give the impression of hesitancy; whatever doubts he might have would be worked out privately, so that his public image was one of total confidence in his own ideas. The ideas or ideology he expounded, as we noted, had for him two crucial aspects: a justification of action and a way of or approach to action. When one envisions cogent and confident arguments being made in terms of these themes one begins to understand the basis of Lenin's dominance over his followers. Lenin would claim for his ideology both rightness and righteousness, correctness and rectitude—and he would make these claims with absolute conviction and an apparent absence of doubt. For any man who was uncertain about either ends or means Lenin was sure to exert a powerful attraction, especially when events, as they did, seemed to follow the course Lenin charted for them. (Also, because he did not act until he felt he thoroughly

---

[15] This discussion relies heavily on the Chapter 5 of Wolfe.
[16] *Ibid.*, p. 95.

understood the relevant theoretical and tactical aspects of a problem, Lenin was less likely than his opponents to be surprised by the arguments of others or the course of events.)

This experience further exemplifies Lenin's tendency to conserve energy and time that others would expend unproductively. Instead of arguing inconclusively over unfinished ideas, he would try to master a problem himself and then produce a straightforward statement of his position. He would save his arguments for those situations where they were most likely to produce tactical advantage; and he would save his energy and strength for the struggle itself, rather than waste it on diversionary encounters.

There are essentially two reasons why Lenin learned his Marxism in this manner, a pattern of learning and action of such efficacious consequences. First, Lenin's basic mistrust, his expectation that the people in his environment would react negatively and/or dangerously towards him, led him to arm himself as plentifully as he could before exposing himself to them; and once he decided to act he would strike hard, attempt to batter down his opponent before he could effectively retaliate. This was especially true when revolutionary activity itself was involved, but it also permeated his relationships with other members of his own cause. Related to this, of course, is that from one sector of his environment—the Tsar and his minions—Lenin had much to fear. Just as for the child any thought of fighting against the father is accompanied by fear and the wish for sufficient strength to withstand overwhelming might, so fighting against the Tsar led to the desire to be well-armed and cautious.

Second, Lenin acted in such a way as to avoid direct, person-to-person argument (but not controversy generally). The conflicts he was trying to rationalize in ideological terms were so intense that they had to be impersonalized as much as possible. The less the participants in debate resembled the members of the familial conflict situation, the less strain such debate entailed. By pushing conflict as much as possible into the realms of abstraction Lenin was able to reduce the tension accompanying personal ties. He could not, of course, impersonalize his intellectual world completely. The frequency with which he split with other socialists is indicative of how unbearable differences were and the commonness of reconciliation of how necessary these men were to one another, despite the ideological imperfections they saw in each other.

In 1893, as his commitment to Marxism and revolutionary action grew, Lenin became increasingly discontented with the inert environment of Samara. Anna reports that one night, after he had read Chekhov's short story, *Ward No. 6,* Lenin told her that he felt as if he, like the man in the story, were locked up. As Anna put it, "I realized that Samara was for him also a sort of Ward No. 6, that he wanted to get out of it almost as desperately as the poor man in Chekhov's story."[17]

The story itself is quite revealing of Lenin's state of mind at this time.[18] It focuses on two main characters, one the inmate of a mental ward (Ward No. 6), the other the doctor in charge of the hospital of which the ward is a part. The inmate, Ivan Dmitritch Gromov, is the son of a deceased nobleman who, after his father's death, was unable to complete his education and who gradually became overwhelmed by persecutory phantasies. He is a man tormented by guilt feelings, but who does not know why he should feel guilty. His lack of self-control, his inability to dominate his fears, has led to his imprisonment in the mental ward. Yet, despite his madness, his mind retains a peculiar lucidity, a profound insight into the corruption and immortality of the hospital, the town, and Russia. He is, moreover, a convinced opponent of political authority, and, in a sense, the story is a parable of the fate of the resister to social and political oppression.

Here, then, Lenin found portrayed the destiny of the man who rebels, and who is guilty just because he does so. Ivan Dmitritch, like Sasha, is a rebel who was not properly prepared for the struggle into which he was thrown by his own sense of justice. He could not control his own impulses and hence was condemned to life in a dreary cell, a veritable living death. No wonder Lenin felt akin to this man, for the story posed for him exactly his own dilemma. To identify with Sasha (Ivan) meant to share their parricidal guilt and their consequent punishment. But if he did not join them in action against the oppressors, he would have to shoulder the guilt growing out of his aggressive feelings towards Sasha. Nor did acquiescence promise relief, as was graphically depicted for him in the fate of the other major character in Chekhov's story, Dr. Andrey Yefimitch Ragin.

Andrey Yefimitch is a character rather like Goncharev's Ob-

---

[17] *Reminiscences of Lenin,* p. 43.

[18] Cf. Anton Chekhov, *The Horse Stealers and Other Stories,* Constance Garnett, trans. (New York, 1921), pp. 29-109. Also see Edmund Wilson's treatment of the story in his *To the Finland Station* (Garden City, N. Y., 1953), pp. 369-71.

lomov—a well-meaning but very weak-willed man of rather liberal inclination. All his life he has been unable to do what he felt was right (namely to try to reform at least some small part of society), and he justified his passivity on quasi-nihilistic philosophical grounds. He does feel dully the intellectual sterility of the town in which he lives, and hence is delighted when he discovers, quite by chance, that one of the inmates of the lunatic ward which he ostensibly supervises, namely Ivan, possesses an original and phil-osophic turn of mind. Fascinated by Ivan, he starts paying frequent visits to the ward. This behavior is incomprehensible to his fellow townsmen, who decide his interest in Ivan must be a sign of developing insanity and eventually succeed in having him locked up in Ward No. 6, to share the fate of the men he had previously condemned to the lifelong brutalization and dehumanization of that desolate room. And the doctor does not develop the energy or will to protest against this treatment until it is too late, until he is on the verge of death, already confined in a house of dead souls.

Thus the story did not provide Lenin with an alternative to revolt. Revolt or not, there seemed to be no escape from guilt or doom. Under the impact of this frightful prospect, in the provincial backwater of Samara, unable to act and thereby find out whether Marxism really provided a way out of this dilemma, Lenin's habitual self-control weakened, and he found himself in need of comforting conversation and escape from himself.

The very fact that Samara provided no opportunity for action is undoubtedly one of the reasons why Lenin was moved by the condition of the confined men in the story. Lenin wanted to escape the intellectually stifling atmosphere of Samara, to come in contact with people who were thinking and doing, not just vegetating amidst "the idiocy of rural life." Just as much, however, it would seem that he wanted to get away from his family. Lenin, it must be remem-bered, felt he bore the double responsibility for the deaths of his father and brother—whom he had wished dead in order that he might possess his mother. Now, when, in a sense, he had his mother to himself the feelings of guilt were sure to be oppressive; each day as he bathed in his mother's solicitude he would feel he was getting it only because the two elder men of the family were no longer there. He could not enjoy his love for his mother or her love for him at this close range; it was better to receive loving letters (and money when he needed it—until her death his mother remained a source of sustenance to him) and give them in turn and thus avoid a direct confrontation with his guilt.[19]

Hence in the fall of 1893 Lenin elected to go to St. Petersburg instead of following the rest of the family to Moscow, where Dmitry was to go to school. By so doing he both escaped from his family and threw himself into the center of revolutionary thinking, if not activity, in Russia. Shortly before his arrival in the capital, and during the first months there, he started to write out his views on Marxism for a reading public. "New Economic Developments in Peasant Life" and "On the So-Called Market Question," his first works, were attempts to demonstrate that Russia was a developing capitalist country and that therefore it was not exempt from the inexorable laws of dialectical development which Marx had formulated. He also wrote a long essay, "Discussion Between a Social Democrat and a Populist," which has not been preserved. In any case, as Wolfe notes, virtually all of Lenin's works until 1900 were a "discussion between a Social Democrat and a Populist."[20] Thus an analysis of his major attack on the populists, *What the "Friends of the People" Are and How They Fight the Social Democrats,* will help us to understand what he found of value in Marxism (the Social Democrats were Marxists), and why he rejected populism.

What the "Friends of the People" Are is an examination of the populist criticisms of Marxism and of the content of the populist program, as it was then being enunciated by N. K. Mikhailovsky and others in the monthly periodical, *Russkoye Bogatsvo* (Russian Wealth). In approach it is imitative of the sarcastic, somewhat heavy-handed polemical style of Marx, on the one hand, and it carries on the attack against the populists begun by G. V. Plekhanov a few years earlier, in *Our Differences* (1885), on the other.[21] In his analysis Lenin attempts to prove that Russia is indeed a capitalist country, and that only revolutionary Marxism provides a guarantee of victory for the oppressed.

It should be noted at the outset that Lenin was careful to

---

[19] Lenin's writings of 1893-94 are found in Vol. I of his *Collected Works* (Moscow, 1960).

[20] Wolfe, p. 97.

[21] Georgy Valentinovitch Plekhanov (1857-1918) was one of the first, and most brilliant, Russian Marxists. He was the principal leader of the Emancipation of Labour group, the first organization of Russian Marxists in exile.

differentiate between two varieties of populism. Although all its forms were viewed as being in error insofar as they did not realize the necessity of Russia's passing through a capitalist phase of development, the earlier Narodism of Chernyshevsky and others, with its dialectical sophistication and activist embodiment in such things as the terrorist sections of the *Narodnaya Volya* (which Sasha and his coconspirators claimed to represent), was treated as a glorious and heroic forerunner of Russian Marxism:

> It required the genious of Chernyshevsky to understand so clearly at that time, when the peasant Reform was only being introduced . . . its fundamentally bourgeois character, to understand that already at that time Russian "society" and the Russian "state" were ruled and governed by social classes that were irreconcilably hostile to the working people and that undoubtedly predetermined the ruin and expropriation of the peasantry. Moreover, Chernyshevsky understood that the existence of a government that screens our antagonistic social relations is a terrible evil, which renders the position of the working people ever so much worse. [22]

Contemporary Narodism, by contrast, is viewed as betraying this heritage:

> Yes, indeed, you [the Narodniks] are besmirching those ideals!
> *Faith in a special order, in the communal system of Russian life; hence—faith in the possibility of a peasant socialist revolution—that* is what inspired them and roused dozens and hundreds of people to wage a heroic struggle against the government. And you, you cannot reproach the Social Democrats with failing to appreciate the immense services of these, the finest people of their day, with failing to respect their memory profoundly. But I ask you, where is that faith now? It is vanished. [23]

In effect, Lenin is saying that not he, but the populists, are defiling the tradition of which his brother was a part. Lenin rejects the accusation that he does not "appreciate the immense services" of his brother, that he has abandoned the faith in "socialist revolution." He views himself as remaining true to the spirit of his brother's

[22] Lenin, *What the "Friends of the People" Are,* in his *Collected Works* (Moscow, 1963), I, 281-82.
[23] *Ibid.,* pp. 263-64.

actions, even if it is now necessary to view the struggle in somewhat different terms.

The earlier Narodniks and his brother can thus be admired because they put the struggle first, because they realized that victory could only be achieved by revolution. This element of their creed can be readily assimilated into Marxism, even if their analysis of the meaning of the struggle must be rejected. But the current crop of populists have abandoned the concept of conflict while retaining the invalid theoretical framework. They have discarded the grain and kept the chaff of the doctrine. Lenin, by viewing them in this light, could condemn them with a clear conscience; his identification with his brother remained intact as long as he viewed the essence of his brother's creed as revolt rather than populist theory. And his brother's political action, after all, was exactly that—an elemental revolt of the son against the father.

As we have seen, however, Sasha's mode of action gave Lenin no assurance of success; in fact, it connoted failure. But Marxism seemed to promise a solution:

> [Capitalism is progressive because] it AWAKENS THE MIND OF THE WORKER, converts dumb and incoherent discontent into conscious protest, converts scattered, petty, senseless revolt into an organised class struggle . . . a struggle which derives its strength from the very conditions of existence of large-scale capitalism, and therefore can undoubtedly count upon CERTAIN SUCCESS.[24]

Marxism thus allowed Lenin to rise above Sasha's "senseless revolt," and above his fate. By becoming a Marxist Lenin not only maintained his identification with his brother, but also conquered him. He, not Sasha, understood the dictates of Marx, the revolutionary father. He, not Sasha, would carry out Marx's program of action and thereby gain history's esteem and victory over the Tsar. In short, Marxism allowed Lenin to identify himself with both Sasha and an image of his father. In Marx Lenin found a benevolent, omniscient father, a wise and methodical teacher, a fit repository for his feelings of love and respect for his real father. And in the Tsar, the perfect embodiment of the vengeful Oedipal father, he found his dangerous opponent, over whom, however, Marx promised victory.

In many ways, this early polemical writing of Lenin's bears the

[24] *Ibid.*, p. 236.

marks of his more mature productions: his emphasis on revolt, on the capitalist nature of Russian society, on tsarism as the "gendarme" of European capitalism;[25] his easy assumption throughout that he is a fit spokesman for the Social Democrats (that is, Marxists); and his thorough, bone-crunching demolition of his opponents' arguments, as well as his blunt, forceful style. All these are already in evidence. But one central Leninist characteristic is missing: his discussion of organization and organizational activity is fuzzy and cursory. The Party, whose role Lenin developed in such great detail later on, here has but a nebulous embodiment. Thus Lenin at this juncture knew what he was fighting for, and that he was fighting; but he did not know quite how to fight.

As was noted earlier, Lenin expected to find in St. Petersburg a chance to throw himself into important revolutionary activity. He was evidently somewhat disappointed at what actually existed. In a famous incident, which Krupskaya records from personal memory, Lenin attended a Social Democratic gathering at which someone was arguing in favor of activity aimed at educating the workers, which would be organized through a "Committee for Illiteracy." When this was mentioned:

> Vladimir Ilyich laughed, and somehow his laughter sounded laconic. I have never heard him laugh that way on any subsequent occasion.
> "Well," he said, "if anyone wants to save the fatherland in the Committee for Illiteracy, we won't hinder him!"[26]

Lenin came to the capital expecting broad-scale activity and found piecemeal work. The very idea of such trivial means for such great ends must have seemed incongruous to him. In the years that followed he would look for better means, but for the time he adjusted himself to the opportunities the city presented—and threw himself into work on the Committee for Illiteracy. He did so, however, with no illusions about the ultimate effect of such activity on the possibility of broad social change.

Lenin used the work of the committee to gather information about working class conditions and worker mentality and to test his powers of communication with this group. The technique that Lenin

[25] *Ibid.*, p. 261.
[26] *Krupskaya*, I, 3.

used for getting across his ideas to the workers is described by Babushkin, a workingman who was one of his "students" at this time:

> He frequently tried to provoke us to speak or to arouse us to start a discussion . . . and then urge us on, compelling each to demonstrate to the other the correctness of his standpoint on a given question. Thus our lectures were made very animated and interesting, and we began to become accustomed to speaking in public. This mode of study served as an excellent way of clarifying a given question for the students. All of us greatly enjoyed these lectures, and were constantly delighted by our lecturer's power of intellect, it being a standing joke among us that an excess of brains had made his hair fall out. At the same time, these lectures trained us to do independent work, and to find material. The lecturer would hand us lists of questions which required on our part close knowledge and observation of life in the factory and workshop.[27]

It is not surprising that Lenin was a *teacher* to the working men—teaching was the family profession. The strength of Lenin's identification with his father is shown by this incorporation of teaching into his occupation of revolutionist. Earlier he had served as tutor, mainly in languages, to other members of the family. Later others were to be struck by his professional manner which was, at the same time, devoid of rhetorical devices and pedantry.[28] The naturalness and simplicity of his speaking—and writing—style came in part from the early absorption of his father's activities. Lenin had been emulating a teacher for so long that he could speak without consciousness of style or gesture. His manner of presentation was an organic part of his personality and by its very lack of pretension captivated his listeners and made them conscious of the intensity of his conviction.[29]

One of the striking things about Lenin was his lack of personal grandiosity, of which his simplicity of speech and straightforward writing style are two examples. In other respects, too, Lenin gave the impression of extreme unselfconsciousness—in the utilitarian-

---

[27] Quoted in Wolfe, pp. 104-105.

[28] Leon Trotsky, *Lenin* (New York, 1962), pp. 32-33. Also Wilson, in his perceptive sketch of Lenin in *To the Finland Station*, refers to him as "The Great Headmaster."

[29] *Ibid.*, pp. 162-71.

ism of his style of dress, his willingness to laugh at himself, and his embarrassment at applause. In comparison with someone as theatrically oriented as, say, Trotsky (or Gandhi, in a somewhat different way) Lenin would appear ordinary; but this very ordinariness was an indication of an extraordinary man. For the lack of self-consciousness upon which Lenin's simplicity was based is a sure indicator of a highly integrated and self-confident personality; and such a personality pattern was extremely rare among the Russian revolutionists, who, on the whole, were relatively unstable individuals. Lenin was at ease with himself, confident in his cause and in his ability to lead it. He did not need theatrical props either to reassure himself of his own importance or to attract the attention of others. He was, in other words, the one man among his contemporaries who really felt comfortable in the role of leader. Because he had salvaged from his childhood enough of his own identification with his father, he could play the role of father for others without feeling that to do so was either presumptuous or incongruous. Trotsky, by contrast, never was able to develop this feeling.

In the summer of 1895 Lenin got permission to go abroad, ostensibly for his health (he did, in fact, try a couple of cures for his chronically nervous stomach), but actually to try to establish contact with G. V. Plekhanov, P. B. Axelrod, and V. P. Zasulich, the leaders of the Liberation of Labour, a Russian Marxist group with headquarters in western Europe. His contact with Plekhanov and Axelrod in particular did nothing to shake his confidence in them; both, but especially Plekhanov, had been the major sources, aside from Marx and Engels themselves, from whom Lenin had learned his Marxism and he treated them with something approaching reverence. He accepted their advice to moderate somewhat his attacks on the Liberals,[30] and returned to Russia bent on maintaining contact with them.

Not long after his return, however, Lenin was arrested and imprisoned. During the period preceding his arrest he had become increasingly conscious of the possibility, and had made a great effort to pass on his knowledge, both of contacts and conspiratorial techniques, to others—and to appoint a successor.[31] Trotsky, in his

---

[30] Haimson, pp. 106-109, also deals with some of the strategic reasons for Lenin's "softer" attitude.

[31] Krupskaya, I, II. Because she was the least known to the police Krupskaya was appointed as Lenin's successor.

first revolutionary efforts, would take no such precautions. Trotsky was, of course, somewhat younger than Lenin at the time of his first imprisonment, but it is nonetheless indicative of his greater involvement in himself and smaller involvement in the cause that he should have given relatively less thought to carrying on the work after his possible removal.

Although he was occasionally bothered by loneliness, Lenin adjusted well to the prison routine.[32] Political prisoners were treated relatively well by the authorities and Lenin was allowed frequent visitors and unlimited access to books. Direct communication on revolutionary matters was not possible, but secret techniques were easily devised for passing on information. Lenin was thus able to maintain considerable contact with the outside world. Soon after his arrest he began work on what was to be *The Development of Capitalism in Russia* and several other pieces as well. In fact, all three of our protagonists found prison very congenial for working; none of them gave in to the melancholia that prison often bred. All three met the challenge of imprisonment by setting themselves a routine. Lenin's consisted of exercising, careful eating, and hard work.[33] He so mastered the environment that he was able to joke, as he left on his leisurely journey to Siberian exile, that "It is a pity they let us out so soon. I would have liked to do a little more work on the book."[34]

The routine of captivity so agreed with Lenin that by the time he reached Siberia he was even rid of his stomach trouble and tendency towards insomnia. Lenin himself attributed the change in his health to the lack of "uncertainty" about his position now that he had been arrested.[35] Manifestly, of course, Lenin's position while still at large in St. Petersburg was uncertain because he did not know if and when he would be arrested. This would be especially trying for Lenin, for he had always lived a highly ordered and organized life, with the days neatly compartmentalized for various kinds of work and the future roughly mapped out. Professional revolutionary activity, by contrast, involved a disorderly life in a constantly changing context. Moreover, it was a fight, a fight against political (and implicitly

---

[32] *Ibid.*, p. 20.

[33] See Lenin's letter to his mother of February 7, 1898, on p. 53 of Elizabeth Hill and Doris Mudie, eds., *The Letters of Lenin* (London, 1937).

[34] Quoted by Krupskaya, I, 20.

[35] Letter to his mother, March 1897. *Letters of Lenin*, p. 27.

parental) authority. Hence, the activity itself was to some extent guilt-inducing; some residual feelings remained that the legal authorities were also legitimate, that rebellion was wrong (although it should be stressed that this seems to have been less prominent in Lenin than in Trotsky; Lenin continued to fear and respect authority but he credited it with less rectitude than did Trotsky). Also, revolutionary activity carried with it the threat of punishment, just as Lenin's earlier coveting of his mother brought with it the threat of paternal revenge. Thus as long as Lenin was free, he would be apprehensive about being caught. Once he was caught he would find, with considerable relief, that the dreaded punishment was not so bad after all and hence bearable. At the same time he would gratify his residual feelings of guilt by bearing the punishment meted out to him. Similarly, while in prison or exile, he would be much less able to participate in revolutionary work, hence the strains attendant on that activity would be held in abeyance. Finally, prison and exile promised an orderly and routinized life similar to the family life of his childhood but without the same tensions.

After spending fourteen months in prison, Lenin was exiled to Shushenskoye in Yenisseisk province, where he stayed until February 1900. While there he finished *The Development of Capitalism in Russia,* and with its completion put an end for the time being to questions of self-definition and goals. From now on, with one or two major exceptions, he was to concern himself with means, not ends. He also did a translation of Webb's *The Theory and Practice of English Trade Unions* and kept up his considerable correspondence with fellow Social Democrats both in exile and in western Russia. His family served as his primary intermediaries in this matter, as well as the suppliers of his various needs, especially books.

Before leaving Lenin, on the verge of returning to Russia and thence to western Europe, with the plans already formed in his mind for an all-Russian Marxist newspaper, some aspects of his personal life must be filled in. While he was in exile he married Krupskaya, who had been one of his earliest companions during the St. Petersburg period. Also, while in exile, Lenin avoided as much as possible the squabbles and conflicts of the other exiles. Conflicts were especially great between the young Social Democrats and the old members of the populist movements who were still in the area. Lenin's solution to this problem was exactly that which he had used earlier himself—a complete break with the older revolutionists.[36]

[36] Krupskaya, I, 38.

Finally, while still in St. Petersburg, Lenin had formed intimate friendships, perhaps the only ones of his adult life, with Martov and Potresov, two Social Democrats of his generation and men who appeared to share his theoretical orientation. As his time in exile drew to a close, he envisioned the three of them, brothers in the revolutionary cause, working together in the new organization he planned. They were to be for the younger generation what Plekhanov, Zasulich, and Axelrod were for the older; he foresaw all six of them cooperating in the mutual effort. The next few years of his life in particular would be devoted to working out his relationship with these people, especially with Martov, his soon-to-be blood brother, and Plekhanov, the father of Russian Marxism.

GEORGE ORWELL

Why I Write

In a subject full of dilemmas of ideas and emotions, it is probably well to include something from the master of clarity in the English language—the "Crystal Spirit," as one of his biographers described him. There are few writers in the twentieth century whose works have been immersed in such bitter recrimination as have those of George Orwell. Every line he wrote from the time of the Spanish Civil War he considered to be "*against* totalitarianism and *for* democratic Socialism." Yet, by the time of his fame after the defeat of fascism, his major works were construed only as attacks upon the totalitarianism of the Left. Together with John Dos Passos, Arthur Koestler, and others, he was thus considered by the Left to be one of the apostates—betrayers, cranky malcontents. That political judgement has moderated only slightly in the passage of twenty years.

The autobiographical cameo which follows, written three years before his death in 1950, outlines the conflict-laden discovery by the artist of his political conscience. Being of service, the long-established civil and humanitarian tradition of the educated classes in England, conflicted with the writer's egoism, aesthetics, and his eye for the truth.

"In a peaceful age," which he would have preferred, Orwell may have written differently, poetry or ornate description rather than polemics. But, he writes, "It is forbidden to dream again," so he infused his politics with art and impassioned his art with purpose.

FROM A VERY early age, perhaps the age of five or six, I knew that when I grew up I should be a writer. Between the ages of about seventeen and twenty-four I tried to abandon this idea, but I did so with the consciousness that I was outraging my true nature and that sooner or later I should have to settle down and write books.

I was the middle child of three, but there was a gap of five years on either side, and I barely saw my father before I was eight. For this and other reasons I was somewhat lonely, and I soon developed disagreeable mannerisms which made me unpopular throughout my schooldays. I had the lonely child's habit of making up stories and holding conversations with imaginary persons, and I think from the very start my literary ambitions were mixed up with the feeling of being isolated and undervalued. I knew that I had a facility with words and a power of facing unpleasant facts, and I felt that this created a sort of private world in which I could get my own back for my failure in everyday life. Nevertheless the volume of serious—i.e. seriously intended—writing which I produced all through my childhood and boyhood would not amount to half a dozen pages. I wrote my first poem at the age of four or five, my mother taking it down to dictation. I cannot remember anything about it except that it was about a tiger and the tiger had "chair-like teeth"—a good enough phrase, but I fancy the poem was a plagiarism of Blake's "Tiger, Tiger". At eleven, when the war of 1914–18 broke out, I wrote a patriotic poem which was printed in the local newspaper, as was another, two years later, on the death of Kitchener. From time to time, when I was a bit older, I wrote bad and usually unfinished "nature poems" in the Georgian style. I also, about twice, attempted a short story which was a ghastly failure. That was the total of the would-be serious work that I actually set down on paper during all those years.

However, throughout this time I did in a sense engage in literary activities. To begin with there was the made-to-order stuff which I produced quickly, easily and without much pleasure to myself. Apart from school work, I wrote *vers d'occasion,* semi-comic poems which I could turn out at what now seems to me astonishing speed—at fourteen I wrote a whole rhyming play, in imitation of Aristophanes, in about a week—and helped to edit school magazines, both printed and in manuscript. These magazines were the most pitiful burlesque stuff that you could imagine, and I took far less trouble with them than I now would with the cheapest journalism. But side by side with all this, for fifteen years or more, I was carrying out a literary exercise of a quite different kind: this was the making up of a continuous "story" about myself, a sort of diary existing only in the mind. I believe this is a common habit of children and adolescents. As a very small child I used to imagine that I was, say, Robin Hood, and picture myself as the hero of thrilling adventures, but quite soon my "story" ceased to be narcissistic in a crude way and became more and more a mere description of what I was doing and the things I saw. For minutes at a time this kind of thing would be running through my head: "He pushed the door open and entered the room. A yellow beam of sunlight, filtering through the muslin curtains, slanted on to the table, where a matchbox, half open, lay beside the inkpot. With his right hand in his pocket he moved across to the window. Down in the street a tortoiseshell cat was chasing a dead leaf," etc. etc. This habit continued till I was about twenty-five, right through my non-literary years. Although I had to search, and did search, for the right words, I seemed to be making this descriptive effort almost against my will, under a kind of compulsion from outside. The "story" must, I suppose, have reflected the styles of the various writers I admired at different ages, but so far as I remember it always had the same meticulous descriptive quality.

When I was about sixteen I suddenly discovered the joy of mere words, i.e. the sounds and associations of words. The lines from *Paradise Lost,*

> So hee with difficulty and labour hard
> Moved on: with difficulty and labour hee,

which do not now seem to me so very wonderful, sent shivers down my backbone; and the spelling "hee" for "he" was an added pleasure. As for the need to describe things, I knew all about it already. So it is clear what kind of books I wanted to write, in so far as I could be said to want to write books at that time. I wanted to write enormous naturalistic novels with unhappy endings, full of detailed descriptions and arresting similes, and also full of purple passages in which words were used partly for the sake of their sound. And in fact my first completed novel, *Burmese Days,* which I wrote when I was thirty but projected much earlier, is rather that kind of book.

I give all this background information because I do not think one can assess a writer's motives without knowing something of his early development. His subject matter will be determined by the age he lives in—at least this is true in tumultuous, revolutionary ages like our own—but before he ever begins to write he will have acquired an emotional attitude from which he will never completely escape. It is his job, no doubt, to discipline his temperament and avoid getting stuck at some immature stage, or in some perverse mood: but if he escapes from his early influences altogether, he will have killed his impulse to write. Putting aside the need to earn a living, I think there are four great motives for writing, at any rate for writing prose. They exist in different degrees in every writer, and in any one writer the proportions will vary from time to time, according to the atmosphere in which he is living. They are:

(1.) Sheer egoism. Desire to seem clever, to be talked about, to be remembered after death, to get your own back on grown-ups who snubbed you in childhood, etc. etc. It is humbug to pretend that this is not a motive, and a strong one. Writers share this characteristic with scientists, artists, politicians, lawyers, soldiers, successful businessmen—in short, with the whole top crust of humanity. The great mass of human beings are not acutely selfish. After the age of about thirty they abandon individual ambition—in many cases, indeed, they almost abandon the sense of being individuals at all—and live chiefly for others, or are simply smothered under drudgery. But there is also the minority of gifted, wilful people who are determined to live their own lives to the end, and writers belong in this class. Serious writers, I should say, are on the whole more vain and self-centered than journalists, though less interested in money.

(2). Aesthetic enthusiasm. Perception of beauty in the external world, or, on the other hand, in words and their right arrangement. Pleasure in the impact of one sound on another, in the firmness of good prose or the rhythm of a good story. Desire to share an experience which one feels is valuable and ought not to be missed. The aesthetic motive is very feeble in a lot of writers, but even a pamphleteer or a writer of textbooks will have pet words and phrases which appeal to him for non-utilitarian reasons; or he may feel strongly about typography, width of margins, etc. Above the level of a railway guide, no book is quite free from aesthetic considerations.

(3). Historical impulse. Desire to see things as they are, to find out true facts and store them up for the use of posterity.

(4). Political purpose—using the word "political" in the widest possible sense. Desire to push the world in a certain direction, to alter other people's idea of the kind of society that they should strive after. Once again, no book is genuinely free from political bias. The opinion that art should have nothing to do with politics is itself a political attitude.

It can be seen how these various impulses must war against one another, and how they must fluctuate from person to person and from time to time. By nature—taking your "nature" to be the state you have attained when you are first adult—I am a person in whom the first three motives outweigh the fourth. In a peaceful age I might have written ornate or merely descriptive books, and might have remained almost unaware of my political loyalties. As it is I have been forced into becoming a sort of pamphleteer. First I spent five years in an unsuitable profession (the Indian Imperial Police, in Burma), and then I underwent poverty and the sense of failure. This increased my natural hatred of authority and made me for the first time fully aware of the existence of the working classes, and the job in Burma had given me some understanding of the nature of imperialism: but these experiences were not enough to give me an accurate political orientation. Then came Hitler, the Spanish civil war, etc. By the end of 1935 I had still failed to reach a firm decision. I remember a little poem that I wrote at that date, expressing my dilemma:

A happy vicar I might have been
Two hundred years ago,
To preach upon eternal doom
And watch my walnuts grow;

But born, alas, in an evil time,
I missed that pleasant haven,
For the hair has grown on my upper lip
And the clergy are all clean-shaven.

And later still the times were good,
We were so easy to please,
We rocked our troubled thoughts to sleep
On the bosoms of the trees.

All ignorant we dared to own
The joys we now dissemble;
The greenfinch on the apple bough
Could make my enemies tremble.

But girls' bellies and apricots,
Roach in a shaded stream,
Horses, ducks in flight at dawn,
All these are a dream.

It is forbidden to dream again;
We maim our joys or hide them;
Horses are made of chromium steel
And little fat men shall ride them.

I am the worm who never turned,
The eunuch without a harem;
Between the priest and the commissar
I walk like Eugene Aram;

And the commissar is telling my fortune
While the radio plays,
But the priest has promised an Austin Seven,
For Duggie always pays.

I dreamed I dwelt in marble halls,
And woke to find it true;
I wasn't born for an age like this;
Was Smith? Was Jones? Were you?[1]

The Spanish war and other events in 1936–37 turned the scale and thereafter I knew where I stood. Every line of serious work that I have written since 1936 has been written, directly or indirectly, *against* totalitarianism and *for* democratic Socialism, as I under-

[1] p. 5, ft. 1.

stand it. It seems to me nonsense, in a period like our own, to think that one can avoid writing of such subjects. Everyone writes of them in one guise or another. It is simply a question of which side one takes and what approach one follows. And the more one is conscious of one's political bias, the more chance one has of acting politically without sacrificing one's aesthetic and intellectual integrity.

What I have most wanted to do throughout the past ten years is to make political writing into an art. My starting point is always a feeling of partisanship, a sense of injustice. When I sit down to write a book, I do not say to myself, "I am going to produce a work of art." I write it because there is some lie that I want to expose, some fact to which I want to draw attention, and my initial concern is to get a hearing. But I could not do the work of writing a book, or even a long magazine article, if it were not also an aesthetic experience. Anyone who cares to examine my work will see that even when it is downright propaganda it contains much that a full-time politician would consider irrelevant. I am not able, and I do not want, completely to abandon the worldview that I acquired in childhood. So long as I remain alive and well I shall continue to feel strongly about prose style, to love the surface of the earth, and to take pleasure in solid objects and scraps of useless information. It is no use trying to suppress that side of myself. The job is to reconcile my ingrained likes and dislikes with the essentially public, non-individual activities that this age forces on all of us.

It is not easy. It raises problems of construction and of language, and it raises in a new way the problem of truthfulness. Let me give just one example of the cruder kind of difficulty that arises. My book about the Spanish civil war, *Homage to Catalonia,* is, of course, a frankly political book, but in the main it is written with a certain detachment and regard for form. I did try very hard in it to tell the whole truth without violating my literary instincts. But among other things it contains a long chapter, full of newspaper quotations and the like, defending the Trotskyists who were accused of plotting with Franco. Clearly such a chapter, which after a year or two would lose its interest for any ordinary reader, must ruin the book. A critic whom I respect read me a lecture about it. "Why did you put in all that stuff?" he said. "You've turned what might have been a good book into journalism." What he said was true, but I could not have done otherwise. I happened to know, what very few people in England had been allowed to know, that innocent men were being falsely accused. If I had not been angry about that I should never have written the book.

In one form or another this problem comes up again. The problem of language is subtler and would take too long to discuss. I will only say that of late years I have tried to write less picturesquely and more exactly. In any case I find that by the time you have perfected any style of writing, you have always outgrown it. *Animal Farm* was the first book in which I tried, with full consciousness of what I was doing, to fuse political purpose and artistic purpose into one whole. I have not written a novel for seven years, but I hope to write another fairly soon. It is bound to be a failure, every book is a failure, but I know with some clarity what kind of book I want to write.

Looking back through the last page or two, I see that I have made it appear as though my motives in writing were wholly public-spirited. I don't want to leave that as the final impression. All writers are vain, selfish and lazy, and at the very bottom of their motives there lies a mystery. Writing a book is a horrible, exhausting struggle, like a long bout of some painful illness. One would never undertake such a thing if one were not driven on by some demon whom one can neither resist nor understand. For all one knows that demon is simply the same instinct that makes a baby squall for attention. And yet it is also true that one can write nothing readable unless one constantly struggles to efface one's own personality. Good prose is like a window pane. I cannot say with certainty which of my motives are the strongest, but I know which of them deserve to be followed. And looking back through my work, I see that it is invariably where I lacked a *political* purpose that I wrote lifeless books and was betrayed into purple passages, sentences without meaning, decorative adjectives and humbug generally.

IV | The European Intellectuals

JOHN M. CAMMETT
The Historical Role of Italian Intellectuals

Whether intellectuals are defined as a class, a club, technocrats, jesters, or custodians of culture, it is clear that they have performed essential mundane functions in European society, both within the establishment and in opposition to it. Antonio Gramsci, the leading theoretician of Italian Marxism, laid some of the groundwork for the modern analysis of that role in his description of the concept of "hegemony." In the following chapter, from *Antonio Gramsci and the Origins of Italian Communism* (1967), John Cammet outlines Gramsci's classification of intellectuals into "traditional" and "organic", distinguished by their relationship to the dominant economic and social structure. Thus, the "organic" intellectual—the manager, administrator, or politician—is incorporated into the concept of the intellectual by virtue of his "directive" role in society. In this definition, Gramsci attempted to add the objective element of "function" in dealing with intellectuals to the more subjective idea of "consciousness" by which the European intellectual traditionally identified himself in society.

Although essentially a Marxist viewpoint, Gramsci's categories are not intended to be rigid or unchanging. Leonard Krieger's idea of the "liberal intellectual" and Ernst Nolte's concept of "transcendence," discussed in the chapters which follow, can be viewed as complementary approaches. Despite many differences, all three, in a sense, attempt to account for the tension which exists in intellectuals between the "inner" and "external" realities.

TYPES OF INTELLECTUALS

GRAMSCI'S ANALYSIS of parties may serve as an introduction to his abiding interest in the role of intellectuals, for him (as for others in our own time) a key cultural and political question. He was dissatisfied with previous criteria for classifying groups as "intellectual" or "non-intellectual" because he believed these criteria were based almost exclusively on comparative evaluations of the cerebral activity involved in any act. On this basis, everyone would be an "intellectual" to some extent: every man, apart from his profession, "exhibits some intellectual activity, . . . shares a world-view, has a conscious line of moral conduct, and therefore contributes to sustaining or modifying a conception of the world." A more precise and perhaps more fruitful method for classifying intellectuals would describe their "social function."

From this "functional" point of view, Gramsci considers as intellectuals all those who exercise "technical" or "directive" capacities in society—e.g., industrial managers, administrators and bureaucrats, politicians, and "organizers of culture" like artists and scholars. Some of these categories are only adapted to the basic activities of certain social groups. Thus industrial managers and foremen are "specialists" in organizing industry for the capitalists. But society also needs men of a larger, broader, or more "political" vision—in short "directors," who will organize society in general to "create the most favorable conditions for the expansion of the class" whose interests they serve.

Besides this "vertical" distinction of intellectual types (the specialists and the directors), Gramsci also makes a "horizontal" distinction between "traditional" and "organic" intellectuals. The "traditional" group is the totality of creative artists and learned men in society, those who are usually thought of as "intellectuals." Their outstanding characteristic is a feeling that they represent a "historical continuity uninterrupted by even the most radical and complicated changes of social and political systems." This attachment to past intellectuals has important political consequences: for example, traditional intellectuals feel that they are "autonomous, independent of the dominant social group."

Gramsci does not attempt to establish the actual degree of coordination between "traditional" intellectuals and the social group that dominates economic production; indeed, he would have rejected any such effort as the purest abstraction. But he does assert that, generally speaking, this relationship is not "immediate," but "mediated" by many elements in society's superstructure. For example, the "traditional" intellectuals of the ecclesiastical hierarchy, as conscious heirs of the apostolic tradition, have never completely shared the world-view of the socially and economically dominant classes. Even so, they achieved—or were granted—a near monopoly of important social activities, such as education, philosophy, and science.

The "organic" intellectual is more directly related to the economic structure of his particular society: new categories of them are, in fact, created by "every social group that originates in the fulfillment of an essential task of economic production." The "organic intellectual" gives his class homogeneity and awareness of its own function, in the economic field and on the social and political levels. The capitalist entrepreneur brings forth the industrial manager, the political scientist, the cultural innovator, a new law, and so on.

Obviously, the two types of intellectuals are not rigidly separated. Every intellectual has some connection with a basic social group, although his interests may not be identical with that group's. For example, the Church, at any given point in its history, has had to come to terms with the dominant socio-economic group; nonetheless, its interests are not *identical* with that group's. The interests of the organic intellectual are, however, more nearly identical with those of the dominant class of the time than the traditional intellectual's. Moreover, when there are many traditional intellectuals hostile to the interests of the dominant class, the dominant class must campaign for their "assimilation and 'ideological' conquest."

Under normal conditions, the organic intellectuals of the "historically (and realistically) progressive class" will be able to dominate the intellectuals of subordinate classes. The result is solidarity among all intellectuals, who are held together by "bonds of a psychological order (vanity, etc.) and often of caste (technico-juridical, corporative, etc.)." As long as a dominant class remains progressive and truly advances the interests of most of the society, this "system of solidarity" is likely to continue.

Geography and class origin provide a third basis, especially in Italy, for classifying intellectuals: differing types derive from urban and rural bourgeoisie. The provincial middle classes "specialize" in producing state functionaries and members of the liberal professions, while the metropolitan bourgeoisie produce technicians for industry. Hence, intellectuals of provincial origin are usually traditional, whereas urban intellectuals are mostly organic. Still, traditional southern Italian society also has some organic intellectuals in the so-called *pagliette* (literally, "straw hats"), who act as middlemen between the peasants on the one hand and the landowners and government on the other.

Although every social group develops its own organic intellectuals, the industrial proletariat has relied mostly on "assimilated" traditional intellectuals for leadership. Gramsci always regarded this as one of the chief problems of the working class . . . . The initial stage in forming the new organic intellectual would be a technical and industrial education obtained directly in the shops. At the same time the select worker would strive to rise above this level: "From technical work he arrives at technical science and historical humanistic views, without which he would remain a 'specialist' and would not become a 'director' (that is, specialist plus politician)."

In classifying intellectuals, Gramsci distinguished two different areas in the superstructure of society, partly following a distinction already made by Hegel, Giannone, and Vico: "political society" is made up of public institutions and organs of coercion (the army, the courts, the State bureaucracy); "civil society" is the totality of private institutions (Church, schools, political parties). While analyzing political parties, Gramsci . . . had pointed out that they were elements of civil society; unlike "political" elements, they tried to obtain free consent to a given economic situation. Organic intellectuals, part of the dominant class, provide personnel for the coercive organs of political society. Traditional intellectuals, important in civil society, are more likely to reason with the masses and try to obtain "spontaneous" consent to a social order.

THE CONCEPT OF HEGEMONY

Gramsci's thoughts on intellectuals led him to consider the Marxist view of the State. As he wrote . . . in 1931, Marxists usually think of the State as "political" society, not as an equilibrium of political society with civil society—the hegemony of one social group over the whole society, "exercised through so-called private organizations, such as the Church, trade unions, schools, etc." A British student of this phase of Gramsci's thought has provided us with a useful introductory definition of the problem: hegemony is "an order in which a certain way of life and thought is dominant, in which one concept of reality is diffused throughout society in all its institutional and private manifestations, informing with its spirit all taste, morality, customs, religious and political principles, and all social relations, particularly in their intellectual and moral connotations." It follows that a hegemony is the predominance, obtained by consent rather than force, of one class or group over other classes. Hegemony is therefore achieved by institutions of civil society.

In its general sense, hegemony refers to the "spontaneous" loyalty that any dominant social group obtains from the masses by virtue of its social and intellectual prestige and its supposedly superior function in the world of production. Thus the Italian bourgeoisie exercised an almost unchallenged hegemony over the workers and peasants from 1870 to 1890, following its successful conclusion of Italian unification and before the birth of the Italian Socialist Party, with a competing and "autonomous" ideology. In a more restricted sense, Gramsci uses the term "hegemony" to refer to projected alliances of a predominant working class with other "subaltern" but "progressive" social elements, especially the peasantry, parts of the petty bourgeoisie, and the intelligentsia. Even in a Socialist state, the term "hegemony" would still be useful to indicate the social (or civil) form of the workers' State based on consent—in contrast to the "dictatorship of the proletariat," based on force, which would be the state's political form.

The development of hegemony depends on the "level of homogeneity, self-consciousness, and organization" reached by a given social class. Mere awareness of economic interests is not sufficient: the class must be convinced that its "own economic interests, in their present and future development, go beyond the corporative circle of a merely economic group, and can and must become the interests of other repressed groups. This is the most purely political phase, which marks the passage from structure to the sphere of complex superstructures." At this point, the class has truly become a party, and it must now fight for its intellectual and moral values, as well as its economic and political ends. The leading class must also coordinate its interests with those of "allied" classes. In this new equilibirium the "interests of the dominant group will prevail," but not to the point of fully achieving only its own "crude" economic interests.

The fundamental assumption behind Gramsci's view of hegemony is that the working class, before it seizes State power, must establish its claim to be a ruling class in the political, cultural, and "ethical" fields. "The founding of a ruling class is equivalent to the creation of a Weltanschauung." This idea, of great theoretical importance for the development of Socialism, was basic to Gramsci's work at least as far back as the days of *Ordine nuovo* and the factory-council movement. For Gramsci, a social class scarcely deserves the name until it becomes *conscious* of its existence as a class; it cannot play a role in history until it develops a comprehensive world-view and a political program.

The "orthodox" school of Marxism, in the late nineteenth and early twentieth centuries, was riddled with "economism" and materialism, a climate that left no room for problems of hegemony. For Gramsci, it was Lenin who revived Marxism as a creative philosophy: Lenin, "in opposition to various 'economistic' tendencies" reaffirmed the importance of hegemony in his conception of the State and gave the cultural "front" as much emphasis as the economic and political fronts. Lenin's struggle against "economism" and "tail-ism" (or "spontaneity") led him to stress the necessity of educating the masses in a revolutionary sense. Moreover, his theory of the political party was founded on the conviction that conscious organization was essential for victory. Perhaps most important of all, he insisted on establishing a "hegemonic" relationship between working class and peasantry as a prerequisite for the revolution.

Still, Gramsci seems to have doubts about Lenin's thoroughness in examining the hegemony of the working class and the "cultural front." In reality, Gramsci went far beyond Lenin in seeing hegemony as a political and cultural predominance of the working class and its party aimed at securing the "spontaneous" adherence of other groups. Hegemony—rule by consent, the legitimatization of revolution by a higher and more comprehensive culture—is the unifying idea of Gramsci's life from the days of *La Citta futura* [1917] to those of the *Quaderni del Carcere* [1927].

In his later work Gramsci stressed the problem of "civil society," hegemony, over the problem of "political society," which is—for Marxists—the dictatorship of the proletariat. The shift in emphasis was caused by Gramsci's increasing awareness of differences between the Russia of 1917 and Western Europe after 1923. Problems of hegemony, said Gramsci, become particularly important in periods that follow a phase of revolutionary activity. Gramsci believed that the class struggle then changes from a "war of maneuver" to a "war of position" fought mainly on the cultural front. The Quaderni were written during such a period, and this partly accounts for their emphasis on hegemony.

In the united front policy Lenin himself, said Gramsci, indicated the need to shift from a war of maneuver, which had succeeded in Russia in 1917, to a war of position, "the only possible one in the West." But the shift was the responsibility of Western Communist leaders because of certain fundamental differences between Russia and Western Europe. "In the East the State was everything, and civil society was primordial and gelatinous; in the West there was a correct relationship between the State and civil society." However unstable the State might have appeared to be, behind it stood "a robust structure of civil society." Under these conditions, the seizure of power by a new class is unlikely to succeed without a prior victory in the area of civil society; hence, the struggle for hegemony, for cultural and moral predominance, is the main task of Marxists in the advanced countries of the West.

NOTES ON THE DEVELOPMENT
OF ITALIAN INTELLECTUALS

Gramsci had a thesis concerning Italian intellectuals: they were in the main "cosmopolitan," "supra-national," and "non-popular" (*non-nazionale-popolare*). These were negative qualities, all the more so considering the great importance that Gramsci assigned to intellectuals in the revolutionary process. It was therefore important to establish in what historical periods and under what conditions the Italian intelligentsia had become detached from the "nation" and the masses.

Gramsci dismissed Mussolini's "Roman tradition" as pure rhetoric. But, although national virtues were totally unrelated to those of ancient Italy, the detachment of Italian intellectuals might have begun in antiquity. Roman intellectuals were originally composed of two main elements: Greek and oriental freedmen who served in the imperial bureaucracy, and a large number of gifted men, deliberately enticed by offers of citizenship to establish their residence in the capital. Italy thus became the center for the cultivated classes of the whole Empire; the intellectuals there were consequently more cosmopolitan than national. Even before the collapse of the Empire, the Church had assured the continuation of this cosmopolitan detachment by taking many intellectuals into its hierarchy—of necessity trained for service to the whole Catholic world. Moreover, Catholicism's dual role as a sacred institution and a secular power determined its opposition to the Italian national spirit.

The history of the Italian written language was a significant reflection of detachment. Latin, as both an ecclesiastic and a learned language, was common to all Europe, but the language gap between the intellectuals and the masses was much greater in Italy than elsewhere, The French clergy, for example, was required to preach in the vulgate as early as the ninth century, but this practice did not become general in Italy until the thirteenth century. The written Italian language had little connection with the masses, owing to its Latin syntax and specifically Florentine vocabulary and phonetics. Italian scholars, with the partial exception of the poets, wrote for Christian Europe, not for Italy. Hence Gramsci concluded that even the tools of the intellectuals—Latin and Italian—were learned languages, and the final supremacy of Italian had little popular importance.

Gramsci asserted that the bourgeoisie of medieval city-states did develop its own category of organic intellectuals—popular poets like Cavalcanti and humanist administrators like Salutati. These men, in many ways, expressed the concrete aspirations of their class. The burghers did not, however, "assimilate" the traditional intellectuals, especially the clergy, or establish a hegemony over other social groups. By their particularism, they attempted to destroy what unity was still to be found in the universal institutions of Church and Empire, and yet were unable to establish a new kind of unity.

Gramsci found a reason for this failure of the early bourgeoisie in its primitive conception of the State—a view limited solely to the economic organization of society which he calls "economic-corporativism." All the institutions and policies of the city-state were accepted or rejected on a purely economic basis. Obviously enough, the classes whose interests countered the policies of the ruling class needed some ideological or political persuasion. Instead of developing ideological tools for obtaining the "consent of the governed," however, the city-state rulers turned to the ready-made formulas of the Church and Empire, despite the basic hostility of these two institutions to the interests of the city-state. This ideological poverty explains why every city in medieval Italy called itself either Guelph or Ghibelline, Papal or Imperial. It was not that the early Italian bourgeoisie and its intellectuals were less capable politically than the same class in France or England; but in countries less burdened with cosmopolitan universalism a national monarchy could be developed as a "superstructure" that adequately met the needs of this early bourgeoisie.

The outstanding political fact of the Italian Renaissance was the final destruction of the particularistic city-states by forces that claimed to represent medieval universalism, the Church and the Empire. From the "national-popular" point of view, the whole movement was regressive: first, because the Italian bourgeoisie, by exhausting itself in impossible attempts to found autonomous states, also lost its economic initiative; second, because even the rudimentary popularism of the city-state intellectuals was then destroyed. From then on, the political capacities of the intellectuals were directed toward personal affairs, toward the maintenance of the family and other concerns of civil society. Intellectual activity was unrelated to Italian political problems, and was commonly regarded as its own justification: it was of no concern to Cellini and Leonardo whether they were employed by an Italian prince or the King of France.

In his discussion of humanism, the major intellectual movement of the Renaissance, Gramsci followed Giuseppe Toffanin's thesis that humanism was an entirely orthodox Catholic development. Through its belief in the universality of culture as embodied in classical antiquity and the Church, humanism only intensified the cosmopolitanism of Italian intellectuals and increased their detachment from the masses. By this interpretation, humanism and the Reformation would be antithetical rather than complementary. Gramsci called humanism "a Counter-Reformation in advance . . . a barrier against a rupture in medieval universalism that was implicit in the city-state."

The Counter-Reformation itself confirmed the aloofness of Italian intellectuals, which the Church increased in two ways: by forcing the emigration of intellectuals who did not wish to submit to her discipline, and by selecting more and more Italian intellectuals for positions in the Church hierarchy, leading these intellectuals to identify themselves even more with the supra-nationality of the Church. The Papacy was forced to begin this transformation to protect itself from domination by the "national" monarchies of Spain and France. But this ostensible "nationalization" of the Church was really very different from a movement like Gallicanism, precisely because its aim was to preserve the universality of the Church. The existing "supra-nationalism" of Italian intellectuals furthered this aim.

For Gramsci, the tradition of "non-popular" cosmopolitanism was a major barrier to the unification of Italy, and seriously hindered twentieth-century Italian intellectuals in performing their proper "hegemonic" role. Niccolò Machiavelli was, however, one earlier Italian intellectual who epitomized qualities that Gramsci thought necessary for establishing a more complete and harmonious state.

NICCOLÒ MACHIAVELLI, "THE FIRST ITALIAN JACOBIN"

Liberation of Italy from the "barbarians" was the goal that led Machiavelli to create an entirely new conception of the State. In the course of his reflections, he developed a specific program for establishing a "modern" Italian State capable of defending its autonomy. Gramsci refers to Machiavelli's theory and his specific political program as a "precocious Jacobinism." Jacobinism as theory is a purely "political" approach to the problems of society, with the aim of radically changing that society. The Jacobin establishes a pattern for society, and then employs all his force to create it; he knows what he wants and how to get it. As a specific political program, Jacobinism would aim at founding a coordinated national state by allying major urban classes, such as the proletariat and the petty bourgeoisie, with the peasants. This alliance can be initiated by establishing a national militia, drawing members from all these classes; it is strengthened by a series of myths (based on reality) that the populace will enthusiastically accept.

This is the abstract program of "Jacobinism." But it is also important to examine the real historical role of the French Jacobins, those "energetic and resolute men," those "creators of irreparable *faits accomplis*" who impelled the bourgeoisie forward with "kicks in the behind." Important in the ultimate success of the Jacobins, said Gramsci, was the heterogeneity of the Third Estate. Its principal elements were an economically advanced but politically moderate group and a "disparate" intellectual elite; thus the class expressed a variety of political positions, depending upon general circumstances. At the beginning of the Revolution, the Third Estate had, in fact, demanded only reforms that interested the "actual physical components" of its social group—that is, reforms that satisfied its immediate "corporative" interests. But this stage was ended by the resistance of the old social forces and by foreign threats to even these limited revolutionary gains.

At this point the Jacobins, "a new elite," stepped forward. They thought of the bourgeoisie as "the hegemonic leadership of all the popular forces." The Jacobins consequently opposed any compromises that might isolate the bourgeoisie from its popular base, and this intransigence gave them a special rôle in the Revolution. They stood for the present and future needs "of all the national groups that were to be assimilated by the fundamental existing group." Particularly important for Gramsci, because of the class structure in Italy, was the acceptance of Jacobin rule by the peasantry, which eventually understood that the Old Regime could be defeated only by a peasant alliance with the "most advanced forces of the Third Estate, not with the moderate Girondins." True, the Jacobins "forced the hand" of the revolutionary movement; but they did this on a solid historical basis by making the bourgeoisie both the dominant class (the class holding State power) and the "hegemonic" class.

Gramsci concluded that "Jacobinism was a categorical incarnation of the Prince," or conversely, that Machiavelli was the first Italian Jacobin. All of Machiavelli's political and historical work should be interpreted in this light; the *Prince* and the *Art of War* are especially relevant. Much misunderstanding and dislike of Machiavelli was occasioned by failure to see him as a man of his age. Machiavelli is often accused of fostering despotism, but considering the political immaturity of the early bourgeoisie and the inherent limitations of the economic-corporative city-states, absolute monarchy was really an instrument of revolutionary progress, an essential element in forming a superstructure organically related to the State's economic life. In reality, the *Prince* was primarily not a systematic treatise on political science, but an appeal for the organization of an Italian State, formulated in a truly Jacobin manner. In the main body of the text, Machiavelli outlined, with scientific detachment, exactly what was necessary to achieve this goal; in the epilogue, he appealed with great eloquence and passion for popular support in fulfilling his plan.

Gramsci also rejects the common notion that Machiavelli was a "visionary" and not a "realist." He was not a realist in the sense that he limited his attentions to the sphere of political actuality. Instead, he was concerned with "what ought to be"—realistically—and therefore applied his intellect and will to projecting a new relationship of classes and institutions in Italy. But these classes and institutions were "real" entities, and Machiavelli analyzed them in a thoroughly "Jacobin" manner: beginning with the actual social structure, he established a goal that was attainable through resolute political direction of forces in the structure. Gramsci, in fact, concluded that only this Jacobin attitude is realistic, because it alone can deal with historical reality.

If the *Prince* indicated Machiavelli's Jacobin attitude, then the *Art of War* was proof of his Jacobin program. In it Machiavelli outlined plans for creating a national militia, a citizen army composed of both urban and rural classes. Gramsci emphasized the Florentine statesman's awareness that neither an effective militia nor a powerful state could be created without bringing the peasants into political life. The similarity of this program with that of the later Jacobins was important evidence that Machiavelli was a sixteenth-century "Jacobin."

It was certainly not Machiavelli's cultural "nationalism" that appealed to Gramsci. This was an old motif in Italian culture, and in any case Gramsci was not a "nationalist." There are, however, three ideas in the *Prince* that are remarkably close to the spirit of Jacobinism. First, the last chapter of the *Prince* was an "Exhortation to Liberate Italy from the Barbarians"; Machiavelli appealed directly to the masses, over the heads of various Italian State governments. This was unique for an Italian intellectual of that time. Second, Machiavelli knew that force alone would not guarantee the success of his political program. Ultimately, the "best fortress [of the Prince] is the love of the people; for although you may have fortresses, they will not save you if you are hated by the people." This was an early statement of the crucial importance of "spiritual" leadership—hegemony—in the political struggle, not unlike that practiced by the Jacobins. Finally, it would be hard to find a better example of the Jacobin propensity to deal with problems in a "purely political" spirit—and with "energy and resolution"—than Machiavelli's introduction to the 17th Chapter of the *Prince*:

> I say that every prince must desire to be considered merciful and not cruel. He must, however, take care not to misuse this mercifulness. Cesare Borgia was considered cruel, but his cruelty brought order to the Romagna, united it, and reduced it to peace and fealty. If this is considered well, it will be seen that he was really much more merciful than the Florentine people, who, to avoid the name of cruelty, allowed Pistoia to be destroyed.

There is a whole new world of politics in this statement. It may not yet be "Jacobinism," but it is even further from the cosmopolitan detachment of intellectuals contemporary with Machiavelli.

LEONARD KRIEGER
The Intellectuals and European Society [1]

H. Stuart Hughes noted the demise of the "system-builders" after the generation of the 1890's. Since then no total, coherent cosmology has re-emerged. Leonard Krieger's article on the modern European intellectual traces some of the consequences of that fragmentation in philosophy—the loss of a describable unity in reality which once allowed the intellectual to function as the seer and interpreter. In the absence of total meaning, Krieger notices, the intellectuals have been reduced from the vanguard to stragglers behind a society running ahead of their comprehension. In phenomenonology, logical-positivism, and existentialism, the dominant philosophical strains when the following article was written, Krieger sees both a confident revision of the nineteenth-century systems and a rather forlorn hope to rediscover the harmonious concretization of philosophy and function enjoyed in the eighteenth century.

In the case of Gramsci's "organic" intellectual, the tension between ideal and reality is relieved in fulfilling the needs of the dominant social structure. For the "traditional" intellectual, for most purposes identical with Krieger's "liberal intellectual," twentieth-century realities are full of paralyzing dilemmas and threats of extinction. Consequently, as both Krieger and Nolte mark, the crisis of twentieth-century thought lies in the vain pursuit of a meaningful contemporary transcendence.

RECENT EVALUATIONS have tended to pass one of two judgments upon the European intellectuals. It has been concluded either that they live in isolation from their society and say nothing relevant to it or that they are entirely submerged in the society and merely reflect it.[2] The facts to which these judgments refer are clear enough. On the one hand, intellectuals have adopted a critical position vis-a-vis all the important social and political forces of the

Reprinted with permission from the *Political Science Quarterly*, Vol. 67 (June 1952), pp. 225-247.

[1] This paper was originally delivered before the European Seminar of Columbia University's European Institute in March 1951. (ed.)

[2] An excellent article which goes beyond these categories is by Kenneth Douglas, "The French Intellectuals: Situation and Outlook", in Edward Mead Earle, ed., *Modern France: Problems of the Third and Fourth Republics* (Princeton, 1951), pp. 61-81.

day, which offer no foothold for their ideas. The continental middle classes have moved into confessional parties in which clerical and economic interests predominate; the secular liberal parties have been reduced to splinter groups of the Right; the working class adheres either to a communism which has a set, unalterable doctrine or to socialist parties which can no longer afford a clear theoretical basis; the organizations of the Resistance are dead—Sartre wrote their epitaph with his withdrawal from the *Rassemblement Democratique Révolutionnaire*, which he had helped to found in their image. On the other hand, intellectuals have adopted an apologetic position vis-a-vis institutional forces—state, party, church, or university—on which they are increasingly forced to depend for their livelihood and for their continued intellectual existence. The factors behind this development range from the bureaucratization of the intellectuals which has grown out of the shrinkage of middle-class inherited incomes and the financial instability of the general periodical—the disappearance of *Horizon* and *Die Wandlung* are outstanding cases in point—to the threat which the Soviet danger poses for freedom of expression as the intellectuals have known it.

These alternative conclusions are susceptible of two rather obvious explanations. The first is that the same phenomenon is judged by different writers from divergent points of view. A prevalence of esoteric themes, for example, can be interpreted either as a product of intellectual isolation or as an evasion of responsibility accruing to the intellectuals' uncritical submergence in society. The second explanation is that the judgments refer to different groups of intellectuals: the liberal intellectuals are in general identifiable as the critics; Communist intellectuals, orthodox religious thinkers, academicians and civil servants are identified as the apologists. But despite the variant judgments and distinctions an important problem remains: what are the general conceptions held by the intellectuals which form the background of their social ideas and on which the judgments of them must be based? Interest in these general conceptions represents more than mere idle curiosity, for it is often the general outlook of an intellectual rather than his social position as such that defines him. Thus, the extent to which a Catholic, an academic, or even a governmental intellectual is subordinated to the institution with which he is associated may well depend not simply upon his association with that institution but also upon his ideas about the nature of reality in general, social reality in particular, and the specific role of his institution in it. This function of ideas permits a variety of social relationships for the intellectuals. Conceptions which allow or encourage intellectuals to find a secure haven with some recognized social or political organization are of little interest, for by and large they come to terms with official doctrines which are well known. Likewise, conceptions which influence intellectuals toward a total unconcern with society supply little substance for an understanding of European society. But those conceptions which imply a tension in the intellectual because they are addressed to social reality and yet are unable wholly to penetrate it—such conceptions are objects of general concern.

The importance of this kind of general conception lies in the promise which it holds out to men that ideas can build a platform out from the world into an absolute realm from which the world can be moved. For an age in which the unitary strands of social experience have tended to unravel and in which tinkering with the resultant parts has been relegated to the efficiency expert, the presence of total views which are somehow connected with experience seems to offer the only possibility of organizing and improving the elements of this concrete existence. To revert to a previous illustration, religious thinkers who seek not so much to rationalize the existing role of faith and the churches by exegeses of traditional doctrine as to interpret anew their function on the basis of the new general insights of the age, academicians who are not content to remain within the framework of their special fields but go beyond them to apply their knowledge and their methods to general problems of humanity—such men participate in the crucial issue before the modern intellectual.

However various its manifestations, this kind of problem may be accounted the problem par excellence of the liberal intellectuals, if liberal be defined for this purpose as referring to that habit of mind which manifests anxiety about the concrete organization of life, is yet dissatisfied with current forms of organization, and is ever open to new ideal impulses which seek to develop this organization beyond those forms. In this sense, "liberal" includes not only representatives of the familiar secular political tradition nor only the intellectuals free of all institutional attachment, but rather all those intellectuals who, whatever their mundane ties, are responsive to general currents which come from beyond those associations and create a tension in them.

The attempt will be made here to deal with some of the general attitudes which form the background for the social and political orientation of European intellectuals who are "liberal" in this broad sense.

II

Some background is required to give an idea of the direction in which European thinkers have been travelling, for twentieth-century thought is composed of such a peculiar melange of old and new elements that only a historical analysis will enable us to discover what is distinctive about it.

Although there is some doubt as to whether the lay intellectual has his origins in the Roman rhetorician or the Italian humanist, we may finesse that issue. The story, for our purposes, begins in the eighteenth century. It is at this point that the social position of the liberal intellectual and the substance of his thought meet in such a way as both to make him an effective force in society and to create the problem which is his main concern today. The position of the intellectual combined two elements: he still carried over from the humanists his consciousness of being a member of an autonomous spiritual estate, with all the critical functions of the *clerc* attributed to this estate by Julien Benda (himself a good eighteenth-century type); but he was at the same time, usually by origin and almost unanimously by conviction, representative of the aims of the liberal aristocracy and the middle classes, so that the standards of his criticism were not simply those of the conscience of the society but entailed a program for a new order. This position of the intellectual manifested itself in the character of his message. In the first place, he had no need to concern himself with "pure thought", since the presuppositions of his thinking had been worked out in the meta-physical and scientific systems of the seventeenth-century, and since, on the basis of this security, he could limit himself to what concerned human affairs. In the second place, the so-called rational synthesis of the eighteenth century was, in content, the perfect meeting-ground for the cosmos and the individual. The external frame of meaning and the goals of the individual were considered to be entirely consonant; reality and ideals were homogeneous. Hence there was no bar to the realization of ideals, and the instrument of this realization was the free society. Consequently, there was no hindrance to the intellectual's immersing himself in social reality, for it was to this arena that he was naturally led, without fear of corruption, even by his contemplation of the eternal verities. And so the intellectual sallied forth to do battle against those phenomena of existence which were malevolent and, in a sense, illusory, thereby fulfilling his traditional function while yet pointing the way for a specific social group with whose material goals he did not identify himself.

The collapse of this rational synthesis, manifested in Immanuel Kant and the French Revolution, brought a real crisis of conscience to the intellectuals. The world of existences had shown itself to be, whether through the Revolution or the reaction, infinitely more complex and less manageable than had been supposed. Nevertheless, despite an initial reaction during the early years of the nineteenth century in which the synthesis was replaced by a confusion of partial complexes of thought, such as romanticism and Destutt de Tracy's sensationalism, and intellectuals recoiled back before the problems of political and social reality (it is not entirely fortuitous that Destutt de Tracy coined the term "ideology" at this time), they soon returned to the charge, built up systematic world-views and operated socially within them. But their ideas and their situation had undergone a significant change. The external framework of man's activity was no longer considered homogeneous with men's purposes; but while not of the same stuff as these purposes, yet it was compatible with them. The cosmic pattern imposed certain limits upon man's activity but yet permitted and even encouraged men to achieve their goals within those limits. But this implied an ambivalent attitude toward the world of existence, and in a sense the emphasis on reality which has been called the hallmark of the nineteenth century was a function of the necessity for careful examination of and abstraction from this reality to secure what was usable for man in it—the rational for philosophical idealists, the lawful and pragmatic for positivists and scientists. History became essential even to systematic thinkers for the working out of the implicit conflict between the two aspects of reality—that is, the external world and the internal ideal.

The immediate consequence of such preconceptions, visible particularly in the middle third of the nineteenth century, was to bring the systematizers into more intense participation in political and social reality than ever before, for their systems demanded man's concrete activity to work out the oppositions within the world (hence the difficulty of classifying men like Comte, Marx, Mill and Spencer within any specific field of thought). While conservative intellectuals appeared upon the scene and underlined the complexity of reality, the bulk of the thinkers continued to plug the same libertarian values, realizable through society, as had been advanced in the eighteenth century. However, as the century wore on into the 70s and 80s, the ever-growing consciousness of the multiplicity of reality began to take its toll. With conflicting material interests coming to dominate the political and social scene in an unprecedentedly unabashed form, the intellectuals tended to split up in a way far more basic than the political or even the philosophical differences between them. One section, perceiving this arena to be impervious to their ideals, withdrew to the Olympian heights of general criticism, while the others subordinated their theories to the interests of the institutions with which they cast their lot and became rooted in a self-consciously middle-class society. The latter tendency was reinforced by the development among academicians of a characteristic type of scholar who lived off the new specialization of disciplines and addressed himself to the study of isolated aspects of existence. Though neither necessarily nor universally definitive of the academic profession, this development, by slighting the general relationships of particular studies, has had the effect of excluding a sizable group of lay thinkers from the ranks of the intellectuals.

III

Even allowing for the inevitable errors of perspective, the thinking of our own century seems infinitely complex. The positions which Western man has taken for the past two thousand years all seem to reappear upon the scene and demand once more to be recognized as ultimate solutions. Religious thought in mystical, eschatological, or humanistic interpretations, rationalism, scientific materialism, idealism, are all in the arena still, not simply as the remnants of intellectual traditions but revivified, almost blatant in their present claims. But this very coexistence bespeaks a common element in the intellectual situation in which they spawn. A frame of reference which permits of so many divergent interpretations is hardly any longer a single frame of reference. Karl Jaspers has said that complete systems of thought are no longer possible, that there is no longer any possibility of comprehending the whole of reality. What has happened is that the reality which was so ambivalently conceived by the nineteenth-century thinkers has lost that aspect which made it rational to man and compatible with his purposes. It has lost its cohesive power and has become fragmented; its total meaning has disappeared. And since reality in this sense is taken to include society as well as cosmos, it would seem that the tendencies exhibited in the latter part of the nineteenth century—hypercriticism, withdrawal, or subordination—have been carried through to their logical conclusions, that the ideas of the European intellectuals tend to escapism or to treason and their consequent position in society to impotence.

Certainly, this seems to be the reigning conception of the present status of the European intellectuals, one that is inherent in the mood of their literature and that constitutes the chief impression from current surveys of the situation.[3] Moreover, there would seem to be good evidence, aside from literature, for such a conclusion. An important segment of European thought between the wars was dominated by a combination of nihilism and activism, by the conception, that is, that a meaningless and mechanized world was closing down upon man and that the only possibility for man's self-assertion in such a world—and this possibility was limited—lay in the powerful deed, in which would be harnessed the primitive life-forces of elemental nature; the very fact of such deeds, rather than their ends, would be the triumph against the encroaching meaninglessness of which men's apathy and powerlessness were considered an integral part.

A corollary was the tendency to adhere to the social unit from which such power could be most effectively drawn and the hierarchical organization of society which would permit it to be utilized. This group, exemplified in the circle of *Die Tat* in Germany, was balanced by those who continued to believe in the values inherited from the eighteenth and nineteenth centuries but who, confronted with the utter imperviousness of reality to those values, could do little but talk of crisis. If the first group moved one step further along the road to immersion of thought in life, the second manifested an extension of the movement of late nineteenth-century criticism in the direction of withdrawal, since they had lost the notion of an essential system of reality which this criticism had had and consequently had lost the toehold in social reality from which to work.

For these movements to be understood aright it must be emphasized that they were reactions against the nineteenth-century systems and particularly reactions against the form which those systems took during the early part of the twentieth century in their

---

[3] For example, *Saturday Review of Literature*, January 13, 1951.

first attempt to accommodate themselves to the new conception of reality; for the period from about 1890 until just after the First World War witnessed the return of the older idealism, in both its philosophical and its general moral sense, to the attempt to impregnate a balky reality with value. This was, significantly, the period of the neo-idealism, with both variants of a neo-Kantianism and a neo-Hegelianism, as well as a revisionism which amounted to a neo-Marxism, both of the Right and the Left.

This was the period, too, in which it was realized that the former conceptions of a rational reality which permitted the realization of the ideal must be replaced by a new synthesis in which the ideal had to be worked, through the intensified activity of man, into a reality which could no longer be conceived systematically and to which consequently concessions had to be made. Thus the new German intellectual liberalism, of the Max Weber-Naumann stamp, combining a social ethic with national power. Thus the Fabian marriage of convenience with trade unionism. Thus the French insistence, in an Alain, a Péguy, a Jaurès, on justice and integrity not as qualifying but as replacing a general system of thought. And thus, on a philosophical plane, the tendency of the neo-Kantians to scrap the *Ding-an-sich* and to proceed to emphasize beyond Kant the activity of human consciousness and particularly the necessity of communal action for ethical ends. For these groups, the nature of reality no longer afforded a coherent totality, but society, which represented the mediating sphere between man and this general reality and partook of elements of both, was still accessible to man. It was the First World War and its aftermath which effectively brought this attempt at reintegration to a close, which lined up society on the side of alien power, and which consequently fed into the undercurrent of general skepticism which had been developing from Nietzsche and Pareto.

This is not the whole story of the period, however. At this point we must distinguish between levels of intellectual activity. The process described above—that is, the new attempt at the realization of ideals and the subsequent combination of disappointment, pessimism and activism—certainly reflected the climate of the age, but at the same time it represented what we may call the secondary stage of ideas: that is, it represented attempts at adaptation by original thinkers and attempts at application by publicizers of ideas developed in a previous period. Simultaneously, however, thinkers began to work on another, a primary, level: apart from the social and the material forces of their age, they began to develop new philosophies to interpret directly, rather than through the medium of older ideas and values, the general experience of their age. That this experience called for a new approach is perhaps evident in the fact that for the first time since Hegel men demanded that philosophy retrieve itself from the function into which it had fallen of examining the methods and assumptions of the special disciplines, notably in the relationship of positivism to the natural sciences, and undertake a new and fundamental examination of reality. Hence some characterization—however superficial—of these new philosophies is probably more appropriate to and revealing of the general assumptions of the age which has produced them than the general mood expressed on other levels of thinking.

What is immediately striking about the new lines of thought is the difficulty of defining them. Not only has none of them achieved any position of predominance but even within each general tendency individual thinkers diverge markedly, thereby testifying to the breakdown of any accepted general framework of reality or of thought. "Schools" of thought, then, in the strict sense, are not to be looked for. With this reservation, however, certain classifications of philosophies of recent vintage can be discerned. The phenomenologists and the logical positivists represent transitions from older types of thought into the present age, the latter, to be sure, only in the logical rather than the chronological sense of transition. Consequently, they contain elements like phenomenology's aim of establishing philosophy as a rigorous science and its assumption of the essential rationality of reality and like logical positivism's self-dedication to explicating the bases and methods of the sciences, which are not wholly typical of contemporary thinking. But in other elements they are truly representative: not only does the phenomenological method, which is radical and dynamic rather than analytic and static, receive widespread current application, but its attitude toward the world of existence, in requiring the suspension of existence for the comprehension of rational essences, recognizes both its potentialities and its obfuscations; logical positivism reveals an implicit tension in its superimposition of "convenient" systems of symbolic logic, for the explication of meaning, upon the empirical basis which is, for it, the only knowable reality and yet of which these systems are structurally independent.

Here these two kinds of thought fall into line with the types of thinking which are peculiarly characteristic of our time: first, the philosophies of experience or process or life, manifested variously in metaphysicians like Alexander and Whitehead, idealists like Croce and Collingwood, and the philosophies of history associated with historicism, with or without their neo-Kantian attempts at an absolute, but generally having in common the rejection of stable concepts based upon an organized reality in favor of approximations to autonomous entities somehow experienced or intuited or pragmatically comprehended in their flight through time and history (the American counterpart would be pragmatism, and only here does this category show a genuine school); secondly, the familiar doctrines of existentialism, in its Christian and secular forms. One might add, of the older schools which have been decisively influenced by this newer thought, the Catholic personalism of Mounier and Marcel,[4] and the Protestant writings of the Barth and Tillich stripe.[5] What, for our purposes, can be said to be common to all these modern philosophies?

The basic attitude which must be emphasized, because it is so

[4] Catholic personalism represents the organization and development of a more general mode of thought going back to the latter years of the nineteenth century. Born in the reaction against the dissolution of the individual by scientific empiricism (particularly in psychology) and objective idealism, the explication of the integral "person" as a central concept found its chief early representatives in Charles Renouvier and Wilhelm Stern, and, in this country, at the University of California from 1919. The concept was taken up by the group of French Catholics around Mounier and Marcel (Denis de Rougemont is the one Protestant prominently represented) as a result of the world depression of 1929, and in this form has found an organ in the periodical *Esprit*, founded in 1932; its German counterpart can be studied in Walter Dirks and his *Frankfurter Hefte*. While this latest form of the concept may be said to be responsible for the "ism" in personalism, the movement is not to be regarded as constituting either a philosophical system or a political doctrine. Its proponents view it rather as an approach, an attitude, with nothing exclusive about it. What is characteristic of this approach is the equal emphasis upon the absolute and the relative, the ideal and the material, the moral and the social, the individual and the community. The "person", for these thinkers, represents the focal point for the necessary interplay of these vital elements: as opposed to the concept of the "individual", now tainted by scientific thought and classical economics, the "person" is the incarnation of totality in disperse and partial temporal history and consequently is the necessary center for any action which is to be both ethically determined and practically effective.

[5] It is, of course, arbitrary to lump recent Protestant thought together in this way. Karl Barth's neo-orthodoxy, for example, is very different in its original from Paul Tillich's religious socialism. In their later development, however, these two movements have drawn closer together, with Barth's provision for a social theory and Tillich's construction of a general philosophy.

contrary to the general conception of modern thought, is its confidence. The fragmentation of reality, the loss of meaning, is to these schools nothing absolute; it is not the mark of failure of nerve or of mind, but rather is the result of errors of previous philosophy which posed a false set of questions and emerged with a false set of answers the illusory character of which is simply being proved in our age. Abjuring systems and arbitrary distinctions, such as the subject-object distinction, upon which systems have been founded, contemporary thought begins from what it considers to be irreducibles—the individual entity and immediate experience. The character of the individual entities varies, of course, with the specific philosophy; in the theories of process and in logical positivism, they are the individual "occasion" and the individual sense-datum which is experienced; in phenomenology and existentialism they are the individual mind or consciousness which experiences. For our purposes, however, these distinctions are not decisive. What is decisive is the common surrender or at least suspension of the conviction that the grasping of reality must be sought through its total coherence in favor of the conviction that the individual entity is a microcosm and is therefore the proper and indispensable basis for a new approach to reality. Moreover, it follows that the very dissolution of reality through the destruction of the absolute subject by history and the destruction of the absolute object by the new science—this very dissolution of reality into process which throws the totality of the process into the realm of the unknown—makes possible an unprecedently certain grasp of the individual constituents of that process; for the knower and the known are integral in experience. Knowledge can be attained only through concrete participation in a life-process which is made up of autonomous individuals. Knowledge then comes, not from contemplation, but from creative activity; this activity concretizes being into individual experience. Thus free, concrete participation makes up, according to this view, the individual life-process which is the basic stuff of reality.

The problem raised by this conception is clear: how does the individual entity, immersed in its own process, get beyond itself, how does it come to a relationship with the other entities and the other processes and thereby attain some knowledge of the whole? How, in other words, is meaning infused into the experience of the individual entity? This, of course, is the decisive question; for, having attained some security of knowledge through transferring the basis of their consideration from the reality of the world in general to the arena of the individual world, this question involves the return to the traditional problem of the general coherence of reality. The issue is not shirked by modern thinkers, who are proud of having escaped, to their own satisfaction, the dangers of solipsism and who extend their feeling of confidence from the comprehension of individual entities to the possibility of building the general structure of reality on this basis. Thus the phenomenological method includes not only a process of reduction, but one of the "constitution of the world", while some logical positivists, at least, reject what they call the "reductive fallacies" of old-fashioned positivism in favor of an "attitude of reconstruction".

The acknowledgement of the problem, however, does not mean that complete solutions have been worked out, but the general lines which such solutions should take have been indicated. In general, the answers given in modern thought revolve around the concept of transcendence, a concept which has undergone a change in meaning along with the general shift in the locus of thinking. Whereas formerly transcendence referred to a reality beyond and above the whole cosmos known by man and was therefore simply descriptive of two realms of reality, it now refers to a reality to be known or created within the cosmos beyond the particular experience of individual men at a certain time and a certain place and consequently becomes not simply a description but an actual power in the lives of men, opening them to the possibilities of action in a meaningful world beyond the here and now. By reason, then, of the individualized basis of reality, the concept of transcendence has become central in modern thought, not only for the question of ultimate reality, but even for the question of this-worldly reality.

The specific interpretations of this concept vary with each thinker, but for our purpose we may distinguish two different types of treatment of the problem of transcendence. In the first type, only faith in God gives assurance of the coherence of all process and consequently of a meaning which can give direction to the individual life-process; that is, which can draw each moment of the process beyond itself and thereby provide not only the goals but also the very basis for continuous creation. Most of contemporary thought expounds or assumes a transcendence of this kind. The second type of transcendence is represented primarily by Heidegger and Sartre: through "conscience" and "decision", man, by an exercise of his sovereign freedom, engages himself in existence, from his interaction with existence he establishes goals for his own action and thereby, by creating being, transcends his immediate situation, his immediate experience. It should be noted that for neither type is the substantive direction of the transcendence clear, save for the specifically Christian section of the divine transcendentalists who fill the gap with revelation. For the others, transcendence seems to represent simply the categorical imperative to go beyond the present; the substance of the absolute thereby postulated seems to be no more than the sum of the individual absolutes which by its richness and diversity manifests the value of human freedom.

IV

This has been a difficult and abstract excursion, but one necessary to uncover the assumptions behind the kind of writing which the intellectuals have been doing since the war; for undoubtedly the chief issue for the intellectual has become that of engagement, and what this means can hardly be understood without reference to the total assumptions of the age. The external evidences of engagement are manifold. Not only do the general reviews intermingle philosophical, literary, political and social articles—with the purpose, as Dolf Sternberger announced in *Die Wandlung*, "of drawing Spirit into practical responsibility and illuminating politics with Spirit"— but leading exponents of the new philosophies have come down into the publicistic and even into the political arena (with the notable exception of Heidegger).

What we have called the primary and the secondary stages of ideas now meet on even terms in the discussion of European social and political problems. Most striking here have been the yearly meetings of the *Rencontres Internationales de Genève*, where philosophers like Karl Jaspers, Georg Lukacs, Nicholas Berdyaev, Merleau-Ponty, Guido de Ruggiero and Karl Barth and men of letters like André Siegfried, Julien Benda, Pierre Hervé, Georges Bernanos, Stephen Spender, Hans Paeschke and Denis de Rougemont have met to discuss problems which live in that intermediate zone of value between philosophy and society—problems like the European Spirit, Technical Progress and Moral Progress, Toward a New Humanism. The temper of these discussions is well illustrated by an incident which took place early in the discussion of technical and moral progress. One participant arose and tendered to the assembly a piece of advice, taken, he said, from an old Eskimo proverb: when you want to hunt the seal in the sea, don't go whistling in the mountains. This admonition to present concrete proposals for action took the conference by storm, thereby revealing the deep-rooted desire of European intellectuals to apply themselves to the solution of political and social problems.

From an external point of view, then, it would seem that the most recent period of European thought has been characterized not so much by the development of new philosophies as by the general recognition of the necessity for the intellectual to engage himself in the political and social arena. This simple interpretation of engagement, however, does not suffice either to explain the concept as the Europeans hold it or to explain what, under its aegis, the intellectuals are trying to do. It might be mentioned, in the first place, that such an interpretation is hardly distinctive, for in the 1840's this kind of engagement was precisely the rallying cry of the Young Hegelians in general and of the young Karl Marx in particular for their revision of Hegel. But secondly, and more important, the injunction to engage in social reality seems rather superfluous to an age which has been thinking along the lines which have been analyzed above: when the individual is so immersed in process, in existence, it is hardly a contribution to tell him to immerse himself still further.

Actually, engagement means two things. First, it states the fact, implied in all contemporary thinking, that men *are engaged* in existence, willy-nilly, and that consequently contemplative, static thought is an illusion. But secondly, it means that men *should be engaged* to transcendence, that is, to the moral purpose which reaches out beyond man's immediate existence and in the light of which he undertakes the creative activity which gives meaning to his life. This double meaning is clear not only in Gabriel Marcel, who, incidentally, seems to have coined the term "engagement" in its contemporary philosophical usage, but in Heidegger as well. The implication of the double meaning of engagement is a dual attitude toward society.

In the first place, the individual *is engaged* in society; the existence of other individuals about him, the existence of social and political institutions, help to make up the total situation which goes to form the experience of the individual and hence to help make him what he is: in this sense, society is on the one hand necessary and on the other neutral or nauseous for the individual.

In the second place, however, the individual *should strive* to transform the original engagement to society into a moral one; through engagement to his own transcendent goal, he opens himself to an absolute (which he either attains or creates) which becomes the ground not only of his own personality but of his recognition of the personality of others and of his essential personal relationship to them.

The fundamental nature of this duality is reflected widely in contemporary thought, for society is seen increasingly as the arena in which the crucial struggles that are to decide man's destiny must be fought out: society is viewed both as an embodiment of the concrete existence in which man is immersed and as an instrument for the transcending of that existence. In the abstract form which much of contemporary German writing gives it, the duality appears in the prevalence of such themes as sleep, silence, phantasy, which are deemed to give man, apart from society, the continuity and the coherence which the broken-up rational articulation of society lacks and with which it must be supplied from outside itself. It appears too in such discussions as the one graced by the Eskimo proverb mentioned above; for, despite the acclaim accorded the demand for practical solutions, the subsequent debate was interrupted periodically by equally urgent warnings of the perils of unremitting social concretion and by demands for purification through discussion of philosophical principles. The duality is striking in Immanuel Mounier's idea of the basically dramatic quality of human history, of the eternal withdrawal and return of Christian faith, characterized at once by transcendence and incarnation, from and to human society, which alternately is fructified by that faith, attracting it into social participation, and corrupts it, repelling it into an extra-social realm for its self-purgation. The duality is evident too in the many current spiral conceptions of human history, which bespeak the alternation between man's creative transformation of his social world and the oppressive weight of this world upon man's freedom. Indeed, in these ideas the infinite drama, with its implications of ultimate imperfection and incompleteness, is not only necessary but desirable, because it provides an ever-recurring challenge to man's assertion of his freedom and of his creative capacities. This line of thought is closely associated with the conception of man's self-alienation and self-recovery which are present in the thought of Hegel and emphatic in the thought of Marx. It is the present relevance of this conception which helps to explain the recent revival, in France at least, of interest in the young Hegel and the young Marx. It helps to explain too why the same climate which leads intellectuals toward existential forms of thought leads so many also to Marxism.

V

Given the emphasis upon engagement, the concern of the intellectuals with specific social and political issues follows naturally, but, since the concept of engagement is part of a general attitude and not of a philosophical system, the applications are not logically consequent. The content of such applications is not given in structured social and political theories. If the ideas in this field contain a pattern, it must be elicited from a series of concrete proposals. Here two examples of such proposals will be examined: on the social problem and on the problem of the nation-state.

The connection between the intellectuals' general concept of man and their judgment upon the present condition of European society lies in their conviction that the present situation represents an epitome in the process of man's self-alienation. There is widespread preoccupation with the problem of the technical civilization in all its ramifications: mechanization of labor, of the state, of public opinion, of war, and even of thought—the last in the form usually of a critique of the older Cartesian basis of scientific thinking. This concern is hardly new, and it must be owned that the solutions preferred are hardly much of a novelty either. They are in agreement on the necessity of what in general seems to be a liberal socialism. What is surprising is, first, the enthusiastic propounding of such a solution, secondly, the general theoretical agreement on the subject, and, thirdly, the basis of their position. For the basic motif is neither democratic nor socialistic, but rather individualistic. And this in two senses: first, that ultimately the highest values to be served are values of the individual, and second, that the only possible means of social salvation are these same values of the individual.

What are these values? The names given them are familiar: humanism, liberty, moral spirit. Only these forces, coming from the inherent creative power of individuals—and particularly intellectuals—can create a society in which these forces will be safeguarded. Where then does the socialism come in? Socialism is simply a required condition of engagement and partakes of the dual nature of engagement. It is considered both as an inevitable aspect of the hostile social world in which the spirit must work and as a portion of the transcendent goal to which the spirit must commit itself if man is to recover control over his destiny. This kind of thinking scarcely constitutes a rigorous political system and actually within its framework there is at least one important distinction. For those who fill the labels humanism, liberty, moral spirit, with a traditional content, the emphasis is upon the individual, upon the liberal in liberal socialism.

This tendency is particularly true for men like Karl Jaspers, whose acceptance of the necessity of socialism is reluctant indeed, and finds its extreme expression in the Moral Rearmanent group . . . . For the Catholic personalists, who seek to infuse traditional Christian values with a radically new interpretation, individualism and socialism are in delicate balance—and tension. For those thinkers, finally, who consider the common labels simply as forms which provide the necessary conditions of social action but which require a new content that cannot be defined in advance, the emphasis tends to be upon the socialism, in the faith that experience will create a new and genuine relationship between the individual and society and will thereby also create a new ethic. Thus when Sartre helped found his political organization in 1948, he defined its program simply to be revolutionary democratic socialism as a transcendent goal arising from the projection of man's freedom in his actual social situation, but at the same time he admitted that a theory which would bridge the gap between the conditions and the goal could be established only through discussion based upon the experience of the association itself. It can be said that this pattern, in which the initial reality is firmly comprehended, the final goal generally envisaged, and the connecting social means entirely confused, is a quality bequeathed to political thinking by the general character of contemporary thought.

The absence of a clear line capable of resolving in action the dual conception of engagement leaves the impression that the European intellectuals feel the need both to take account of and yet carefully to skirt around every vital force in European society. The repeated injunction that men remain "open" to all possible experience, the conviction that all systems contain partial truths, the emphasis upon attitude as opposed to doctrine, with the concomitant striving to penetrate all groups and parties rather than to form parties themselves (hence the recent emphasis on the "Rally" and the "Movement" as against the "Party")—all these ideas testify to the eclecticism of contemporary political thought.

At the same time, however, it must be said that the vagueness of the social thinking by European intellectuals today is at least in part attributable to the conviction that the social problem is not, as such, the ultimate one in the current political scene. This consideration brings us to our second illustration of the results of the intellectuals' engagement—their proposals concerning the nation-state; for what does seem to be ultimate, for them, is the general problem of transcending the old nation-state and of achieving a new level from which European society may take a new start and on which the old formulas may assume new meanings. The prevalent concern with European unity is, for the intellectuals, not so much an issue in itself as a possible wedge into the solution of this general problem. Silone has written that the old distinction between Right and Left, as measured in political or social terms, is an anachronism, and must give way to what is today the essential distinction—pro-union and anti-union of Europe—on the grounds that the social problem cannot be resolved within the traditional framework given by the national state.

As far as the international relations of the intellectuals themselves are concerned, the problem of European integration seems to present no great obstacles. Writers of different nationalities meet together in discussion, write in one another's journals, and study one another's output. Again, although no system of thought exists to which intellectuals of various nationalities can subscribe—save possibly Catholic personalism, and this has obvious limitations for unity—the break-up into various schools has not followed national lines. It is true that the empirical tradition remains strongly dominant in England—and this must be accounted an element in the general position of England vis-à-vis Europe—but on the continent the influential role of existentialism in France and Germany, and of Crocean idealism in Italy, is hardly exclusive. In any case, the day has long passed when adherence to a philosophy implied a definite political position or vice versa, and the general presuppositions behind contemporary thought are sufficiently uniform and sufficiently flexible to permit the kind of agreement on general social and political principles such as those discussed above. . . . . .

VI

What, then, can we conclude from this analysis of the European intellectuals?

First, they are convinced that they can understand the reality of our world and our society and that this reality, by reason of its very discontinuity, can be acted upon, within limits, by man.

Second, as their difficult concept of engagement attests, they are making the effort themselves to come to grips with political and social reality while avoiding submergence in it. In this respect they are trying to steer a difficult course in order to arrive at a position approximating the one held in the eighteenth century.

Third, they differ markedly from the eighteenth-century intellectuals in that their political and social ideas do not lead society but rather seem to lag behind it. Despite the new context which they bring to values like humanism, the person, liberty, progress, they do not have sufficient content to distinguish them from the same hackneyed terms which are used in the official language of everyday politics and which are no longer whole-heartedly believed in.

Fourth, one of the reasons for the lack of new content is the incomplete status of contemporary thought—incomplete particularly in the absence of an effective social theory.

Fifth, the absence of new social and political theory is in part the consequence of the fact that the intellectuals do not know to what particular social forces they can engage themselves in order to concretize their general ideas. Sartre's withdrawal from the organization on which he depended to develop a social theory, on the grounds that he felt there was no place for it in the contemporary world of politics, is a case in point.

Finally, then, the intellectuals seem to have completed the circle started in the eighteenth century. Once more, they are the middle-class liberals par excellence. But now their prominence seems to be that, not of the vanguard, but of the stragglers. It is hardly surprising, then, that the theme of political and social engagement has already been labeled the theme of the 1940s and that other intellectual developments, suitable to the new decade, are anticipated.

ERNST NOLTE
The Concept of Transcendence

Ernst Nolte describes the purpose of his study of three European forms of fascism (the Action Française, Italian Fascism, and Nazism) as an attempt "not to present the picture of the era but a concept of it as far as this can be derived from the nature of fascism." The selection which follows contains merely his summary remarks regarding the conceptual nature of fascism on the "least accessible and the most fundamental" level: fascism as a metapolitical phenomon, as resistance to "transcendence." The analysis of fascism on this level ranges beyond the internal political context of "anti-Marxism" and the basic external struggles of nations and classes, to which the bulk of Nolte's study is devoted, into the "hidden foundations of the structure" of fascism viewed in purely philosophical terms.

Although Nolte employs highly disembodied abstractions, in particular the concept of "transcendence," they are meant to be understood within the more concrete framework of fascist thought, psychology, and action. Thus, "theoretical transcendence" can be related to Charles Maurras' concept of "anti-nature" as the pernicious tradition of Western philosophy and religion (for example, the Gospels of St. Paul or Rousseau's notion of liberty) and "practical transcendence" to the threat inherent in modernity—technology, science, and all the changes in the social process which the fascists feared would destroy "the familiar and the beloved." At this level of abstraction the fascist movement which dominated the era of the world wars—and whose mood, Nolte suggests, still persists—can be understood as a response to liberal society's misappropriation of the theoretical and practical freedoms acquired through "transcendence."

MARX: PHILOSOPHICAL DISCOVERY AND CRITIQUE OF BOURGEOIS SOCIETY

IF EVER THERE WAS A JUNCTION if the history of ideas, it was the point at which Marx stood. After the new philosophical departures of Kant, Fichte, and Hegel, and the evolution of the classic

From *Three Faces of Fascism* by Ernst Nolte. Translated by Leila Vennewitz. Copyright © 1963 by R. Piper & Co. Verlag, Munich. Reprinted with permission of Holt, Rinehart and Winston, Inc., pp. 429-454.

concept of political economy by Smith, Malthus, and Ricardo which was relevant at best to popular philosophy the time was ripe for the discovery of the total process of practical transcendence taking place in bourgeois society. In one single vast schema (which, however, for methodological reasons may be split up into its components), Marx discovers the revolution of bourgeois society, criticizes it from the standpoint of the individual human being and his universal nature, and postulates a second revolution which will eliminate the destructive schism.

1. Never has any work of political economy extolled bourgeois society and its leading class to such an extent as the *Communist Manifesto*. It sweeps away all the scruples and inhibitions which prevented Kant and Hegel from proclaiming bourgeois society as the dominant reality of the age.

The bourgeoisie was the first to prove what human activity is capable of: its achievements outshine and Pyramids of Egypt and the Gothic cathedrals. It constantly revolutionizes tools of production and thus all social conditions. It agglomerates the population, centralizes means of production, and concentrates property. It thereby draws all nations, even the most barbaric, into civilization: "The old local and national self-sufficiency and seclusion is being replaced by communication in every direction, by an all-round interdependence of nations."[1] Thus a world market is established and a world literature made possible. At the same time, all that is "indigenous" is being increasingly dissolved; if the workers have "no fatherland"[2] this means that, like the upper bourgeoisie, they will be dependent no longer on the next-to-last form of historical development, but solely on the most recent and all-embracing form of this development.

By dissolving all indigenous and "narrow-minded relationships

---

[1] Marx-Engels, *Ausgewählte Schriften*, I, 27.

[2] Most of the indignant reactions to this, probably the most famous of all Marx's sayings, overlooks the fact that is is immediately followed by the demand that the proletariat first form itself "into a nation." That Marx and Engels did not lack understanding of the problem of nationality is shown by their attitude during the Franco-Prussian War, when they stressed the priority of a war for national existence over the temporary possibilities of the workers' movement. The fact that they even, at least for a time, inclined toward radical German nationalism is documented by their articles in the *Neue Rheinische Zeitung* with what is sometimes startling clarity. Cf. also the extraordinary letter from Engels to Marx of May 23, 1851 ("Wrest from the Poles in the West what one can; ... send them into the fire, eat their land bare ... !"), *Historisch-kritische Gesamtausgabe*, Part III, Vol. I.

and achieving a genuine unification of mankind, bourgeois society is merely acting in accordance with the law of human nature. For in his early work Marx never tires of stressing that man is a universally producing and hence free creature that relates to himself and simultaneously annexes all of nature as an inorganic part of his body. Nature as a whole becomes his creation in that he "re-creates himself not only intellectually and consciously but also actually and actively, and hence sees himself in a world which he has created."[3] And this is just what the bourgeoisie does: "It creates a world after its own image."[4]

The way has now become open for the discovery and definition of that of which philosophy has never so much as been aware: "We see now the history of industry, and what has become the objective existence of industry is the open book of natural human forces, the physically present human psychology, which until now was never regarded in its relation to the *nature* of man but always only in an external utilitarian relationship, because we could only grasp— operating within the state of alienation—the general existence of man, religion, or history in their abstract and universal aspect, in the form of politics, art, literature, and so forth, as the reality of human natural forces and as human generic acts."[5]

First of all, then, Marx's work signifies the philosophical discovery of the economic and industrial universality of bourgeois society and hence the development of a more general concept of practical transcendence in its homology with theoretical transcendence, the only hitherto known form.

2. In Marx's earliest period the premise of his critique of bourgeois society is that bourgeois society is incapable of providing the individual with a congruent universality. He adopts Hegel's concept that the state is the sphere of universal reason whereas bourgeois society is the realm of *bellum omnium contra omnes*, in which "man behaves as a private individual, regards others as means, debases himself to being a means, and is at the mercy of foreign forces."[6] But while Hegel perceives in this difference the reasonably and organically articulated concept, for Marx it is always the mark of untruth and unreason. For man is a universal creature: he is only

[3] Karl Marx, *Nationalökonomie und Philosophie*, edited by Erich Thier (Cologne and Berlin, 1950), p. 150.

[4] Marx-Engels, *Ausgewählte Schriften*, I, 27.

[5] Marx, *Nationalökonomie und Philosophie*, p. 192.

[6] Karl Marx, *Der Historische Materialismus—Die Frühschriften* (Leipzig, 1932), p. 237.

Truly a man when participation in the whole is the stamp of his individuality. As long as he can only fulfill this nature of his within the state, his existence is "abstract." He lives as a "common creature" in the "heaven" of the political world, while in the earthly existence of society he is a self-seeking, narrow-minded atom. The materialism of bourgeois society stands in sharp contrast to the nonmaterialism of the state.

Marx's problem during this early period may be summarized as follows: How can the divided individual return, on the new level of practical universality created by bourgeois society, to that harmony with his world which existed in ancient and medieval times? For the Marx of that time the key is the realization of philosophy. He takes a momentous step by discovering in the proletariat a class of human beings which is the special product of bourgeois society while yet no longer part of that society because, due to its universal suffering, it possesses a universal character also in the subjective sense: "Philosophy cannot be realized without the elimination of the proletariat, the proletariat cannot be eliminated without the realization of philosophy."[7] But Marx only hit on the proletariat because he was looking for it. Marxism does not spring from the contemplation of reality or a sense of outrage: it is a philosophical construct seeking to fuse the newly discovered sphere of the universal but unaware bourgeois society with the reality of the individual and the philosophical concept of man as a universal being.

What bourgeois society does to the individual emerges in a new light during Marx's second period, exemplified by his first sojourn in Paris, his study of political economy, and the composing of *Die ökonomisch-philosophischen Manuskripte*. Now the concept of "alienation" moves into the spotlight; not only does bourgeois society fail to elevate the individual to genuine universality: it also deprives and "denatures" him.

This is the situation of the worker in such a society: "The more the worker exhausts himself, the more powerful becomes the alien objective world which he creates, the poorer he and his inner world become, the less belongs to him. . . . Hence the greater the activity, the more objectless the worker."[8] True, he receives the subsistence he requires to maintain physical existence; but this is just where the worst of all perversions lies, for he is a man, that is to say, a living

---

[7] *Ibid.*, p. 280.
[8] Marx, *Nationalökonomie und Philosophie*, p. 142.

being, capable of producing universally. If all his efforts are directed toward maintaining bodily existence, he turns his essence into a mere means of existence: hence he must do to himself with his own hands what Kant had forbidden man to do to his fellow man. However, what Marx sees is not the injuries men do to each other but the inhumanity of a system in which "the devaluation of the human world increases in direct proportion to the exploitation of the material world."⁹ Bourgeois society is the living contradiction. It creates a world of commodities, but only because the creators in this world have become commodities themselves; it makes leisure possible, but only because all leisure is withheld from its lower stratum; it is universal, but only because the majority of its members have been deprived of human universality.

The more the concept of "division of labor" becomes central for Marx—*The German Idealogy* marks this stage in his progress—the more strongly does a third indictment of bourgeois society emerge: it disfranchises the individual. This accusation, of course, reaches back far beyond bourgeois society: division of labor has been a primary factor throughout history, and indeed he puts all history on trial. For prior to all known history there existed the condition in which man's relationship to things was "in order." In that state the only thing which belonged to an individual was what he had produced himself. Here the product of labor remained unmistakably something which had its appointed subordinate place in man's life process. This relationship could be called the closed production cycle. In it the subject dominated the object, the producer the product, in keeping with his true nature. But this production cycle is isolated and hence "narrow." Not until man alienates himself from his product and hands it over to someone else does he emerge from his isolation. But the forfeiting of barriers means the forfeiting of possessions. It means a limitation to activity, and human dependence on material relationships. What had been the subject is now the object. The production cycle of a collective has no subject which is its equal or its superior. The rulers consume, the ruled produce: both are dehumanized, made subservient to the product and its laws. As the universal production cycle, bourgeois society is the clearest manifestation of this cleavage. *All* individuals stand powerless and helpless in the face of the uncontrolled and senseless movement of the world of commodities. But this disfranchisement began in the

⁹ *Ibid.*, p. 141.

earliest historical times. Consequently he says in *The German Ideology:* "For as soon as work begins to be divided, each person has one particular circle of activity imposed upon him from which he cannot escape. . . . This immobilizing of social activity, this consolidation of our own product into an impartial force over us, which grows away from our control, cuts across our expectations, nullifies our calculations, is one of the chief elements in all historical development to date.[10]

There is no denying the radical-reactionary trait in Marx's critique of bourgeois society.[11] It emerges very soon in Marx's high estimation of ancient and medieval times (in which the life of people and state were identical, albeit restricted), it appears again in Engels' latter-day predilection for the prehistoric tribal constitution.[12] But it is the philosophical concept of subjectivity which seems to substantiate this feeling, and it is the Hegelian concept of dialectic which reconciles this feeling with history.

It is a mistake to believe that with *Das Kapital* Marx's critique of bourgeois society changed its character and became scientific rather than philosophical. True, terms such as "generic nature" and "true reality" give way to highly specialized analyses of profit rates and land rents, accumulation and crisis. It is also true that many critical descriptions go no further than what had already been observed by other socialist writers and some time later was to become the commonplace of every critique of culture: that the manufacturing system imposes a crippling abnormality on the worker by a hothouse forcing of specialized skills and by turning him into the automatic mechanism for producing a single part.[13] But despite its scientific garb, the underlying philosophical conception keeps cropping up.

For what is "capital" but the alienated reality of human universal-

---

[10] Karl Marx, *Diedeutsche Ideologie* (Berlin, 1932), pp. 22f.

[11] No doubt a study of "Marx in socialism" would yield significant results with particular reference to this trait, provided this study refrained from the misleading distinction between "utopian" and "scientific" socialism. Compared to Fourier, Saint-Simon is an outright realist—and Marx is much closer to Fourier than to Saint-Simon. Fourier, this enemy of "commerce," this anti-Semite and opponent of "morality," who was born in 1772 and who had practically no knowledge of industrial capitalism, is an excellent example of the confusing intertwining of "progressive" and "reactionary" (or more accurately, primitivist) trends from which no form of socialism has remained entirely free.

[12] Cf. also Marx, *Das Kapital*, I, 5th ed. (Hamburg, 1903), 54: "Such a condition of mutual separation did not, however, exist for the members of a primitive society."

[13] *Ibid.*, p. 325.

ity which has become master of its own origin? Capital would not exist if "surplus value" were not continually draining into it: surplus labor, contributed by the worker, in excess of his own value as a commodity and without pay. His ability to create in excess of the mere value of his productive power (the production and reproduction costs of his physical existence) is what stamps him as a human being. "Surplus value" is not primarily an economic category: it is the worker's objectivized "surplus existence," that is, "human existence." Only because generations of workers have had to renounce the realization, within and for their own lives, of their creative power that exceeds mere physical existence, are their grandsons faced with the alien and opaque world of means of production, a world to which they are admitted only on certain conditions and for limited periods. Only because the unlived lives of countless human beings are absorbed by capital has *it* now become the real life on which all existing things depend. It only *appears* to bring profit and pleasure to its owners, the capitalists, who can in fact only survive in a pitiless struggle against each other if they become mere exponents of the productive forces. What counts now everywhere is not the human being but an inhuman being which, although dead, "comes to life like a vampire by sucking in living labor,"[14] and which is actually an object although it is the dominant subject of the age.

When this perversion becomes the absurd mumbo jumbo of the "paper world" of the credit system, it has its origin in the "fetishism" of the simplest commodity which causes human beings to view "the social characteristics of their own labor as the objective characteristics of the products of labor themselves."[15] Hence for human beings today "their own social action takes the form of the action of objects, which rule the producers instead of being ruled by them."[16] It is doubtlessly true that today man is living for the first time in one world; but this world is perverted in its roots because man is divided and alienated from himself and the world has become something of which he is deprived rather than, as it should be, something of which he is possessed.

How can we doubt that the powerful breath of this critique is philosophical and not scientific? It is of incalculable significance that

[14] *Ibid.*, p. 194.
[15] *Ibid.*, p. 38.
[16] *Ibid.*, p. 41.

the philosophical discoverer of bourgeois society was at the same time its most passionate critic. But the sole *telos* of this critique is the individual, whom Marx regards, in contrast to Hegel, as a reality; in contrast to Adam Smith, as universal; and in contrast to Kant, as self-alienated in history.

3. What, then, would a society have to be like in which the real human being per se was universal and at the same time had regained the primordial obviousness of his relationship with his products?

He would have to live in a universal society and no longer be subjected to division of labor. He would have to feel the sum total of social production to be his own work in which he joyfully participated in various capacities and which in any case he could see in its entirety. He should not require either the compulsions, consolations, or illusions of the old society.

In fact Marx's critique of bourgeois society suddenly becomes the blueprint of the no-longer-bourgeois, the classless, society, a blueprint which had implicitly always underlain his critique. In the various periods of his life he gave it various formulations in which the inherent unity of the idea keeps reappearing, not always with equal clarity but always recognizable.

In his earliest period he deals with "human emancipation" and describes it thus: "Only when the real individual human being takes back the abstract citizen in himself and as an individual human being has become a generic creature in his empirical life, his personal work, and his personal relationships, when man recognizes his *forces propres* as social forces and has organized them and hence ceases to separate social force from himself in the form of political force, only then has human emancipation been achieved."[17]

In *Die ökonomisch-philosophischen Manuskripte* he speaks of communism as the "reintegration" of man and defines it as follows: "This communism is as perfect naturalism humanism, as perfect humanism naturalism, it is the *genuine* resolving of the struggle between existence and being, between objectivization and confirmation of self, between freedom and necessity, between the individual and the species. It is the answer to the riddle of history, and is aware of itself as this answer."[18]

In its sweeping claim this definition proves the following: if Kant saw the priority of practical transcendence in the interminable

[17] Marx, *Der Historische Materialismus*, p. 255.
[18] Marx, *Nationalökonomie und Philosophie*, p. 181.

striving of a "nonsocial-social creature of irreducible finiteness," if for Hegel the schema of the dialectic of fulfillment could only be carried to completion in theoretical transcendence, then Marx brings the poles together and comes up with the proposition of an achievable practical transcendence. This is defined in such a way that those extremes which are the universal prerequisites for the very existence of history are conceived of as one. Scholasticism defined the nature of the angel as the union of individual and species; Marx uses theological methods to construct the communist man of the near future.

There is no comparable boldness in *Das Kapital.* There are only sporadic instances of dealing with future education, for example, or "absolute availability for changing labor demands"[19] which the future worker will have to possess. Only once does Marx deal with a concrete problem of future society, and that is the controlling of investments, which in capitalist society is mechanically conducted by market automatism based on the profit principle. The problem is reduced, according to Marx, "simply" to the fact that "society" must calculate in advance how much labor and means of production it can apply to long-range projects without suffering impairment.[20] This would be a superficial answer even if offered by someone who merely suggested that the economy should be controlled by a wise bureaucracy instead of the unconscious market; but coming from a thinker who desires to abolish division of labor, it is positively irresponsible. Who, after all, constitutes the "society" which calculates? How is the calculation carried out? How does the individual participate in it? Is not the projected absence of domination already in its theoretical roots turning into a new domination of man over man?

A discussion of the concept of the classless society would be incomplete without considering its underlying principles and its ultimate significance.

According to the schema of the dialectic, the underlying principle is that the existence of the proletariat is "alienation which hastens toward completion and hence its own elimination."[21] It is the compulsion of his speculative basis that leads Marx to his "theory of progressive pauperization," to that part of his doctrine which was

---

[19] Marx, *Das Kapital,* I, 453.
[20] *Ibid.,* II, 288.
[21] Marx, *Nationalökonomie und Philosophie,* p. 215.

the first to be visibly exploded with the most far-reaching consequences.[22]

The ultimate significance of the classless society lies in the fact that it is called upon to replace theoretical transcendence. For Marx is far from declaring, as was often done during the Enlightenment, that religion and philosophy are a delusion and a fraud perpetrated by priests. The much-quoted words about religion being the opiate of the masses do not in any way stress the poisonous nature of opium. True, religion is merely the "realization in fantasy of human nature," but it is nevertheless man's sole legitimate existence as long as this existence possesses no genuine, that is, earthly, reality: "Poverty in religion is simultaneously the expression of real poverty and the protest against real poverty. Religion is the sigh of the oppressed creature, it is feeling in a heartless world, just as it is the spirit of nonspiritual conditions."[23] It is not of utilitarian world-reformers and clever technicians that Marx inquires as to the nature of man, but of theologians and philosophers. And it is precisely for this reason that the classless society can be *essentially* atheistic, because, instead of combating and supplanting religion, it makes religion's legitimate intention a reality, thereby rendering it superfluous.

With the aid of these concepts, the philosophical content of Marxism can be summarized as follows: from bourgeois society's "abstraction of life" (which is merely unconscious and collective practical transcendence), the individual, who after the proletarian revolution has attained genuine universality, regains his original sovereignty and home in a self-sufficient production cycle, with the result that the various types of theoretical transcendence in which the individual had hitherto to confirm his existence are doomed to extinction.[24]

This philosophical content represents the core of Marxism. Here for the first time the secular problem of the age, man's relationship to his new world, to "industry," is profoundly and passionately

---

[22] Although "pauperization" in the strict sense of the theory must be regarded as relative, the word itself speaks a different language, as does the theory of catastrophe. Cf. *Das Kapital*, I, 728.

[23] Marx, *Der Historische Materialismus*, p. 263.

[24] It must not be overlooked that there is a subsidiary current in Marx's thought which casts doubt on this monumental and fantastic unity of theoretical and practical transcendence.

explored. That it did not proceed by observation and empiricism goes without saying.

Of course, this is not the whole of Marxism. As is usually the case, the significant concept met with more response even in daily life than the pallid understanding of the workaday world. Its transcending nature formed the historic link with the most recent social phenomenon, the still oppressed but already emerging proletariat, thus enabling it to become Europe's most recent faith. At the same time Marx managed to weld into his doctrine scientific theories which had existed long before him.[25] It was this apparently monolithic unity which engendered that widespread fear and hatred without which fascism could never have arisen, for in its negation fascism took this unity with desperate seriousness, although it was the obvious flaws in this unity that contributed to the triumph of fascism.

NIETZSCHE: THE PREBOURGEOIS SOIL OF "CULTURE"

However, it was not so much the structure of this unity as the philosophical core which, long before Maurras and Hitler, made of Nietzsche the most significant and radical adversary of Marxism.

This proposition may come as a surprise, for the younger man never knew the older one other than indirectly,[26] neither does the

---

[25] The theory of concentration and exploitation, for instance, had been developed by Sismondi, and the doctrine of the progressive diminution of profit rates goes back to Ricardo. It is well known that the doctrine of the value of labor is a feature of classical national economy as a whole.

[26] In a letter to his friend von Gersdorff written in 1868, *Historischkritische Gesamtausgabe-Briefe*, II (Munich, 1938), 182, the young Nietzsche relates that he had acquired from a little book a good deal of information "on the state of the social-political parties," and that it, too, radiated "the irrational greatness of Lassalle." It would seem impossible to write a book on Lassalle without describing his relationship to the author of the *Communist Manifesto*. The author of the little book (Joseph Edmund Jörg) was able to—so forgotten was Marx the year *Das Kapital* was published. He is mentioned only once in a trivial and misleading context; Nietzsche is not to blame for not following up this reference. Later Nietzsche frequently referred to the works of Eugen Dühring, which he called "a whole trembling world of subterranean revenge" (*Werke*, VIII, 435). Dühring, *Geschichte der Nationalökonomie und des Sozialismus*, which Nietzsche studied attentively, contains a lengthy chapter on Marx, although without any quotations and written in such a dry, pedagogically critical style that Nietzsche apparently found no reason to pursue his efforts. Nevertheless, these points of contact are quite enough to credit Nietzsche with an intuitive knowledge of the basic intentions of Marxism.

thematic material of their work seem to display much similarity. From first to last, Nietzsche was concerned with "culture," and for him this was no less than man's communion with himself in philosophy, art, and religion—in short, theoretical transcendence. The discovery of the Dionysian background of tragedy, the defense of genius against the masses, the insistence on the necessity of slavery, serve no other purpose than to explicate the elements of genuine culture: its background, reality, and basis. They are developed along with the indictment of the enemies of culture; science and its logical (Socratic) optimism, mass emancipation and its shallow utilitarian outlook, revolution and its pernicious effects. But although almost all his ideas foreshadow the future (especially his attack on Parmenides and the latter's overwhelming abstraction of thought), on the whole the young Nietzsche discovers the incompatibility of "culture" with "industry," of theoretical with practical transcendence, so naively and undialectically that he cannot be regarded as a true opponent of Marx. After all, Marx was anything but a complacent extoller of modern achievements like David Friedrich Strauss, who was torn to shreds by the young Nietzsche in a brilliant and high-spirited attack.

There is little that anticipates the outline of future developments as markedly as the fact that Nietzsche could only arrive at Marx's level after allowing his oldest enemy to reign in his own heart for a time, leaving traces which never quite disappeared. During his so-called period of enlightenment, the son of the pastor and royal tutor[27] caught up with a whole century's history of ideas in one swift and violent development. With a determined gesture he sacrifices religion and art to science, genius to the competent average, antiquity's state of freemen and slaves to modern democracy. The despiser of the modern became the spokesman of a scientifically emancipatory mass culture, which he evidently interpreted as practical transcendence. But as a steady accompaniment to all this, a note of dissension becomes audible, attesting to the continuing influence of his early days. Nietzsche's late philosophy was born the

---

[27] Nietzsche's father was not only for a time tutor to the princesses at the ducal court in Altenburg: he also gave his son the names Friedrich Wilhelm as a mark of gratitude toward an "exalted benefactor"; and in 1848, on hearing the news of the king of Prussia's humiliation at the hands of the revolution, he spent days in deep despair and complete seclusion.

moment this influence finally gained the upper hand, and the short period of enlightenment together with the new perspectives of ecumenical breadth and modern austerity became the basis for the triumphant resurrection of his youthful problems and attempts at solution. However, what had then been rudimentary and sketchy had now become a coherent system of thought which rejected or transformed most of what the young Nietzsche had esteemed and loved. And it is this which places him and even the most subtle concepts of his philosophy in such diametric opposition to Marx that probably no two thinkers have ever stood in such close yet opposite proximity, like mask and face, negative and print.

Nietzsche had now grasped that the abstraction of life dominating European existence and manifesting itself as science, industry, mass democracy, socialism, constitutes a single phenomenon and *as such* is inimical to culture. In its trend toward a closed cycle of production and knowledge, it cuts the ground from under the feet of creative genius, the ground of "reality," in which all "life" is rooted. That which for Hegel was "progress in the consciousness of freedom," for Marx alienation but at the same time realization, becomes for Nietzsche an *Attentat*, a crime, the origin of which goes back to earliest times.

He now develops more firmly the idea that abstraction of life ultimately springs from abstraction of thought, the earliest schema of Western metaphysics, which contrasted "being" with "becoming" and believed it had thereby achieved a standpoint outside reality and hence had arrived at an attitude of judgment toward life. This metaphysical approach has been carried on in Christianity; socialism, which believes itself capable of altering the very essence of reality, is merely its most radical consequence. The nature of European "horizon-consciousness" leads to the autonomy of the universal cycle of knowledge and production which levels all men, absorbs them as parts of itself, and hence destroys culture. This life-negating synthesis of theoretical and practical transcendence Nietzsche calls "morality." In so doing he regains a context which Hegel took for granted but which Marx had in his turn pushed back into the darkness. At the same time, however, he sets himself the task of developing an entirely new form of "horizon-consciousness." For if "everything which has hitherto been known as truth" is recognized as the most harmful and insidious form of lie, as the "ruse for sucking out life itself and making it anemic," if "morality" appears as "vampirism,"[28] then a new truth and a new philosophy are required. Its content is the doctrine of the "eternal recurrence," its reality is the "superman," its soil is created by the "lords of the earth."[29]

But it also requires the unrelenting struggle against destruction and the *Attentat*. And since Nietzsche seeks to interpret life-inimical morality more and more as a deficient and inferior form of life itself, *his* concept of life becomes, contrary to its original meaning, more and more biological. Thus he is forced to offset *décadence* with the completely sound and healthy life: the concept of the "blond beast" is not a freak—it is the logical result of Nietzsche's thought.

It might be said that Nietzsche continually aims his big guns, from every side and every distance, at one single target: Marx's "Thesis on Feuerbach"—that the important thing was to change the world. For this does not merely envisage a political revolution or even a superficial dynamism: it postulates a change of "reality," of the essential structure of the world. The possibility of denying and refuting such a change, of detesting and unmasking its champions, is the passionate and compelling need controlling all Nietzsche's thought. Such a change would destroy culture, while to the very end culture remains for him "the most important thing."[30]

The glorification of *this* reality, with all its terrors, wars, exploitation, and affirmation of the here and now, is the meaning of his doctrine of the eternal recurrence. Only when all things, and within them man, eternally recur exactly as they are now, will it cease to be possible to transcend them toward a goal, toward a "beyond"; at last a new metaphysic encounters *this* life with powerful emphasis, in the "great noontide" of life, every apparent, that is, criticizable, world fades away with the "true" world. And that is what will deprive those who are unable to endure this present, real life—the underprivileged and the pariahs—of their worlds of consolation and their supports, of their yearning gaze into an ultimate realm either here or beyond. The beloved name of the god Dionysus rises to Nietzsche's lips once more when he describes the condition "in

---

[28] Friedrich Nietzsche, *Ecce homo*, in *Werke* (Leipzig: Taschenausgabe, n.d.), XI, 385.

[29] The cosmology which Nietzsche later developed from his concept of the "will to power" (and which undoubtedly contains some important and stimulating ideas) resembles "dialectical materialism" inasmuch as its secondary and derivative character is very evident.

[30] Nietzsche, *Götzendämmerung*, in *Werke*, X, 288.

which man feels himself in every way to be a deified form and justification of nature."[31]

But the price Nietzsche has to pay for his metaphysics of the glorification of life is a high one. It implies the immortalization of the contradiction *in* the world, all transcendence in man becomes petrified in the total affirmation of the world as it is, and this doctrine becomes *nolens volens* the exact counterpart of the concept of the perfect classless society: and culture in Nietzsche's original sense is as impossible in one as in the other.

Properly interpreted, the "superman" is not a biological species but the creator in the new culture. "To create" means for Nietzsche primarily to give "meaning" and define values. The superman not only provides peoples and times with their tables and values: he creates "meaning" for the earth as a whole and for all aeons to come. "He who defines values and controls the will of millennia by controlling the most superior natures, is the supreme man."[32]

The most superior natures are the "lords of the earth," the tools of the superman. Hence his rule is superior to any rule hitherto: it is neither common and direct, like that of statesmen in the past, nor indirect and disguised, like that of philosophers in the past. Consequently he can set the supreme goal for his creation; he no longer works in matter or pure spirit: he is able to "shape man himself as an artist."

Such shaping is fulfillment, and yet again merely a precondition of his creating. For the ruthlessness with which he destroys failures permits, after thousands of years of mediocritization, the re-creation of that ancient and terrible soil out of which supreme creation alone can find fulfillment. For Nietzsche this is the meaning of tragedy: "That new party of life which undertakes the greatest of all tasks, the improvement of mankind, including the ruthless destruction of all that is degenerate and parasitical, will make possible again that excess of life on earth from which the Dionysian condition must once more grow. I promise a tragic age: the supreme art in the affirmation of life, tragedy, will be born again. . . ."[33]

That is Nietzsche's testament as presented in *Ecce homo*, a few months before his collapse: a gloomy and clairvoyant prophecy

---

[31] Nietzsche, *Wille zur Macht*, in *Werke*, X, 217.
[32] *Ibid.*, p. 187.
[33] Nietzsche, *Ecce homo*, in *Werke*, XI, 325f.

which errs only where it loves. Here it becomes quite plain what he means by the superman—he is the man who can even create the soil of life, that soil hitherto provided by nature only: the terrors of existence as the underlying basis of culture.

It is already clear to what extent the concept of destruction[34] must inevitably become the center of Nietzsche's late philosophy. For if history amounts to nothing more than the petty and sterile calculation of the last "squinting" men, who neither obey nor rule and desire to be neither poor nor rich, then the most mighty effort is required to force them back into the state of slavery which is their rightful place. The unmasking of their origin is the first essential.

Consequently, all Nietzsche's late work is dominated by a shrill, frenzied voice, the voice of one seeking to pass judgment on and negate, not "life" as it is imagined but history as it really is.

Everything in the European tradition which is not classical Greek or Roman antiquity is interpreted as morality's revolt of the slaves, beginning with the Jews, "the sacerdotal people of *ressentiment par excellence*,"[35] and continuing via Christianity, the "wholesale revolt of all the downtrodden, the poverty-striken, the failures, the under-privileged,"[36] to their "daughter and continuer," the French revolution. Today, however, the democratic movement has become the legacy of the Christian movement: everything is imbued with "the pessimism of indignation," with the "instinct against caste, against the well-bred, against the last-remaining privileges,"[37] and together with the democratic movement the "emancipation of women," anarchy, and socialism are part and parcel of the phenomenon of the "total decadence of mankind."[38]

Nietzsche's real enemy is obviously the concept of realization; it

---

[34] It might be objected that the idea of destruction is not specific, that it is equally present in Marxism, in which history is seen to destroy the bourgeoisie. It is true that the middle classes saw themselves threatened politically with destruction by the socialist program. But it is equally true that it was a legacy of Marxism if scarcely anywhere did the socialist parties attempt to bring about such a destruction (even in Russia they did so only hesitantly and in the struggle for their own survival). For Marxists regard "expropriation of the expropriators" rather as the radical removal of an already tottering obstacle than an actual battle, and certainly not as physical extermination. It is precisely Nietzsche's thought which proves that the fascist idea of destruction must not be regarded primarily as a homogeneous reaction.

[35] Nietzsche, *Genealogie der Moral*, in *Werke*, VIII, 335.

[36] Nietzsche, *Götzendämmerung*, in *Werke*, X, 282.

[37] Nietzsche, *Wille zur Macht*, in *Werke*, IX, 145.

[38] Nietzsche, *Jenseits von Gut und Böse*, in *Werke*, VIII, 139.

is at this that he aims such terms as *ressentiment, décadence,* and "total decadence." From a philosophical standpoint there is clearly only one unassailable counter-concept: that of the wholly nondecadent man, the "beast of prey, the magnificent roaming blond beast lusting for booty and victory,"[39] the magnificent animality of "the pack of blond beasts of prey."[40]

In practice, however, Nietzsche allies himself with certain phenomena of his day, and these bear little resemblance to the bourgeois society of Smith or Kant: "The maintenance of the military state is the ultimate means of resuming or preserving the great tradition of the supreme human type, the strong type. And as a result all concepts which prolong the state of hostility and distinction of rank between states appear to be sanctioned (for example, nationalism, protective tariffs)."[41]

The fantastic alliance of philosophy and proletariat under the banner of the reintegrating "changing of the world" is confronted by the desperate comradeship in arms of the martial society and the culture proceeding from it with its battle cry of "salvation" and "annihilation."

Not the "decayed ruling classes,"[42] but the future lords of the earth as the "spiritual and physical aristocracy,"[43] as the "ruling caste with the most spacious souls,"[44] know how they have to change the world that it may remain as it is.

"The Biblical commandment, 'Thou shalt not kill,' is naive compared to the seriousness of the life commandment to the *décadents*: 'Thou shalt not reproduce!'"[45] "The weak and the failures shall be destroyed: first lesson of *our* love for our fellow man. And we must help them on their way."[46]

" . . . If his strength rank still higher in the hierarchy . . . , it is not sufficient for him to be capable of cruelty merely at the *sight* of much suffering, perishing, and destruction: such a man must be capable of himself creating pain and suffering and experiencing

---

[39] Nietzsche, *Genealogie der Moral,* in *Werke,* VIII, 322.
[40] *Ibid.,* p. 382.
[41] Nietzsche, *Wille zur Macht,* in *Werke,* X, 8.
[42] *Ibid.,* p. 22.
[43] Nietzsche, *Modernität,* in *Werke,* XI, 95.
[44] Friedrich Nietzsche, *Die Unschuld des Werdens,* edited by Alfred Baumler (Leipzig, 1931); *op. cit.,* II, 405.
[45] Nietzsche, *Wille zur Macht,* in *Werke,* X, 12.
[46] Nietzsche, *Ecce homo,* in *Werke,* XI, 360.

pleasure in so doing, he must be cruel in hand and deed (and not merely with the eyes of the spirit)."[47]

In fact, Nietzsche's whole thought represents the very antithesis of the Marxist conception, and the idea of destruction is the negative aspect of its core. For if history is not realization but an *Attentat* thousands of years old, then only the destruction of the perpetrator of this crime can restore things to their true balance. Nietzsche is not in any obvious sense the spiritual father of fascism;[48] but he was the first to give voice to that spiritual focal point toward which all fascism must gravitate: the assault on practical *and* theoretical transcendence, for the sake of a "more beautiful" form of "life." Nietzsche was not concerned with magnificent animality for its own sake,[49] nor was destruction per se Hitler's goal. Their ultimate aim was a "supreme culture" of the future. Yet it was inevitable that the positive concept of both men, in its fantastic abstractness (for what is "culture" without the acknowledgment of real history?), was completely outweighed by the concrete aspect of their negative will. Many decades in advance, Nietzsche provided the political radical anti-Marxism of fascism with its original spiritual image, an image of which even Hitler never quite showed himself the equal.[50]

However, although this most radical of all antitheses takes place on the soil of bourgeois society, it is not the appropriate expression of opposites immanent in it. Marxism is not the spontaneous self-consciousness of the proletariat: it is above all a doctrine, by means of which a powerful mind grounded in classical German philosophy desired to utilize bourgeois society's most recent product for his boundless hopes for a reintegration of mankind. Nietzsche's thought is not an ideology of the bourgeoisie: on the one hand it is a deeply disturbed protest of the artistic temperament against the general world trend, on the other it is the violent reaction of the

[47] Nietzsche, *Die Unschuld des Werdens*, in *Werke*, I, 252.

[48] There is no direct connection whatever. Nietzsche's only immediate "pupils" were an apolitical musician (Peter Gast), a Jew (Paul Ree), and a Russian woman (Lou Andréas-Salome).

[49] In this context it has been possible to pick out only one—albeit a fundamental—line from Nietzsche's thought. Consequently this study is far from doing justice to Nietzsche's highly complex philosophy as a whole or even to the man himself.

[50] For Nietzsche had none of that German provincialism which was part and parcel of National Socialism. One has only to recall how Nietzsche always stressed the great future role of Russia—the Russia of the "lower classes" (*Werke*, XI, 11 f.; cf. also *Die Unschuld des Werdens*, in II, 433, 436).

feudal element in bourgeois society at being threatened. So although both doctrines could establish a close relation with basic social phenomena and the movements arising out of them, and to some extent accurately voice these trends, essentially they extended far beyond them and were both revealed as the products of that unrestrained intellectual stratum which, in the interplay of its unauthoritative and hence particularly daring schemata, represents the self-consciousness of bourgeois society. What distinguished these two doctrines from all others was their ability to push the society which was their soil to the outermost limits of its existence: to the eschatologically envisaged reality of the universal community of labor and exchange toward which it was heading—to the non-transcendental self-assertion of the sovereign, martial, and inwardly antagonistic group of which it was the offspring.

MAX WEBER: THE THEORETICIAN OF BOURGEOIS SOCIETY BEFORE FASCISM

What stronger evidence in favor of this thesis could there be than the fact that Max Weber, in defiance of every probability of a hypothetical development, is much less close than Nietzsche to fascism? Yet this son of an upper class family was very much part of the imperialist Germany of the turn of the century, and he was certainly no stranger to all the trends and characteristics of the age pointing back to Nietzsche and on to Hitler. Indeed, his inaugural speech at Freiburg University in 1895 abounds in phrases which, in meaning and sometimes even formulation, could have appeared in *Mein Kampf.* Nevertheless, this same speech contains the starting point of a distinction which, when further developed, makes it possible to see him as representing the basic anti-Hitler potential of German politics.[51] For our purposes only one element need be singled out: his attitude toward Marx and Marxism and thus indirectly his relationship to Nietzsche and the spiritual core of fascism. It happens to be a highly important element; moreover, it throws light on his position toward and within bourgeois society.

Max Weber knew nothing of the fear of the socialist movement which is the wellspring of fascism. He had only contempt for the cowardice of the bourgeoisie when confronted by Social Democra-

---

[51] Cf. Ernst Nolte, "Max Weber vor dem Faschismus," *Der Staat*, Vol. II, No. 1 (1963), pp. 1-24.

cy, but he also despised the potential obverse of this cowardice—a rank brutality. He sees socialism as a manifestation of bourgeois society which has to find a place within this society. He formed the concept of the "workers' aristocracy" long before Lenin.[52] Hence in 1907 it was natural for him to ask why the Social Democrats should *not* rule the communes. As for himself, he says, he is convinced that the attempt would be more dangerous for the ideologists among them than for bourgeois society.[53] It is the "discovery of the reality of the proletariat" which gave him this confidence, the discovery which was then being made in many places and which opened the first cracks in Marx's speculative thesis of the homogeneity of the world proletariat (without eliminating it, for its continued existence was still a *sine qua non* of fascism).[54]

Max Weber does not stop at a substantiated assumption. He seeks to prove empirically what Marx had established by philosophical premises: As a result of technical innovations, will qualified workers be replaced by people of lesser or higher qualifications? Is the working class moving toward qualitative and economic differentiation or toward uniformity? What is the relationship between the upper working class and the petite bourgeoisie? Not only does this provide him with evidence for his view that, broadly speaking, the West European working class is a section of the bourgeoisie (a view, incidentally, which Engels had anticipated by half a century);[55] he also makes it possible for himself to divide the scientific elements in Marx's work from the nonscientific. In this way he contributes to the dissolution of the synthesis of mass appeal, science, and philosophical concept which had constituted the real effectiveness of Marxism and yet had been an all too vulnerable element of it.

More important, however, is Max Weber's attitude to the core of Marx's thought. For Weber's real subject is identical with Marx's: practical transcendence.

[52] In the inaugural address, Max Weber, *Gesammelte Politische Schriften,* 2nd ed. (Tubingen, 1958), p. 23.

[53] Max Weber, *Gesammelte Aufsätze zur Soziologie und Sozialpolitik* (Tubingen, 1924), pp. 407f.

[54] "Homogeneity" or the lack of it is a fact and can in principle be empirically ascertained. However, whether the political alternative must necessarily mean the inclusion of the working class in the nationalism of a section of the bourgeoisie is by no means certain. The internationalism of the workers' movement was not necessarily dependent on the correctness or otherwise of the Marxist theory.

[55] Max Weber, *Wirtschaft und Gesellschaft,* Half-Vol. I, 4th ed. (Tubingen, 1956), p. 35.

He seeks to trace "the unfolding of an efficient economy from its beginnings as an instinctive reactive search for food,"[56] that "process of rationalization and socialization whose progressive reaching out into all communal activity must be pursued in every field as the essential motivating force of evolution."[57] If the disintegration of original family communism and the increasing trend toward calculativeness are merely two aspects of the same thing, then today, in "universal market integration," the production process has largely detached itself from its dependence on the individual and the terms of organic existence, and has created social conditions of extreme impersonality, complexity, and differentiation. Hence the West is characterized merely by one particular most advanced stage of a universal process of which the rudiments are to be found everywhere, and which Max Weber paraphrases by such terms as "systematization," "sublimation," "rationalization," "intellectualization." Thus Max Weber is concerned with bourgeois society within the framework of the world-historical process, exactly like Kant, Hegel, and Marx. But he discards some dogmatic premises which are typically Marxist.

He does not accept the later thesis of Marx that at no time have religious forces played an important role in this process. On the contrary, his most significant analyses serve to clarify the connections between theoretical and practical transcendence, so that actually he restores a link which Kant, Hegel, and Nietzsche took for granted and which figured also in the work of the young Marx, and even in later intimations,[58] although these were not elaborated.

He does not adopt the unclarified Marxist concept of productive force. The term "development of the productive force" merely poses a problem without offering any solution to it. Max Weber's answer is to be found in the concept of "charisma" which, although the most polyvalent word in all his writings, in essence means the underivable power of "invention."

He does not share Marx's belief that only total alienation would produce a sudden total restoration of human nature. He was not without sympathy for Marx's concept of the "history of alienation," but because he augments it—separation of the producer from the

---

[56] *Ibid.*, p. 195.

[57] In *Das Kapital* there are frequent scornful references to the puritanical nature of English capitalism.

[58] Weber, *Wirtschaft und Gesellschaft*, Half-Vol. I, p. 119.

means of production took place also in armies and was now taking place in universities—he sees it as an irreversible process which can never achieve a "higher unity" with the individual. It is not based on the private ownership of the means of production; a socialist economy would not reverse the expropriation of the workers—it would only augment it by the dispossession of the owners. Because in a socialist economy a struggle for "positions of advantage"[59] would inevitably begin and real power of disposal would only rest with a few, that "iron shell"[60] which modern times have built around the individual is bound to become even more solid and unbreakable. The trend toward "minimization"[61] of rule, displayed by some forms of democracy and particularly by socialism, was something Weber never quite believed in; essential to his own struggle for the parliamentary system and internal political freedom was the conviction that the power of bureaucracy would become ever more firmly rooted and impossible to dislodge, and that one could merely strive to ensure a minimum of control and individual freedom of movement. History, he says, inexorably gives birth to new aristocracies; neither the fear nor the hope (according to one's outlook) existed that there would ever be too much freedom in the world. Weber shares with Marx his evaluation of the present trend and also his fear of the "parceling" of man; but where Marx had seen a recovery, Weber sees a deterioration, because he recognizes that "socialization" is bureaucratization and regards the notion of universal, reintegrated man who is no longer subjected to division of labor as nonsensical wishful thinking.

Thus Max Weber corrects that "irresponsibility" with which Marx allows "the" society of the future to carry out its plans, and with the concept of the dialectic of perfection tears the very heart out of Marxist faith. We can only shake our heads sadly over the question of whether he or Marx gauged bureaucracy more accurately. Max Weber had not been dead ten years when Trotsky, the most important surviving leader of the Russian revolution, began to indict the bureaucratic degeneration of the state, and Weber's posthumous star witness was no other than Stalin when the latter evolved his theory of a "revolution from above," for which there is absolutely

[59] Weber, *Gesammelte Politische Schriften*, p. 242.
[60] Weber, *Wirtschaft und Gesellschaft*, Half-Vol. I, pp. 169f.
[61] In "Wissenschaft als Beruf," *Gesammelte Aufsätze zur Wissenschaftslehre*, pp. 578f.

no foundation in Marx's thought. The only possible objection is that the concept of bureaucracy is an equivocal one, and that Weber based his ideas too much on the Prussian-German form. But the interesting question here is not whether, where, and to what extent Max Weber was right as opposed to Marx. The heart of the matter is something quite different.

The very fact that Max Weber turns a penetrating and rational gaze on the inconsistencies of Marx's theories is what divides him by an abyss from the radicalness of Nietzsche's antithesis and even more so from Hitler's mythicizing search for "agents." He has no intention of "destroying" Marx intellectually, or even of replacing the materialistic view of history with a nonmaterialistic doctrine of the priority of religious attitudes in history. To interpret his works on religious sociology in this way is to misinterpret them. They are far more of an augmentation than a refutation. For Max Weber, Marx always remains the great fellow thinker, and there exists a broad range of insights and evaluations common to both.

For Weber, too, class struggle is a fundamental reality of the age, capitalism means the dispossession of the producer, and the cleavage of society into bourgeoisie and proletariat is the chief hallmark of modern times. His description of industrial conditions often recalls those of Marx. However, this congruity, far from being imitative, brings to light the simple fact, yet one which is often overlooked, that only a small part of "Marxism" stems genuinely from Marx: the theory of class struggle, the economic view of history, the analysis of capitalism—all these had been developed before and side by side with Marx by "bourgeois" theoreticians, and Weber simply took back what belonged to the theory of bourgeois society.

Hence he does not show even a trace of that sweeping "doctrine of the enemy" and its cogency, which is as central for Maurras and Hitler as for Nietzsche. He acknowledged having political enemies, of course, and he fought them with intensity and determination. But when he discloses their historical origin they become more understandable instead of more alarming; they never appear in a line of descent more or less identical with European history.

Max Weber is thus not tempted to repudiate his own assumptions and to conceive a "history of decay." He leaves no doubt that he regards himself as the heir to those Puritans whose ethical rigorism and world-conquering faith gave birth to modern capitalism; no human type provided him with as much guidance and support as the

Jewish prophets, with whom that anti-magical and rationalistic reshaping of the world began which is the fundamental trait of the history of the West. As a result he expresses himself quite favorably concerning the great Western revolutions, including the French.

It is equally true, of course, that Max Weber repeatedly shows a strange vacillation toward just those principal phenomena to which he gave his closest attention. In his eyes, rationalization is not merely typical of the West: it is also the root of his torturing anxiety as to whether man has even the strength to withstand the fearful rupturing effects of the irrevocable perversion of all natural conditions within the "apparatus" of the modern world. The concept of "progress" entirely loses its traditional positive accent; its use is frankly stated to be "inopportune." Most revealing of all, perhaps, is the use of the term "disenchantment," which in the total context of his work has a quite positive meaning and yet in one of Weber's best-known utterances is imbued with the melancholy sound of Stefan George's laments.[62]

This vacillation of such a man as Weber is possibly more indicative of the profound change in the intellectual climate favoring fascism than all the books written by Bergson or Klages. But at the same time it makes it clear that there is more to this change than a purely sociological "escape into irrationalism."

And finally, a simplified interpretation does not exhaust what the Weber doctrine contains of the fateful and inconclusive battle of the various "gods," that is, scales of value, and thus in the last resort of the various manifestations of theoretical transcendence. For the thesis that fate, rather than science, holds sway over these gods and their battles[63] sounds very curious coming from a man whose lifework culminated in the insight that there is no more fateful power today than science and the rationalization associated with it. This proposition can only be understood against the background of that uncertainty vis-à-vis his own central concept, an uncertainty which, although it notes the reality of "progress," has begun to doubt the desirability of progress. However, can it really be taken for granted that other scales of value—"gods"—present themselves as alternatives, which the specific social movement has not created but which are left behind and endowed with an extremely intensive self-awareness? Is this perhaps the strangest characteristic of

---

[62] *Ibid.*, p. 588.
[63] Lenin, "Staat und Revolution," *Ansgewählte Werke*, II, 190.

bourgeois society in its relation to the forms of theoretical transcendence?

OUTLINE OF A TRANSCENDENTAL SOCIOLOGY
OF THIS PERIOD

A "transcendental definition of bourgeois society" is now no longer a strange-sounding postulate: it has been contained, although sometimes only by implication, in the thinking of Marx, Nietzsche, and Max Weber. All that remains is to summarize, with the aid of the concepts previously developed, avoiding the specific definitions of each thought system, and then to apply this to the new phenomena of bolshevism and fascism, which at this point can only be seen in unity although not *as* a unity. Fascism, although it is still the theme, requires but a few sentences; for if . . . the era was only to be interpreted by examining fascism, in the same way the metapolitical method of observing fascism only becomes definable within a context far transcending fascism.

Typical of the transcendental nature of bourgeois society is that within it practical transdendence has developed to an undreamed-of efficacy, without supplanting the traditional forms of theoretical transcendence. The politico-sociological aspect (which is superficial when isolated) may be formulated as follows:

Bourgeois society is that form of society in which the leading class performs its task of establishing the technical and economic unity of the world, and emancipating all men for participation in this undertaking, in ever new political and intellectual compromises with the hitherto ruling powers: it is the society of synthesis. Hence in bourgeois society the historically new and specific—that unprecedented expansion of the practical scope of mankind and the revolutionary change in the status of the individual and all groups within society as a whole which is summarily known as "industrialization"—is proceeding almost clandestinely and without the consent of considerable sections of its own intellectual stratum, whose spiritual home is after all theoretical transcendence, however arbitrarily and undogmatically they may interpret it.

The thesis that when threatened this stratum ultimately aligns itself with bourgeois society and *its* class and that its thinking is therefore dependent on its environment, is, although generally speaking correct, nevertheless remarkably naive. For its relative (and in some cases absolute) disengagement is precisely what is so astonishing, so singular, and so much in need of explanation.

Bourgeois society gave birth to practical transcendence, at the same time endowing it with a guilty conscience. Its self-consciousness is only precariously derived from the contest of a plethora of modes of thought of which the most extreme are a utopian reaching into the future, or a glorifying emphasis on certain typical features of the past. This character of bourgeois society is without doubt associated with the fact that within the state private entrepreneurs have initiated the movement of this society and kept it going: but presumably it could also be "socialistically" organized, without sacrificing its transcendental nature, provided the starting point was abundance and not want, and that power did not fall into the hands of dogmatists. For bourgeois society did not remain unchanged in its structure; within its own framework it produced that new class, the "technical intelligentsia" which Marx had completely ignored and which combined on various levels with the older classes, turning out to be the most productive and expansive group within this structure. It is advisable, therefore, to abandon the narrow term "bourgeois society" and to speak instead of "liberal society."

Liberal society is a society of abundance—all forms of theoretical transcendence can develop independently, although not without being affected externally; a self-critical society—the attainment of practical transcendence remains subject to criticism; an uncertain society—it is continually subject to self-doubts.

Kant's and Hegel's ideas show how unquestionably the early self-image of this society is rooted in philosophy; Marx and Nietzsche mark the extremes of this self-doubting—which is, of course, a product of their philosophical detachment. For the obvious possibility of a nontranscendental yet advantageous subordination of individuals in the social process—the basic supposition of classical political economy—is rejected by both with equal fervor. Their antithetical solutions were adopted by social structures which are transcendentally distinct from liberal society. But Max Weber's work demonstrates that this society need not necessarily be driven in directions where it will retain mere fragments of its uncurtailed self.

Bolshevism achieved power in Russia in defiance of the acknowledged premises of the Marxist doctrine, and it modeled itself on the master's more esoteric expectations for a short time only. Nevertheless, it is to some extent entitled to invoke Marx as its authority.

Lenin found it difficult to forsake the orthodox assumption that what was really on the agenda was the revolution of the Western European proletariat, and that his own enterprise was historically premature. At first he was still convinced that the functions of power-wielding were by that time so simplefied that they were open "to every nonilliterate,"[64] and that the age of nonrule was hence rapidly approaching: "Under socialism *all* will rule in turn and quickly get used to the fact that no one rules."[65]

But it was not long before the Marxist postulates were replaced, both in practical measures and a number of theoretical utterances, by a complete mobilization, directed by a single will, of the cluster of races that is Russia in a grim struggle for existence. He realized it was not a matter of setting mankind an example of a higher and better way of life—the crossroad at which the country now stood was more commonplace, more ruthless: "Go under, or forge full steam ahead. That is the question put by history."[66] It was a matter of "catching up," of struggling up out of backwardness, lack of culture, want, and poverty in the midst of a hostile world. In their overwhelming simplicity and conviction, a great number of utterances from his latest period leave no doubt whatever that this more modest interpretation represents Lenin's final insight rather than this or that bombastic pronouncement about the victory of socialism over capitalism.[67]

Thus the "day-to-day problems of the economy" became "the most important affairs of state." It is easier to grasp the nature of bolshevism from any front page of any Soviet daily newspaper than from the most shocking reports of famine and barbarism. Famine and barbarism have always existed; but never since the existence of a bourgeois society and of newspapers had the headlines dealt with production records, reports on working methods, and appeals for increased productivity. Bolshevism signifies the dominating emergence of the element that had remained half-hidden in bourgeois society: it is the most unequivocal affirmation of material production and at the same time of practical transcendence. Society[68] thereby loses its spiritual wealth and the spur of self-criticism, and acquires

---

[64] *Ibid.*, p. 250.

[65] Lenin, "Die drohende Katastrophe und wie man sie bekämpfen soll," *ibid.*, p. 130.

[66] E.g., Lenin, "Über die Naturalsteuer," *ibid.*, p. 830.

[67] Lenin, "Die nächsten Aufgaben der Sowjetmacht," *ibid.*, p. 377.

[68] Here "society" means not the totality of its members but the leading group.

an unshakable complacency and a hitherto unknown enthusiasm in its sense of historical necessity.

But in this case all that remains, if anything, of Marx's own special and personal concepts, which in his eyes alone justify the unique quality of practical transcendence, is a propagandistic semblance. As a result, bolshevism's battle with the orthodox Marxists in its own ranks is among the most tragic and moving chapters of the history of our time. And yet the Soviet Union has conformed to Marxist thought in so far as it has always regarded the emancipation of its own peoples (that is, their adaptation to the exigencies of industrial society) in terms of a higher world process. True, the concept of "world revolution" has led more than any other to the defeats of bolshevism in its confrontation with developed bourgeois society; at the same time, it constitutes a hallmark of world-historical distinction, since it is evidence of a relationship not only to a selfishly interpreted "industrial production" but also the total process of practical transcendence. For this very reason the term "development dictatorship" is inadequate as applied to the Soviet Union and, despote all structural similarities, the difference as against fascism is fundamental. The fact that, alone among non-Western powers, the Soviet Union could complete its industrialization[69] on the strength of its own initiative and to a large extent under its own steam; that, in spite of the known harshness of its methods of government, it enjoys what often seems a mysterious prestige among the underdeveloped nations; that it was the first state to succeed in penetrating outer space—these are all closely related facts which become intelligible when seen against a background of transcendental definition.

It has now become evident what fascism actually is. It is not that resistance to practical transcendence which is more of less common to all conservative movements. It was only when theoretical transcendence, from which that resistance originally emanated, was likewise denied that fascism made its appearance. Thus fascism is at the same time resistance to practical transcendence and struggle against theoretical transcendence. But this struggle must needs be concealed, since the original motivations can never be entirely dispensed with. And insofar as practical transcendence from its most superficial aspect is nothing but the possibility of concentration of

---

[69] "Industrialization" is also meant here as a total process and hence distinguished from feudal Japan's purely technical adoption of industrial forms of production.

power, fascism pursues its resistance to transcendence from within that transcendence and at times in the clear consciousness of a struggle for world hegemony. That is the transcendental expression of the sociological fact that fascism has at its command forces which are born of the emancipation process and then turn against their own origin. If it may be called the despair of the[70] feudal section of bourgeois society for its traditions, and the bourgeois element's betrayal of its revolution, now it is clear what this tradition and this revolution actually are. Fascism represents the second and gravest crisis of liberal society, since it achieves power on its own soil, and in its radical form is the most complete and effective denial of that society.

It is precisely in this broadest of all perspectives that the observer cannot withhold from fascism that "sympathy" of which we have spoken. This sympathy is directed not toward persons or deeds, but toward the perplexity underlying the colossal attempt to overcome that perplexity, which is the most universal characteristic of an era whose end cannot be foreseen . . . For transcendence, when properly understood, is infinitely remote from the harmlessness of safe "cultural progress"; it is not the couch of the finite human being, but in some mysterious unity his throne and his cross.

Nevertheless, fascism as a metapolitical phenomenon still serves as a means of understanding the world today: only when liberal society, after steadfast and serious reflection, accepts practical transcendence as its own although no longer exclusive product; when theoretical transcendence escapes from its ancient political entanglements into genuine freedom; when Communist society looks at itself and its past with realistic but not cynical eyes and ceases to evade either one; when the love of individuality and barriers no longer assumes political form, and thoughy has become a friend of man—only then can man be said to have finally crossed the border into a postfascist era.

[70] It is no doubt clear from the foregoing that here the definite article is used not collectively but hypothetically.